Coaching Psychology in

Coaching psychology is a distinct branch of academic and applied psychology that focuses on enhancement of performance, development and wellbeing in the broader population. In *Coaching Psychology in Schools*, Mark Adams demonstrates how psychological principles and approaches can be applied in schools to enhance the performance of education practitioners, teams and settings, with corresponding benefits for the children under their care.

Coaching Psychology in Schools aims to put psychology in the hands of the reader, imparting psychology-informed coaching strategies that can enhance effectiveness in supporting others to learn, change and develop. The book challenges traditional notions of how psychology can contribute to education and illustrates how better outcomes for children can be achieved by helping adults to unlock and utilize their resources. The book covers how coaching psychology can be applied to:

- Develop classroom practice
- Improve teacher performance
- Support Continuing Professional Development
- Enhance practitioner and team performance, confidence and wellbeing
- Support practical problem-solving
- Develop individual and organizational resilience

Real-life case examples are used throughout to illustrate practical coaching methods and techniques that are underpinned by established psychological approaches, including solution-focused coaching, cognitive-behavioural coaching, motivational interviewing and many more.

Coaching Psychology in Schools will be essential reading for coaches, psychologists and education practitioners who have an interest or investment in helping others to move forward, including school leaders, teacher coaches, CPD co-ordinators, advisers and consultants. It will also be of interest to those working in other professional contexts who are interested in finding out more about coaching psychology and its potential applications.

Mark Adams is a Chartered Psychologist with fifteen years' experience of working in education as a teacher, educational psychologist and coaching psychologist. He is the Director of Adams Psychology Services, Bristol, providing consultation, coaching and training services to education settings and practitioners, while also supporting others to develop proficiency in coaching skills. Mark is passionate about applying psychology to support others to learn, achieve and develop.

Coaching Psychology
Series Editor: Stephen Palmer

Coaching psychology is a distinct branch of academic and applied psychology that focuses on enhancement of performance, development and wellbeing in the broader population. Written by leading experts, the **Coaching Psychology** series will highlight innovations in the field, linking theory, research and practice. These books will interest professionals from psychology, coaching, mentoring, business, health, human resources and management as well as those interested in the psychology underpinning their coaching and mentoring practice.

www.routledgementalhealth.com/books/series/COACHPSYCH/

Titles in the series:

Coaching Psychology in Schools
Enhancing performance, development and wellbeing
Mark Adams

Coaching Psychology in Schools

Enhancing Performance,
Development and Wellbeing

Mark Adams

Routledge
Taylor & Francis Group

LONDON AND NEW YORK

First published 2016
by Routledge
2 Park Square, Milton Park, Abingdon, Oxon, OX14 4RN

and by Routledge
711 Third Avenue, New York, NY 10017

Routledge is an imprint of the Taylor & Francis Group, an informa business

British Library Cataloguing in Publication Data
A catalogue record for this book is available from the British Library

Library of Congress Cataloging-in-Publication Data
Names: Adams, Mark, 1973–
Title: Coaching psychology in schools : enhancing performance, development
and wellbeing / Mark Adams.
Description: East Sussex ; New York, NY : Routledge is an imprint of the
Taylor & Francis Group, an Informa business, [2016] | Includes
bibliographical references.
Identifiers: LCCN 2015019701| ISBN 9781138776012 (hardback) | ISBN
9781138776487 (pbk.) | ISBN 9781315762630 (ebook)
Subjects: LCSH: Teachers—Psychology. | Educational psychology. | Teacher
effectiveness. | Effective teaching. | Motivation in education. |
Teachers—In-service training. | Personal coaching.
Classification: LCC LB2840 .A294 2016 | DDC 370.15—dc23
LC record available at http://lccn.loc.gov/2015019701

ISBN: 978-1-138-77601-2 (hbk)
ISBN: 978-1-138-77648-7 (pbk)
ISBN: 978-1-315-76263-0 (ebk)

Typeset in Times
by Keystroke, Station Road, Codsall, Wolverhampton
Printed in Great Britain by Ashford Colour Press Ltd,
Gosport, Hants

For Eliza, Alice and Charlie, who have made me rich.

Contents

Illustrations

Figures

Tables

Boxes

Foreword

Stephen Palmer

The practice of coaching psychology focuses on enhancing performance and wellbeing in individuals, organizations and communities. Taking an evidence-based approach, the models, frameworks and techniques can be used in one-to-one, team or group coaching. This exciting book, *Coaching Psychology in Schools: Enhancing Performance, Development and Wellbeing*, launches the new Routledge *Coaching Psychology* series. Educational Psychologist Mark Adams demonstrates how coaching psychology theory and practice can be applied within a community that is often larger than a small country village – a school. This innovative book is the first coaching psychology book specifically concentrating on working within schools and will be of interest to professionals who wish to develop their knowledge and skills in order to enhance the performance, development and wellbeing of anybody within this community. Classroom practitioners, educational psychologists, school leaders, advanced skills teachers, managers and consultants are all likely to find this book a useful addition to their resources. And there is also a bonus: the models and techniques covered in this book can also be applied to self-coaching so that as professionals facilitate growth in their client groups, they can start to use the same strategies on themselves.

Professor Stephen Palmer, Ph.D.
Institute of Work Based Learning, Middlesex University
President of the International Society for Coaching Psychology

Preface

Coaching psychology has a different starting point. Rather than dysfunction, the implicit assumption is a desire to grow, develop and improve: to gain new skills, and to hone existing ones. It reaches out to a new clientele, offering the benefits of psychology to people and organisations wishing to make the most of the resources that lie within the individual.

(Miller, 2007, in Palmer & Whybrow, 2007, p. xviii)

To the reader

Since the early 2000s, the use of workplace coaching as a tool for enhancing performance, development and wellbeing has become increasingly prevalent in education. Across the UK, the USA and Australia, coaching is taking place in schools in a variety of forms and for a diverse range of purposes (van Nieuwerburgh, 2012). Its emergence has been accompanied by the parallel development of *coaching psychology* – a specific subdiscipline of academic and applied psychology that focuses on the enhancement of performance, development and wellbeing in the broader population.

Whereas psychology has traditionally been associated with disorder, pathology and the amelioration of distress or dysfunction, coaching psychology takes established psychological approaches and puts them to work in the service of enhancing the lives of everyday people and institutions. As such, coaching psychology represents a vehicle through which the benefits of applied psychology can be experienced on a much larger scale. Nowhere does this have more significance than in the places where we equip and prepare the future members of our society: our schools and education settings. If coaching psychology can be applied in schools in order to enhance the educational experience of the children and young people within them, surely this is something we cannot afford to ignore.

So, is this the case? Can psychology be applied in schools to this effect? My contention is that it can, and I intend to demonstrate that in this book. In the coming pages I will present a range of ways in which coaching psychology has been applied to support the performance, development and wellbeing of *adults* in schools, with corresponding benefits for the children under their care.

My hope is that this will lead to increased demand for coaching psychology services in education, and also an increase in the numbers of psychologists who offer coaching to schools as part of their professional services. So that is the first aim of this book.

My second aim is somewhat broader and more ambitious in nature. As well as demonstrating applications of coaching psychology and their impact, I wish to leave you, the reader, better equipped to practise coaching yourself – should you so desire, of course. Psychology has much to offer to the practice of coaching in the form of a host of principles and models that can underpin and bring depth to the coaching relationship. However, such approaches are not the exclusive province of psychologists and can, in fact, also be utilized by other people or professionals who have an interest or investment in helping others to move forward (e.g. teacher coaches, school leaders). Furthermore, many of the principles can be applied in the context of self-coaching so we can improve our own professional and personal effectiveness. The more people there are in education who are skilled at supporting the performance, development and wellbeing of themselves or others, the better, so I would like to hand these approaches over to you so that you can incorporate them into your own life and practice. Therefore, when documenting examples of how coaching psychology has been applied in schools, I will use a case study format that makes visible the detail of the methods and principles used. In that sense this is also very much a 'how-to' book, with the emphasis being on imparting practical tools and principles that can support you in becoming more effective at helping other people (or yourself) to learn, grow and develop.

Who is this book for?

This book is intended to speak to the following audiences:

*   People who wish to find out more about what coaching psychology is and the ways in which it can be of benefit to schools.
*   People who work in education and who wish to develop their proficiency at enhancing the performance, development and wellbeing of others.

This could include, for example, school leaders; middle managers; school coaches; mentors; Continuing Professional Development (CPD) co-ordinators; classroom practitioners; Advanced Skills Teachers; Specialist Leaders of Education; consultants; Educational Psychologists; Trainee Educational Psychologists; and coaching psychologists.

Due to the broad applicability of the approaches and principles described, the book will also be of interest to those working in other professional contexts who would like to find out more about coaching psychology and its potential applications.

While the case studies presented have all taken place in a UK context, the methods and principles used are transferable and so are relevant to readers outside the UK.

A word on style

For the most part, I will speak to you directly and adopt a more personal style of writing. The exception to this is the case study narratives, where you will notice that I switch to the third person ('the coach' rather than 'I'). This is because the case studies are not about *me,* they are about the methods and principles used, and I do not want anything to detract attention from that. Plus, I think they read better that way.

The other stylistic point of note is the use of references. While I want this book to be an engaging and practical read for you, I also want to signpost you to further reading material and demonstrate that the methods described are grounded in the existing literature and research base. Therefore, where appropriate, I have used references in the text to indicate my sources.

Learning objectives

By reading this book, you will learn:

- What coaching psychology is and how it can be of benefit to schools.
- How psychology can supplement and enhance core coaching skills.
- How coaching psychology has been used to address real issues in schools (e.g. classroom practice, leadership performance, staff wellbeing).
- Specific methods that can be used to support the performance, development and wellbeing of education practitioners.
- How we can work with others in a way that makes change more likely.

You will also be given the opportunity to think about how you can incorporate the methods and principles described into your own practice.

How those objectives will be achieved

The book is divided into three parts.

Part 1: Foundations

This sets the context for the book while outlining the core principles, concepts and skills that run throughout the approaches described in Part 2.

The Introduction opens the book with an overview of the key themes, explored through the lens of a personal narrative in order to set the book in context and to bring some life and heart to the material. If you are short of time, you can simply skip to the bullet-point summary at the end of the Introduction where the key facts are summarized.

In order for you to: (i) understand how psychology can enhance core coaching skills, and (ii) apply coaching in your own practice, you will need to be familiar with core coaching skills and principles. The next three chapters are therefore devoted to this topic. Chapter 2 defines the aims and principles of coaching, while the core skills needed to facilitate a coaching conversation are described in Chapter 3. Chapter 4 emphasizes the importance of structure in coaching, while outlining one of the most well-known coaching frameworks (I-GROW).

Chapter 5 illustrates how coaching practice can be supplemented and enhanced with psychology, and provides an overview of the psychological approaches that inform the practices in Part 2.

Part 2: Applications

Part 2 presents a range of ways in which psychology can be applied through coaching to enhance the performance, development and wellbeing of education practitioners. Each chapter will demonstrate how coaching psychology has been brought to bear on a real-life school issue. Some of the coachees' details have been modified to protect anonymity.

Chapter 6 introduces a non-judgemental approach to teacher observation that can support the self-directed learning of classroom practitioners. You will see how the approach was used to support a teacher to reduce low-level disruption in the classroom.

Chapter 7 demonstrates how coaching can be applied to support practitioners to move towards identified performance standards, in this case showing how a secondary school science teacher was supported to improve the quality of teaching and learning in his lessons.

Chapter 8 illustrates the value of coaching as an individualized form of CPD, enabling a senior leader to discover that the capacity to lead and manage others effectively was something that already existed within her own resources.

In Chapter 9 we see how coaching can be applied to enhance practitioner wellbeing, in this case supporting a primary school practitioner to overcome anxiety about speaking in public.

Chapter 10 demonstrates how coaching was used to support a new-to-role Special Educational Needs Co-Ordinator to manage some of the practical and emotional demands of role change.

Chapter 11 provides an example of how a coaching approach can assist practitioners and schools with practical problem-solving, in this case supporting a primary school team to problem-solve how to provide for a number of young children with significant Special Educational Needs.

Chapter 12 shows how coaching can be used to support the performance, development and wellbeing of teams, and introduces a solution-focused coaching model (ENABLE) which I have developed in the course of my practice.

Chapter 13 focuses on how psychological principles can be imparted on a larger scale to support the members of an organization to develop and apply resilience-enhancing strategies.

To support you in extracting the key learning points and further incorporating the principles and methods into your own practice, each chapter in Part 2 will conclude by addressing the following questions:

1   How was coaching applied to support the improvement of performance, development and/or wellbeing?
2   What coaching skills, models or techniques have we covered?
3   How else could this approach or these principles be applied?
4   What can we learn about how to help others to change?
5   How could you apply these skills or principles in your own practice?

Part 3: Reflections, conclusions and future directions

Chapter 14 pulls together the learning points that have emerged throughout the book, before we consider the future of coaching psychology in schools in Chapter 15.

Whether you are a psychologist, a coach, an education practitioner or other interested party, I welcome you to this book and hope you find it helpful.

Acknowledgements

There is a range of people to whom I would like to express my sincere gratitude, who have contributed either directly or indirectly to the writing of this book.

My first acknowledgement goes to Eliza, my wife of five years and friend of twenty-three, a person of many remarkable qualities and a source of friendship, fun and support to all who know her. My rock, my anchor, my love. That she can also provide high-quality professional support and advice is an added bonus I take advantage of not infrequently. To paraphrase Richard Ayoade: Thank-you, Harold, for more than everything.

I would next like to pay tribute to the motivating and life-enriching influence of Alice and Charlie, our beloved children who keep all else in perspective. I am incredibly proud of them both, and am confident that the world is a better place with them in it. My thanks also to my parents for their continued support on my journey.

Beyond my immediate family, I must next acknowledge the contribution and support of those who have variously read drafts and offered feedback throughout the writing of this book: Eliza Adams, Brigid Allen, Claire Banks, Nic Garrick, Pam Harris, Lynne Hindmarch, Jack Humphreys, Jak Lee and Susie Weaver. I am grateful to them all for being so generous with their time and thoughts. Any faults or misjudgements in the final text remain entirely my own. My thanks also to Susannah Frearson of Routledge for her supportive, pragmatic assistance.

Into the professional domain, my warmest thanks are extended to the clients of coaching whose case studies feature in this book. They have courageously allowed the content of their confidential sessions to be shared in the interests of furthering the learning and development of others, and I am very grateful to them for that. There would be no book without them.

My journey into coaching psychology began with my secondment to the Improving Behaviour in Schools coaching service (later 'IBIS Coaching & Training'), and I will always fondly remember the learning, enjoyment and sense of contribution I experienced as part of it. Thank you to my friends and former colleagues – Dr Jak Lee, Antony Fugill, Jo Trott and Zoe Stephens – as well as Nigel Harrisson, Chris Wardle, and Lesley Kaplan for innovatively creating and developing the team into the exceptional example of applied psychology practice that it was. Thank you also to Bristol Educational Psychology Service for supporting my secondment.

To the schools and education practitioners of Bristol, I would like to express thanks to Hilary Harris, Coral Harper and Alison Goddard-Jones – all long-time advocates and supporters of coaching in schools. I am grateful also to the many other practitioners I have worked with over the years who are too numerous to name but who have each taught me something about what it means to be helpful – yes, even you, Mr Barnes.

I would like to recognize the contribution of the team at the Centre for Coaching, London – particularly Stephen Palmer, Siobhain O'Riordan and Nick Edgerton – for providing some of the most inspiring, affirming, stimulating and useful professional (and personal) development opportunities of my career to date. Their influence, I hope, can be detected in the pages of this book. For providing an emerging psychologist with necessary stimulation and direction, I am grateful to the Special Group in Coaching Psychology, the International Society for Coaching Psychology, and those practitioners who have contributed to the birth and maintenance of both.

This section would not be complete without acknowledging the influence of Dr Anthony Grant and his colleagues at the University of Sydney, whose work led to the emergence of coaching psychology as a discipline.

And so to Jack Humphreys: one-time colleague, unofficial mentor and lunchtime compadre; a man of rare intelligence and values, who has been a source of invaluable support and challenge through times of both difficulty and success, and who has been a confidante, companion and, above all, friend, for the best part of a decade. The sum of your contribution to my life, career, and personal and professional growth cannot be captured here. Suffice to say, comrade, that if I can ever give back to you even a *fraction* of what you have given to me, I will be deeply memnooned.

Finally, my thanks to Iain Forsyth and Jane Pollard, two people I have never met but whose film provided the necessary jolt of inspiration that helped me to get this book over the line.

Mark Adams
January 2015

Part 1

Foundations

Chapter 1

Introduction

> I have almost invariably found that the very feeling that has seemed to me most private, most personal . . . has turned out to be an expression for which there is a resonance in many other people. It has led me to believe that what is most personal and unique in each one of us is probably the very element which would, if it were shared or expressed, speak most deeply to others.
>
> (Rogers, 1961, p. 26)

In the very first chapter of his classic work *On Becoming a Person*, Carl Rogers, an eminent psychotherapist and arguably the most influential psychologist of the twentieth century, observes how hungry people are 'to know something of the person who is speaking to them or teaching them' (Rogers, 1961, p. 4). This is an observation that I was at first determined to ignore while writing this book, querying the place of my voice and electing instead to write in third-person journalspeak that would effectively keep me out of the picture. However, as the book has developed, the need to engage *you*, the reader, through the use of a personal voice has become increasingly apparent to me. This realization has also coincided with the emergence of a growing belief that my giving away of something of my personal experience is something that will add value to this book and make it more engaging. Take this introduction, for example. In order for you to understand the purpose, context and spirit of this book, there are certain core questions I need to address:

- What is the value of psychology?
- How can psychology be applied in education?
- What is coaching?
- How is coaching used in education?
- What is coaching psychology?
- How can psychology inform coaching practice?
- What are the aims of this book?

Of course, I could readily cover those themes through the provision of some basic facts and a series of concise and impersonal bullet points; however, while that approach may have its merits, I believe that in doing so I might overlook a valuable opportunity. As Rogers notes, sometimes it is that which is most personal and unique in each of us that speaks most deeply to others, and I believe that there are aspects of my own experience in relation to the above questions that, if shared, may resonate with something inside you. It is therefore with Rogers' advice in mind that I open this book with something of a personal introduction.

Psychology: a subject for life

Psychology – the scientific study of how we think, feel, behave, learn, interact and develop – has been the subject of my heart since I was 17. I find psychology fascinating because it speaks to us about our everyday existences, what it means to be a person, and how, for better or for worse, we function and interrelate as human beings. While I was first attracted to psychology by an interest in pathology and dysfunction, over time I have become increasingly drawn to what psychology has to say about what is *right* with people, our strengths and qualities, and the conditions under which we can perform to our optimum potential. Indeed, psychology has much to tell us about such matters. But the value of psychology extends beyond mere description, however interesting that description might be. In offering us theories, lenses and language that can support us to make sense of and navigate the messy, complex and dynamic world of human experience and interaction, psychology is a subject that equips us for life itself. And it is here where the true value of psychology lies – in its potential to make a positive contribution to lives and society through real-world applications. *This* is what drives my passion.

A broader impact of psychology in education

Psychology can be applied in any number of the domains of life and work, from sports contexts to businesses to clinical settings. Personally, I work as an Educational Psychologist, which means that I apply psychology in my work with schools and families to support them to improve the quality of educational experience for the children under their care. Sometimes this involves doing assessment work with children; often, it involves supporting the planning of interventions for children with Special Educational Needs and Disabilities; however, it also sometimes involves work with teachers and schools in order to support them to improve the quality of their provision on a broader scale. I find this latter form of work particularly satisfying since it greatly increases the numbers of children who can benefit from my efforts: apply psychology to support a teacher to improve the quality of their practice (e.g. how they develop a constructive learning environment, how they facilitate learning, how they motivate the children, or how they manage behaviour) and it thereafter potentially benefits every child that teacher comes into contact with. What is more, the added bonus is that the teacher may then become more effective at providing support to their colleagues. As you can see, the potential benefits of such work are significant in terms of their ripple-effect impact on the overall capacity of the organization to provide for the children under their care; therefore, as an emerging psychologist in the early 2000s, I was keen to develop this aspect of my practice. It was with this mind-set driving my ambitions that I discovered the practice of *coaching*.

What is coaching?

Coaching is a way of working with people that focuses on supporting them to improve their performance, learn and develop, and/or experience greater wellbeing. It is, in essence, a form of helping relationship, where one person builds a relationship with another (or a team or group) with a view to supporting them to make positive changes in their life and situation. As a psychologist with an interest in helping people to unlock their strengths and apply their skills to everyday challenges, I was naturally drawn to coaching as a discipline. What I found was an area of practice that not only seemed to be effective in helping myself or others to move forward but was, moreover, closely aligned with my own core values and principles (e.g. respect, aspiration, appreciation, collaboration, individuation, and an emphasis on the importance of learning). Coaching and I were a natural fit at both the practical and philosophical levels.

What is coaching psychology?

At some point in 2003 I received a mailing from the British Psychological Society (BPS) asking members to vote on whether the BPS should form a Special Group in Coaching Psychology (SGCP) for those interested in this area of practice. I didn't know what coaching psychology was, but I was enthusiastic about coaching and so did a little homework. It didn't take much research to discover that coaching psychology was an emerging discipline of academic and applied psychology in which qualified psychologists would apply their skills in the context of coaching to support performance and wellbeing in the broader population. An area of professional practice that would align my passion for psychology, my enthusiasm for coaching, my core values and principles, and my desire to have a broader impact in schools? You can imagine my response. Thankfully, I was not alone in my views. The SGCP was formally launched in the autumn of 2004, and continues to provide a home within the BPS for those people (not just psychologists) who are interested in applications of psychology to coaching practice (www.sgcp. org.uk). From this point on, I also considered myself to be an aspiring coaching psychologist, and was soon fortunate enough to be able to begin delivering such services in my work with schools.

How is coaching used in education?

Coaching seems to have gradually permeated the educational landscape since the early 2000s, when it was advocated by the Department for Education and Skills as a strategy for supporting schools to increase their collective capacity for sustainable change and improvement. My first formal experience of coaching in education was in a specialist service of psychologists and teachers that used coaching methods and principles to support classroom teachers to develop their behaviour management skills. I was immediately struck by the ways in which coaching could have a positive impact on teachers' performance and wellbeing, and how it seemed to have genuine practical value in helping teachers to make adjustments to their day-to-day practice that would benefit many of the children they came into contact with. However, coaching has much broader applicability. Throughout the 2000s, a number of publications emerged that indicated a growing recognition of the range of possible applications for coaching in schools, with school leaders noting that they might use coaching for a variety of purposes, including addressing pupil behaviour; improving teacher performance; developing lesson planning; supporting a new head teacher; creating an inclusive school; spreading good practice; and growing the organization (Creasy & Paterson, 2005, p. 19). Over time, the practice in our team developed and diversified until we were coaching about a broad range of themes with a number of client groups (e.g. developing motivational practices, coaching for wellbeing, and coaching for senior leaders).

Since then, the use of coaching in education has continued to grow and evolve, and as such it is likely that an education practitioner will encounter a variety of different coaching relationships. This could include formal coaching from an external specialist; in-school coaching from a trained coach in their own organization; a line manager or other professional adopting a coaching style; or peer-to-peer coaching from a professional in a similar role in their own or another school. Indeed, with the advent of 'Teaching Schools' and the increased emphasis on school-to-school and peer-to-peer support in the United Kingdom, coaching is now more relevant to education than ever. There is also a gradually accumulating evidence base regarding the impact of coaching in education, demonstrating a range of positive outcomes for children, young people, teachers and organizations, including increased goal attainment; reduced stress; enhanced wellbeing; enhanced resilience; improved performance; improvements in student attainment; and the implementation of new practices following professional development experiences (see van Nieuwerburgh, 2012, for a summary).

How can psychology inform coaching practice?

In the course of my work I began to note how my own practice as a coach was greatly enhanced by the application of psychological principles and approaches, such as an understanding of how people move through the change process or specific techniques and frameworks that could be used to support people on their developmental journey. Over the years I have been inspired and influenced by the person-centred approach, Solution-Focused Brief Therapy, cognitive-behavioural psychology, Self-Efficacy Theory, the 'stages of change' model, Self-Determination Theory, Motivational Interviewing, positive psychology, and research into the factors that influence the outcomes of helping relationships. All of these influences have enhanced my practice and made me a more effective agent of change; my hypothesis is that they may make *you* more effective, too. Indeed, my contention is that these principles and approaches can be applied by a broad range of people and professionals to enhance their own personal effectiveness and their proficiency at supporting others to learn, grow and develop.

What are the aims of this book?

Ten years on from my first encounters with coaching I remain as passionate about and committed to the practice as ever, having repeatedly seen the impact it can have on practitioners and teams in schools. Indeed, one of my aims in writing this book is to capture some of that impact so that others can see what coaching and coaching psychology can offer to education. If you work in education, then I want you to see close-up the benefits and opportunities that coaching can present: to watch as a person grows in confidence as they discover that they do, in fact, have the personal and practical resources they need to achieve their goals; to see a teacher recognize and challenge the negative conclusions he has drawn about himself that give rise to anxiety; to see a team find the will and the way to create a new special educational provision from scratch for the children of their community. All these examples, and more, will be explored in Part 2 of this book. What I find most appealing about these examples is that in all cases change has come about by working with people in a way that respects their skills and experiences, demonstrates belief in their capacity to change, and empowers them to move forward with renewed confidence and vigour. My hope is that seeing the evidence of such impact will encourage more people in education to take up or make use of these principles and practices.

This brings me on to my broader aim: as well as demonstrating the impact that coaching and coaching psychology can have, I want to leave you, the reader, armed with a collection of psychological principles and tools that can inform your practice. Yes, I am speaking to psychologists here, but my intention is for these ideas to also reach beyond that audience. Coaching is a practice that has relevance to many roles in education, and psychology is a tool that can inform such practice and make it more effective. Therefore, my grander ambition in writing this book is – to borrow the words of psychologist George Miller – to *give psychology away* so that you can use it in your own lives and practice to support the performance, development and wellbeing of yourselves and others.

You might be a senior leader who wishes to consider how best to enhance the performance of individuals or teams, or is thinking about how to move your organization forward; or you might be a classroom practitioner who provides development opportunities to your peers through in-school support mechanisms. You might be an in-school coach or CPD co-ordinator who works with practitioners in your own or other settings; or you might be a middle manager who has moved out of the classroom and suddenly found yourself experiencing the demands of a role in which you need to provide support and challenge to others. You might be an Advanced Skills Teacher, a Specialist Leader of Education, a Local Leader of Education, an Executive Principal – the list goes on. I believe that if you have any interest in understanding how to work with others in a way that makes their growth and development more likely, coaching and psychology have relevance to you all. At the same time, you may wish to use some of the principles and practices described in this book to support self-reflection on the goals you want to achieve, how you might go about achieving them, and how to overcome any obstacles you might encounter on your path. Indeed, I continue to draw upon them myself on a regular basis (not always successfully).

In sharing my personal intentions and experiences, I hope that I have given you a sense of what this book is about, what I want to achieve, and why that is important to me. More importantly, I hope that what you have read may have resonated with you in some way, and that it might stimulate your interest in discovering more about either coaching or the psychological principles and practices outlined in this book. As you can see, I am passionate about psychology, and I hope that, after reading this book, you will be too. Whoever wields it, psychologist or teacher, psychology is a tool that can be applied to improve the quality of educational experience for the children under our care. What other imperative do we require?

Summary

- Psychology – the scientific study of how we think, feel, behave, learn, interact and develop – offers us theories and models that can support us to improve our personal and interpersonal effectiveness.
- Applied in the context of education, psychology can support teachers and schools to improve the quality of their provision on a broad scale. Coaching is one example of such an application.
- Coaching is a way of working with people that focuses on supporting people to improve their performance, learn and develop, and/or experience greater wellbeing.
- Coaching psychology is a distinct subdiscipline of applied psychology in which psychology-informed coaching models are used to support enhancement of performance, development and wellbeing in the broader population.
- Coaching has a diverse range of applications in education, including improving teacher performance, supporting the development of leaders, and developing schools as organizations.
- The practice of coaching can be informed by a range of psychological theories and approaches, including the person-centred approach, Solution-Focused Brief Therapy, cognitive-behavioural psychology, and many more.

- This book aims to demonstrate the impact that coaching psychology can have in schools, while imparting a collection of psychological principles and practices that can be utilized by others to enhance their own personal effectiveness and their proficiency at supporting others to learn, grow and develop.

Chapter 2

What is coaching?

> Coaching is recognized as a powerful vehicle for increasing performance, achieving results and optimizing personal effectiveness.
>
> (Bachkirova *et al.*, 2014, p. 1)

'Coaching' is a term that has traditionally been associated with promoting excellence in sport, and that is indeed where the origins of modern-day life and workplace coaching are located. In 1974, Timothy Gallwey wrote a landmark book called *The Inner Game of Tennis*, which transformed approaches to coaching by de-emphasizing the importance of skill instruction in favour of supporting players to manage and reduce internal states that might be interfering with their performance (e.g. fear, doubt, inattention, distraction). Gallwey's ideas were then adapted and applied to business contexts, leading to the emergence of workplace coaching as a method for supporting executive and employee performance and career development. Then, in 1992, the publication of Sir John Whitmore's *Coaching for Performance* popularized Graham Alexander's now-famous GROW model (Goal, Reality, Options, Will) and led to a further proliferation of the use of coaching approaches for supporting enhancement of performance and development in people's work and personal lives.

Since then, coaching has evolved into an estimated US$2 billion industry worldwide with applications in executive development, business, human resources, education, and personal improvement, to name but a few (ICF & PricewaterhouseCoopers, 2012; Law, 2013; Skiffington & Zeus, 2003). A number of institutions exist which are dedicated to the advancement of the coaching profession, including the Association for Coaching (AC), the International Coach Federation (ICF), and the International Society for Coaching Psychology (ISCP). In many contexts, coaching is being increasingly recognized as a powerful vehicle for improving performance and optimizing personal effectiveness (Bachkirova *et al.*, 2014). It is clearly a part of the fabric of modern society. But what is it?

The AC (2014) advocates the definition of coaching suggested by Anthony Grant, as follows:

Coaching is a collaborative, solution-focused, result-oriented and systematic process in which the coach facilitates the enhancement of work performance, life experience, self-directed learning and personal growth of individuals from normal (i.e. non-clinical) populations.

(Greene & Grant, 2003, p. xiii)

While this definition may be accurate – and, indeed, is in many ways merit-worthy – it has been noted that 'attempts to define coaching as designed [purely] for the "mentally healthy" clientele group are now seen as unsatisfactory for many practical and ethical reasons' (Bachkirova *et al.*, 2014, p. 3). Moreover, the definition is perhaps not the kind of in-a-nutshell explanation one might use to explain what coaching is to the layperson. Instead, for the purposes of this exploration, we will use the following definition offered by Myles Downey: 'Coaching is the art of facilitating the performance, learning and development of another' (Downey, 2003, p. 21).

Notwithstanding that Downey's description does not explicitly refer to the enhancement of wellbeing, this concise definition is adequate for our purposes. So, if coaching is about facilitating the performance, learning and development, and/or the wellbeing of another person, how exactly does one go about that? And how does that opportunity come about?

Let us consider that a person is experiencing some kind of problem in their work or personal situation that they would like to resolve, and they would like to talk it through with someone else in confidence. It should be emphasized at this point that coaching need not be problem-focused – for example, the person may instead have a goal that they wish to achieve, a development area they wish to pursue, or a dilemma they wish to explore – but for the sake of illustration, the example of a person with a problem is a good place to begin. The person happens to know of a coach, and so contacts them to arrange for a coaching conversation to take place. If the person works for an organization, there may be an in-house coach that the person can use; alternatively, the person may be able to contract an external provider of coaching services. From hereon, we will use the term 'coachee' to refer to the person who wants the coaching conversation (we will avoid the term 'client' since there can be multiple client relationships in any given engagement; see Appendix 1).

Coaching conversations

Coaching takes place primarily through the medium of conversation. In essence, the role of a coach is to create a conversational space in which the coachee can reflect on aspects of their professional and/or personal life or situation with a view to solve problems, explore and resolve dilemmas, attain greater clarity, develop insights, achieve greater emotional wellbeing, and/or move towards desired goals. Sir John Whitmore, one of the worldwide leaders in the emergence and development of workplace coaching, suggests that two of the primary aims of coaching conversations are to raise awareness and to develop responsibility (Whitmore, [1992] 2002).

Raising awareness

Awareness has two components: the coachee's awareness of what is happening in their surrounding context, and their self-awareness of what they are experiencing internally. A key function of the coach is to facilitate the coachee's exploration of their situation so that it enhances the clarity of their perception, enables them to determine what is relevant, and increases their degree of self-awareness with regard to their own emotions, desires and interpretations.

Developing responsibility

Similarly, there are a number of components to responsibility. First, the coach is careful to ensure that the coachee retains ownership of the problem or situation – that is, the coach does not take the monkey from the person's back by assuming responsibility, taking the load, and trying to solve the problem for them. Instead, the emphasis is on creating a space in which the person can talk through their situation with the coach acting as a sounding board rather than an expert fixer. Throughout the conversation, the coach works with the coachee in such a way so as to support the person in maintaining focus on those aspects of their internal or external situation that they can control or influence. Finally, the coach works to ensure that the coachee retains ownership of any actions they do or do not decide to take as a result of the conversation. *Choice* is paramount, and the coach respects the person's right to determine the path they would like to take. This is important for strengthening commitment to any actions undertaken, while also recognizing that the coachee retains responsibility for any consequences – positive or otherwise – which occur as a result of their actions. It is the person who must continue to live with their situation once the coaching conversation or engagement has ended, and we must never lose sight of that.

If these are the aims of a coaching conversation, the question then becomes: how are those aims achieved? What skills can a coach use to facilitate the coaching conversation towards those outcomes? There are a number of core tools that the coach can draw upon, but before exploring the detail of those, it is first important to capture something of the broader essence and spirit of coaching. These crucial principles are more about the manner in which the coach approaches the engagement and the beliefs they have about people than they are about the exercise of any specific technique.

The spirit of coaching

Coaching conversations can be broadly characterized as collaborative, non-directive, facilitative and future-focused. However, with the exception of collaboration, each of these principles comes with an important caveat, as we shall see below.

Collaborative

Coaching typically takes place within an egalitarian, non-hierarchical relationship, with neither party occupying a 'one-up' or 'one-down' position in terms of status or authority (Grant & Stober, 2006; Starr, 2003). Instead, the focus is on the development of a collaborative alliance between coach and coachee in which goals, perspectives and solutions can be co-constructed (Zeus & Skiffington, 2000). The coach respects the coachee as an equal partner who brings resources, views and experience to the engagement. In contrast to a mentoring relationship, the coach may not have expertise in the specific problem or area of learning being worked on, and may or may not have occupied a similar professional role to the coachee; however, the coach will bring a set of skills, principles and approaches that can be brought to bear on practical and/or psychological aspects of the coachee's life or situation.

Non-directive

This is a term that merits some scrutiny. In counselling and therapeutic contexts, 'non-directive' is a term used to denote approaches in which the counsellor or therapist follows the client's lead, allowing them to explore their thoughts and feelings while actively listening and communicating empathy and understanding (e.g. Rogers, 1961). Coaching *is* predominantly non-directive in this sense, since in the majority of circumstances the coachee will determine the topic for discussion and throughout the conversation the coach will listen, reflect and empathize. However, the purely non-directive counsellor or therapist does not teach the client a particular therapeutic approach, nor do they introduce specific techniques that the client can use. In this sense, coaching may depart from the non-directive principle in that, at points in the conversation or engagement, the coach may introduce more steer to the conversation or share particular techniques or methods that the coachee can apply to their situation to support their reflection and planning.

Crucially, coaching is also non-directive in the sense that the coach does not tell the person what to do; rather, the coach focuses on creating a conversational space in which the coachee can explore different perspectives and options before making their own decisions about the way forward they wish to pursue (Downey, 2003; Starr, 2003). In this way, the coach maintains and demonstrates respect for the coachee's right to self-determination (Ryan & Deci, 2000; see Chapter 5). Indeed, depending on the nature of the engagement, the coach may not be in a position to offer instruction or expert advice about the matter under discussion, and may not be in possession of 'the answer' that the coachee may be looking for. The coach respects the fact that the coachee is the partner in the relationship who has more knowledge about themselves and their own unique situation, and is better placed than the coach to know what will and will not work for them (Starr, 2003).

Facilitative

A fundamental assumption of coaching is that the coachee is a capable person who brings strengths and resources to the engagement and has the ability to develop their own insights. The role of the coach is to help the person to tap into this potential, using a range of skills to facilitate the coachee's active engagement and reflection. As noted by Timothy Gallwey, one of the forefathers of the modern coaching approach: 'Coaching is unlocking a person's potential to maximize their own performance. *It is helping them to learn rather than teaching them*' (cited in Whitmore, 2002, p. 8, italics added).

At this point it is important to clarify that an emphasis on non-directive facilitation does not mean that there is no room in coaching for the coach to share perspectives, ideas or suggestions with the coachee. A common misconception about coaching, which arises partly as a result of the emphasis placed (correctly) on facilitation, is that all solutions, perspectives or insights must be drawn from the coachee through the coach's questioning, and that the coach should not offer any observations or suggestions of their own. Certainly, there are dangers associated with being overly directive in a helping conversation or relationship, and one would typically expect the majority of a coaching session to reflect the facilitative style previously described; however, there may be moments within a conversation or engagement where it may be helpful for the coach to shift their approach and to draw on other skills to support the coachee in moving their thinking forward (e.g. making a suggestion or giving an opinion). Of course, this is where it can sometimes be helpful for the coach to have some prior experience of the theme that is the focus for coaching. For example, if coaching teachers how to develop behaviour management skills, then the coach having some knowledge of effective strategies is potentially an asset to the conversation, as long as the coach knows how and when to use such knowledge without short-circuiting the coachee's reflective process or seeking to impose their knowledge upon them. This will be explored further in Chapter 3.

Future-focused

The engagement is typically focused more on helping the coachee to articulate and move towards a desired alternative future, with less time spent on analysis of their past history (c.f. counselling or therapy). However, there may be occasions when an exploration of the past may be instructive in order to make sense of the present, to understand patterns of thinking or behaviour, or to inform planning of future actions. Furthermore, there are (frequently) times during coaching sessions when the coachee simply has a need to tell their story and be heard. In such circumstances, ignoring this need or forcing the client to explore a future-focused question they are not yet ready to explore would not be helpful.

Coaching for learning

A coaching engagement is essentially a personalized learning experience, an opportunity for the coachee to reflect on aspects of their performance and development with a view to deepening their understanding and facilitating further professional and personal growth. But what is learning? And how can a coach facilitate it?

The learning process

One of the most well-known models of the learning process is that described by David Kolb (1984), who defines learning as 'the process whereby knowledge is created through the transformation of experience' (p. 38). In Kolb's model, learning progresses through a four-stage cycle in which the learner first has a concrete experience, then reflects on that experience, derives general rules to try to describe and understand their experience, and then engages in active experimentation to try to test out their learning and hypotheses.

Applied to coaching this means that, to facilitate learning, the coach needs to engage the coachee in:

- *attending* to the relevant features of their experience;
- actively reviewing and *reflecting* on their experience;
- deriving *learning* from their experience;
- *planning* how to create new ways of acting as a result.

At each stage, the learner's active engagement is an essential driver of the process; indeed, research demonstrates that learning is more likely to last if the learner has

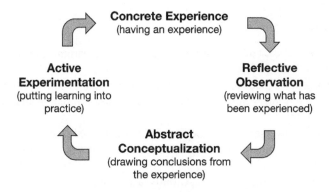

Figure 2.1 Kolb's learning cycle (adapted from Skiffington & Zeus, 2003)

been an active participant in the process, and has engaged in sufficient depth of processing to facilitate the establishment of new neural pathways (see e.g. Bransford *et al.*, 1999; Gross *et al.*, 2010; Michael, 2006; Ramsden, 1992). In other words, the coach needs to operate in such a way to enable the coachee to *work*. The dispensation of prescriptions or advice to a passive recipient is less likely to result in learning, and even less likely to result in learning that lasts.

Principles of adult learning

While children can benefit from coaching, the focus of this book is the application of psychology to work with the *adults* in schools.Therefore, our understanding of how to make coaching a constructive learning experience can be further enriched by an awareness of how adults learn. Skiffington & Zeus (2003) summarize the following principles of adult learning as applied to coaching, derived from the work of Malcolm Knowles (Knowles, 1978):

1   Adults are self-directed and learn best when the coach facilitates and guides them in the acquisition of knowledge.
2   Adults need to connect their new learning to their life experiences.
3   Adults are goal-oriented and need to clearly understand the benefits and value of coaching.
4   Adults learn when they have a reason to do so; therefore, coaching should be tailored to the individual's or group's requirements.
5   Adults tend to be pragmatic and focus on those aspects of a learning situation that are most useful to them in their daily work and personal lives.
6   Adults demand respect for their knowledge and experience.

The above principles of learning arguably underpin all adult-focused coaching engagements (Bachkirova *et al.*, 2014), while their application in practice is demonstrated throughout the case studies described in Part 2 of this book.

Summary

- Coaching is the art of facilitating the performance, learning and development, and/or wellbeing of another person.
- Coaching takes place primarily through the medium of conversation.
- Two of the primary aims of coaching are to raise awareness and to develop responsibility.
- Coaching conversations can be broadly characterized as collaborative, non-directive, facilitative and future-focused (with caveats on three of those principles).
- A coaching engagement is essentially a personalized learning experience which facilitates the professional and personal growth of the coachee.

- The process of learning is driven by the coachee's active engagement, and in work with adults is informed by an understanding of the characteristics of adult learners.

If these are the aims, spirit and principles of coaching, what skills does the coach require to realize them? The foundation skills for facilitating a coaching conversation are covered in Chapter 3.

Suggested reading

Downey, M. (2003). *Effective Coaching: Lessons from the Coach's Coach.* Thomson-Texere.

Chapter 3

Core coaching skills

> It is not an easy thing to permit oneself to understand an individual, to enter thoroughly and completely and empathically into his frame of reference. It is also a rare thing.
>
> (Rogers, 1961, p. 18)

> We have two ears and one mouth so that we can listen twice as much as we speak.
>
> (Epictetus, 1st century AD)

There is no shortage of books on the market describing the core skills that a coach needs in order to facilitate the performance, learning and development of others, and I have personally found the following to be particularly helpful, informative and accessible examples: Downey (2003); Gross Cheliotes & Reilly (2010); Starr (2003). However, while these skills have been frequently documented, it is important to capture them here in order to lay the foundation for the approaches that will be introduced in Chapter 5 and Part 2. The skills may be familiar to many readers, but it is always beneficial to refresh and revitalize the fundamental core aspects of practice.

Let's return to our example of the person who has a problem in their work or personal situation that they would like to talk through with someone else in confidence. What do we want to happen in the conversation? Well, first, we want them to talk, since this can help them to clarify what it is that is on their mind. Often, the very act of articulating what is going on inside and simply getting it out can make a significant difference to a person's feelings. Then, we would like to ensure that they feel heard and understood, and that they believe the coach has an accurate sense of what their experience is. We would like them to have some space to think through different aspects of their situation, and we would like them to leave the conversation a little clearer about, for example, what the key issues are, how they would like things to be different, and how they might go about moving forward after the conversation has finished. Remembering the two primary aims of coaching advocated by Whitmore (2002), we would also like them to be aware of relevant factors in their external environment and inner experience, and we would like them to take responsibility for their chosen course of action rather than abdicating or deferring to the coach. Crucially, all of this must take place within a workable, constructive interpersonal context/climate, and so skills for building rapport are essential. To support achievement of all these aims, there are a number of core skills that the coach can draw upon.

Downey (2003) locates coaching skills on a spectrum ranging from the *non-directive* (those which allow the coachee to think through and solve their problem, e.g. listening) to the *directive* (in Downey's parlance, 'solving someone else's problem for them' by e.g. instructing or giving advice). The concept of a non-directive/directive continuum is a very useful one, so we will borrow that here; however, I am going to use a different meaning of 'directive', and will also be introducing some additional skills not featured in Downey's original framework. Importantly, from hereon we will consider the term 'directive' to refer to *the extent to which the coach's own thoughts or ideas are brought into the conversation* (Gordon, [1970] 2000). This allows for the use of methods in which the coach does, in fact, introduce something else to the conversation (e.g. offering an observation or suggestion), but in a style that respects the coachee's position as an equal collaborator who is free to determine, first, whether they want the contribution and, second, the extent to which they agree with it or otherwise. The key distinction is that, while we may share thoughts or suggestions with the coachee, we do not 'solve the problem for them' but instead sometimes bring alternative ideas or perspectives to the conversation for them to consider. We will expand on how to do that in a moment. For now, we will begin with the least directive skills – i.e. those that do not introduce any of the coach's thoughts – and then gradually move down the continuum.

Core skills

Giving space

One of the least directive (and often most helpful) things a coach can do is to give the coachee space to think, reflect and talk. In school contexts especially, time is at a premium, and opportunities to devote quality attention to a troubling issue can be scarce. A coach can give people the gift of space so that they can articulate what is on their mind and talk things through for themselves with the help of an attentive sounding board. In the course of the discussion, the coach will not attempt to fill the conversation with talk, but will sit comfortably with pauses as the coachee reflects on aspects of their situation. The coach will also deliberately remain silent at points as the coachee considers a particular question or observation. As an indication, I estimate that the coachee should do more than 60 per cent of the talking in the vast majority of coaching conversations.

Attentive listening

If we want someone to talk and feel heard, the first thing we can do is to actually pay attention and *show* that we are paying attention. This means focusing on the person and what they are saying, and it isn't always easy. Do you ever find yourself listening to someone and then realizing that you have 'wandered off' for a few seconds and missed key words or points? How often do our own thoughts or other distractions interfere? Are you just waiting for your turn to speak with your words at the ready? It will show. You may well know what it feels like to be on receiving end of this: stop and think for a moment about how *you* feel when you are talking to someone and they are clearly only half with you, in contrast to how it feels when you know you have someone's full attention.

Attentive listening means that we give the person our total attention and show that we are listening with our non-verbal behaviour (e.g. eye-contact, posture, position, use of hands). At the same time, we are careful to ensure that we do not behave in ways that suggest that our attention may, in fact, be elsewhere (e.g. checking the phone, staring out of the window, reading a poster on the wall). Of course, we are all human, and lapses of attention are inevitable – sometimes for good reason. If that happens, then the best thing we can do is to acknowledge it – sometimes explicitly – and treat it as a cue that we need to refocus. Attentive listening can be supported by trying to visualize what the person is saying, or making a mental note of the key points with a view to summarizing them later.

Encouraging

Encouragement to keep talking can either be verbal (e.g. 'Yes', 'Go on', 'I'm listening', 'I hear you', 'Tell me more') or non-verbal (nodding, mm-hmm, etc.). The key is that the person gets some sort of cue from the listener that they are interested, engaged, and would like the speaker to continue.

Reflective listening

Reflective listening is an art – and, done well, it is indeed an art – of communication in which the listener focuses attentively on what the person is saying and then communicates that understanding in the form of a statement. This demonstrates that the listener has heard and understood the key message in what the speaker is saying, while also enabling both parties to check that they are on the same page. Communication is a potentially messy process, and meanings can be misarticulated and misinterpreted; reflective listening circumvents this danger by giving both partners the opportunity to collaboratively shape between them the meaning of what has been said. Reflective listening statements most usually take the form of a sentence that contains the word 'You . . .', or some variant (e.g. 'You sound like you aren't sure where to go next from here', or 'You're excited about the new opportunity this presents', or 'As well as being concerned about the situation, you're also worried about how others will react') and might encapsulate, for example:

- An experience the person has had.
- How an experience has impacted on them.

- The person's point of view.
- What the person is thinking.
- How the person is feeling.
- A dilemma or decision the person is facing.
- An idea the person has had or an action they plan to take.
- Something of importance to the person.
- Something the person wants to achieve.

The skill of reflective listening is described in countless books, but the two accounts that I have found particularly helpful in developing proficiency with this vital life skill are those by Gordon ([1970] 2000) and Miller & Rollnick (2002). Thomas Gordon introduces the idea of 'roadblocks' to communication, pointing out the usual communication patterns that we tend to use when responding to someone (e.g. reassuring, judging, advising, disagreeing, moralizing) which prevent us from 'staying with' the other person and truly understanding their meaning. If you have not read Gordon's work before, I strongly recommend that you do, but be warned: it is a sobering wake-up call as you recall all the times you have responded in such ways. You may also begin to notice how often the roadblocks occur in everyday interactions (so many opportunities for connection missed); as Carl Rogers notes, empathy can be a rare thing indeed. The other side of it is that, however, if you can learn to connect with people in this way it is genuinely life-changing and life-enriching.

Sometimes, novice reflective listeners simply mirror what has been said, and find that this feels both unnatural and unhelpful. Indeed, such parroting requires little skill on the part of the listener, and involves little expenditure of effort in the service of understanding the speaker's meaning. However, in their seminal work on *Motivational Interviewing,* Miller & Rollnick (2002) point out that there can be different 'layers' of reflective listening, starting with those where the listener uses words that literally echo what the speaker has said, through to those which add meaning and momentum to the conversation by getting to the real message that underpins the words on the surface. They point out that, if it feels like the conversation is going nowhere, the problem may well be one of insufficient depth of reflection on the part of the listener. Different layers of listening are indicated in Table 3.1.

The danger of providing examples is that they all sound very mechanical, whereas genuine, authentic reflective listening is really anything but. Examples are provided purely to illustrate the point about different depths of reflection, rather than suggesting prescribed scripts for the coach to use. Reflective listening needs to be authentic, genuine, sincere, and above all, natural. To make this come alive, and to see how a person reacts to being listened to in this way, I invite you to watch a YouTube video of Carl Rogers working with a patient called 'Gloria'. If you are interested in seeking further guidance on how to listen reflectively and receive people empathically, you can also investigate Marshall Rosenberg's work on *Non-Violent Communication* (Rosenberg, 2003; www.cnvc.org). Rosenberg provides us

Table 3.1 Layers of listening

Mirroring Repeating back exactly what has been said, either in whole or in part.	*Example* Coachee: 'It's been a tough week.' Coach: 'You've had a tough week this week.'
Paraphrasing Using different words to rearticulate the person's meaning.	*Example* Coachee: 'It's been a tough week.' Coach: 'This week has been particularly challenging.'
Continuing the paragraph Venturing the next sentence on the basis of the cues the person is sending.	*Example* Coachee: 'It's been a tough week.' Coach: ' … And it's hit you.' Or … Coach: '… But you've come through it.'
Reflecting feelings Empathizing. Guessing at the feeling that underlies the spoken words.	*Example* Coachee: 'It's been a tough week.' Coach: 'You're feeling exhausted.'
Reflecting needs Guessing at the need that underlies the feeling.	*Example* Coachee: 'It's been a tough week.' Coach: 'You're feeling exhausted and you need some space and rest to recharge.'

with a vocabulary of feelings and core human needs that we can use to make sense of a person's (or our own) experience, and a style of communication that can be used to hear and articulate the feelings and needs that underpin a person's talk. For Rosenberg, it does not matter if we attempt to communicate understanding and are wide of the mark, as the person will correct us; what matters is that we *try.*

The coachee's experience or feelings can also be validated by the coach through expressions such as 'How upsetting!' or 'I understand that being really important to you' or 'What a difficult situation'. While these introduce more of the coach's own perspective, it makes sense for them to be included in the discussion about reflective listening since they are another way of communicating understanding of the coachee's experience and building rapport between coach and coachee.

Clarifying and elaborating

Sometimes in the course of a conversation the coachee's meaning may not be clear, and we may need to ask them to clarify ('How do you mean?', 'Do you mean x or y . . .?', 'I think you mean . . . Is that right?', 'In what way?'). Clarification becomes even more important when we recognize that we can all have a tendency to make inaccurate interpretations about the meaning of something someone has said on the basis of our own assumptions, prior experiences and expectations. A useful strategy to support clarification is *elaborating*, in which the coach gets a bit more information by asking the coachee to expand on something they have already said: 'Can you tell me a bit more about . . .?'.

Summarizing

At suitable moments in the conversation, the coach can group together and summarize the key points that the coachee has made before the discussion continues further: 'So what I'm hearing so far is ...', 'So far we've discussed ...' This further reinforces the message that the coachee has been heard, adds focus and momentum to the conversation, and enables both parties to make sure that they are on the same page. When the coach is summarizing, the coachee has the opportunity to hear their story rearticulated, to step back from their thoughts, to re-evaluate them, and to think about where they might wish to take the conversation next. It also gives the coach an opportunity to take stock and think about other questions or avenues of exploration that might be helpful. It is a valuable intervention, especially if one is feeling stuck about where to go next. When in doubt: summarize!

Questioning

Questions are one of the most important tools in the coach's toolbox, since they engage the coachee in actively thinking about their situation, their internal and external experience, and what they might eventually do. There are a number of different styles of question the coach might use, and different writers use slightly different terminology to describe them (see e.g. Downey, 2003; Starr, 2003). There are *open questions*, which are pure enquiry and encourage open exploration (e.g. 'What's going on for you?'); *closed questions*, which limit response options (e.g. 'Is that the most important thing for us to focus on?'); and *steered questions*, which take the coachee's thinking down a certain avenue (e.g. 'How would you like things to be different?'). It is typically more helpful to begin with open enquiry and then to introduce a greater degree of steer to the questioning as is appropriate to the situation and the needs of the coachee; of course, there are always exceptions to this rule. Some categories of question that a coach might draw on are indicated in Table 3.2.

Note the use of a range of question stems – e.g. What?, Where?, When?, Who? and How? We will return to areas of exploration that a coach might use questioning to explore at various points in Part 2.

Drawing attention

Here, the coach can use questions or statements to draw the coachee's attention to particular aspects of their story or situation, for example: 'What was happening there, do you think?', 'Tell me more about how he reacted', 'What was going on inside you at that moment?'. In this way, potentially important aspects of the coachee's experience can be brought to their awareness.

Noticing

Noticing is a strategy where the coach offers an observation about, for example, something that has happened in the coachee's story or something they have noticed

Table 3.2 Categories of question

Questions that ...	Example
Initiate	'What would you like to talk about?'
Elicit	'What happened?' 'How did you feel?' 'What are your thoughts about it?'
Clarify	'What exactly was it about it that pleased you?' 'Specifically, what did he say?' 'What did you see?' 'Where would you notice a difference if you achieved this change?' 'Who else would notice?' 'When did it happen?' 'How did that happen?'
Check-in	'Are we talking about the thing that is most important to you?' 'How is this conversation going for you?' 'Is this helpful?' 'Am I understanding you correctly?'
Invite action	'What are your options?' 'What do you think you might do?' 'When might you do that?' 'How might you go about that?' 'Who might be able to help you?'
Support reflection	'What was the benefit of that?' 'What have you learned from that?' 'What are the key points you can take away from that experience?' 'What might you do next time?' 'How can you apply that learning in future?'

about the coachee's behaviour in the session. For example: 'I've noticed that's twice now you've come back to that point' or 'I noticed that you gave yourself some time before acting there.' This is one way in which the coach can draw the coachee's attention to aspects of their behaviour or situation, and gives the coachee the opportunity to determine whether or not the observation is of significance. If so, it can be explored further. If not, the conversation can move on.

Wondering aloud

Sometimes open questioning does not lead to helpful insights, and the coachee may benefit from their thinking being drawn to a particular possibility by the coach. Wondering aloud, or musing, provides more steer to the coachee's reflection by the coach explicitly sharing their inner thought process with the coachee, for example: 'I'm wondering if, maybe, he was a bit unsure about how to react', 'I'm wondering if there's a way to tap into those resources . . .', 'I'm wondering if you might be telling yourself something like . . .'. This is not to say that the coach's line of thinking will be helpful, but the act of (tentatively) modelling the thought process enables the coachee to consider it and evaluate its relevance and usefulness.

Giving information

On some occasions the coach may be in possession of a piece of information that it might be helpful to signpost to the coachee – for example, the coach may know of a particular book, website, or some other source of guidance that may be relevant to the coachee's situation. In such circumstances, the key is to make sure that the information is wanted ('If you like, there is something I could share with you . . .?'), to be tentative ('Something that's been helpful to others sometimes is . . .'), and to then give the person space and time to think about what they make of it and how they might (if at all) make use of it ('What are your thoughts?').

Making suggestions

The use of suggestions in coaching – and, indeed, in any helping conversation – merits careful consideration. Certainly, a number of dangers can be associated with suggestions that are offered too quickly, too often, or delivered in a directive style, as follows:

- Suggestions can stop the person from thinking for themselves.
- It can put the person in a 'one-down' position, making them the recipient of the coach's proposed solutions.
- The person may not be receptive to a suggestion offered before they are ready for it.
- The coachee, having not invested in the development of the solution, may not 'own' the solution and may be less committed to carrying it out, especially if the coach has offered the suggestion too soon, without the coachee's thinking having developed to the point where they are ready for it.
- Suggestions can leave the person feeling a bit deskilled ('You didn't think I could get there by myself?').
- If we are not careful, we can assume responsibility for the strategy and whether or not it is successful.
- Offering suggestions can lead to a frustrating wrestling-match conversation in which the coach keeps offering ideas and the coachee keeps batting them back.
- The suggestion may lead to a goal that the coach has in mind, but the coachee doesn't.

Clearly, we must tread cautiously when entering the territory of suggestions. Having said that, there are also times when the coachee may benefit from being able to give consideration to a suggestion that the coach has in mind about, for example, a way of approaching a situation. To avoid the aforementioned dangers, the coach must pay particular attention to the conditions under which the suggestion is offered, including the *timing* of the suggestion, whether the suggestion is wanted, the style in which the suggestion is offered, and what is done after the suggestion has been made. Before offering suggestions, the coach can have the following questions in mind:

- Has the person had an opportunity to think things through for themselves?
- Do I have a suggestion that may be helpful?
- Does the coachee want to hear a suggestion? Have I asked permission to share?

If the above conditions are satisfied, the suggestion can be offered in a tentative, non-directive style, before then seeking the coachee's opinion about the relevance of the idea to their situation. Rather than 'What I think you should do is . . .', the style is more akin to: 'One option you might consider among the others you are thinking about is . . .' or 'Something I have seen work for others is . . . I don't know if that would be of help to you . . . What do you think?' This enables the coach to add ideas to the pool of options being considered, while respecting the coachee's position as an equal partner in the collaboration and inviting them to *actively evaluate* the suggestion offered. Later in the conversation, the coachee will determine exactly how they want to proceed, and they may or may not make use of all or part of the coach's contribution.

Giving feedback

Feedback is information about one's actions and/or their impact in relation to a goal one wants to achieve (Schein, 1988), and in some circumstances the coach may elect to offer this to the coachee if it is considered appropriate. Feedback stands a better chance of being positively received if it is: wanted; well-intentioned; given in the right context; refers to a specific action and circumstance rather than a general trait; describes the impact of that action; and is constructive, i.e. it affirms what they are doing well or offers an alternative course of action to the coachee that may support them in attaining their desired outcome. The coachee's opinion can then be sought about the feedback, while emphasizing their right to take or leave as much or as little of it as is desired so as to respect their autonomy. For example: 'I noticed that you went away and thought about it before acting, which seemed to help you approach it coolly and make sure your own needs were met. Is that fair?', or, 'I noticed that when you gave the task instruction the group started moving before you had finished talking . . . I wondered if it might help you to create the calmer atmosphere you want if you started instructions by first saying "When I say 'Go'" or something like that . . . What do you think?' We will return to the theme of feedback in Chapter 6.

Giving opinion

As a general rule, the coach's opinions should be kept out of the conversation as the whole point is to support the coachee to form their own opinion about their situation and what they might do. However, there may be occasions when the coachee specifically asks for the coach's opinion – in which case, the coach may consider whether they have an opinion or not and, if so, authentically share it with the coachee. Alternatively, the coach may invite the coachee to consider whether they would like to hear an opinion. Either way, the style and manner in which this is done is important. The coach can explain the rationale for their opinion so that it is open to the coachee's scrutiny, emphasize that it is *just* opinion, and then immediately consult the coachee as to their view about the contribution.

Self-disclosure

In some circumstances, the coach can deliberately offer something of their own history for the coachee to consider. This can be useful where drawing parallels helps to make sense of the coachee's situation, or where sharing personal stories may help to build rapport, normalize the coachee's experience, or offer a springboard for further thought. Of course, since the session is about the coachee rather than the coach, this is a strategy to be used sparingly. The other way in which self-disclosure can be helpful is if the coach is willing to authentically share what is going on for them during the session – for example, if the coach is feeling confused there may be work to do to achieve greater clarity of focus, and putting this on the table may provide the coachee with helpful feedback.

To give another example of the value of self-disclosure, I was recently in a coaching session with a senior leader in a secondary school who had concerns about being called to attend a Special Educational Needs Tribunal as a witness. They had not been through the process before, did not know what the process would involve, were unsure how they should approach their role, and understandably had some concerns about this. The person then moved on to begin talking about another subject, at which point I noticed that my mind was not fully with them and was partially lingering on the subject of the tribunal. I decided to put that on the table and to check in with them, assuring that if they wanted to continue talking about the new subject that we would do so – and they would have my full attention on it – but that we could also return to the discussion about the tribunal if desired. They decided that, actually, talking about the tribunal would be more helpful and so we returned to discussing that theme.

Using the skills in practice

With such a broad spectrum of skills that can be called upon, it can seem a little daunting if one starts wondering what may be the 'right' thing to do at any given moment. Having a sense of which skill it might be helpful to draw upon at different times and in different situations is something that comes with practice and experience, but even then no one always gets it right, and there is no way of knowing what will be helpful in advance of doing it; the only thing you can do is use a skill and then determine from the coachee's reaction and the feel of the session whether you were along the right lines or whether you need to change tack. Viewed in this way, as Myles Downey (2003) notes, unless you do something that irrevocably damages the relationship, it is almost impossible to fail: all you get is feedback.

A key principle to remember when drawing from the toolbox is that the aim is to stimulate the coachee's active engagement and reflection and, as far as possible, to keep out of their way. For this reason it usually helps to begin with the skills that inhabit the non-directive end of the continuum, and to then move down the spectrum as befits the needs of the coachee and the situation. Sometimes 'dropping down' more quickly may be appropriate, but there are no hard-and-fast rules as to when that might be the case. Whatever is done, the coach does no more than is necessary, and is always respectful of the coachee's experience and their status as an equal partner in the conversation. The coach maintains an autonomy-supportive style, which seeks the coachee's view about the contribution being offered and emphasizes their right to take or leave as much or as little of it as is desired (Miller & Rollnick, 2002).

There is another core skill that coaches require, which does not neatly fit into the directive/non-directive continuum outlined in this chapter. This is the skill of *reframing*, in which the coach supports the coachee to change the meaning they make of a particular event in order to change the impact it has on their feelings and behaviour; this is achieved by, basically, putting a different spin on the event or changing the context – the 'frame' – in which it is interpreted. For example:

- Reframing a 'failure' as a *learning experience.*
- Reframing a 'failed attempt to change' as a *try.*
- Reframing a 'problem' as an *opportunity.*

Of course, the coach cannot necessarily reframe an event *for* a coachee, since it is the coachee who needs to see the event differently; however, they may be able to introduce or scaffold this process by asking questions such as, for example: 'I wonder if there is a way of reframing this . . .?' or 'I wonder if it's possible to see it in a different light?' The aim is to generate a new way of construing the event so that there is a constructive impact on the individual's thoughts, feelings and behaviour.

Finally, a word of caution: it is impossible to totally capture in print the subtle nature of effective rapport-building and communication skills. These are all just examples that provide some form of guidance, but they cannot be used mechanically and they are no substitute for genuine, authentic interaction. In sessions, I often find myself connecting and communicating with people in ways that are not listed here, which have never appeared in a coaching or psychology textbook and which I would struggle to put into words in a meaningful way. The reality is best understood by watching the process in action, since the true essence of what contributes towards or detracts from a meaningful connection between any two unique individuals is something that transcends the written word.

Summary

Coaches have a broad toolbox of skills that can be drawn upon to build rapport, communicate understanding, facilitate reflection, and support coachees in their thinking and action planning. These range from those skills that are purely non-directive in nature (e.g. giving space, attentive listening), to those that introduce more steer to the conversation (e.g. steered questions), or those that involve the coach sharing thoughts or perspectives of their own (e.g. making suggestions, self-disclosure). The continuum of skills encompasses the following.

Non-directive (following the coachee's thoughts)

- Giving space
- Attentive listening
- Encouraging
- Reflective listening
- Clarifying and elaborating
- Summarizing
- Questioning (open, closed, steered)
- Drawing attention
- Noticing
- Wondering aloud
- Giving information
- Making suggestions
- Giving feedback
- Giving opinion
- Self-disclosure

Directive (introducing the coach's thoughts)

The emphasis in coaching is on non-directive facilitation, but that is not to say that there is no room in a coaching conversation for the coach to offer thoughts or contributions of their own. The over-use of such methods should be avoided, but if used judiciously, timed well, and delivered in the appropriate style, they can form an important part of the coach's repertoire. Successful coaching requires the coach to be adept at using a range of skills and, moreover, to have the ability to judge when it might be helpful to draw upon them according to the needs of the situation and the coachee. In this way the coaching conversation is a collaborative exploration, with the coach acting as a facilitator and a resource, but with the coachee retaining responsibility for the direction and nature of change.

We will bring this chapter to a close with a piece of self-disclosure: in the very first coaching session I facilitated, I exercised a number of the above skills, many of them well, and yet the conversation meandered and didn't really go anywhere. As an analogy, it was as if I was very good at hammering nails into pieces of wood but was not paying attention to the overall shape of the construction that we were building. At the end of it, all that was left was a number of bits of wood on the floor with nails sticking out of them, and a rather dissatisfied client. This was a powerful learning point and emphasized the importance of using structure to add shape, direction and momentum to coaching conversations. A classic framework for structuring a coaching conversation will be described in Chapter 4.

Suggested reading

Downey, M. (2003). *Effective Coaching: Lessons from the Coach's Coach.* Thomson-Texere.
Starr, J. (2003). *The Coaching Manual.* London: Prentice Hall.

Chapter 4

Structure in coaching

> It is very important to structure the coaching conversation, otherwise it is just a conversation, a friendly chat which may lead nowhere. Coaching is essentially a structured, goal-directed conversation that aims to bring about positive purposeful change.
>
> (Greene & Grant, 2003, p. 100)

In the context of coaching, a structure is an overarching framework that outlines the different areas that might be explored in the course of a coaching conversation, with the aim of helping the coachee to move towards their goals or achieve change (Greene & Grant, 2003). This chapter will provide a detailed overview of one of the most well-known generic coaching structures: GROW or I-GROW. Other guiding frameworks drawn specifically from the domain of coaching psychology (e.g. SPACE – Edgerton & Palmer, 1995; ABCDE – Ellis, 1988) will be introduced later in the book.

Structures have a number of benefits, as follows:

- They can guide the coach's questioning, suggesting discussion areas that might be helpfully explored.
- They can provide shape, direction, progression and momentum to the conversation.
- They can act as an aide-memoire to the coach who might be wondering how next to be of help to the coachee. Recall of the structures is often facilitated by the use of an acronym, so they are accessible even in times of confusion or panic.
- They are a useful tool for supporting both coach and coachee to take stock of what has and has not been discussed in the session, and the extent to which different aspects have been covered.
- They can be explicitly shared with coachees so that they can use the structures independently outside the context of the coaching session.

There are also some cautionary caveats to bear in mind about the use of structures, which will be discussed later in the chapter. For now, we begin with what is probably the most well-known coaching model.

The GROW (or I-GROW or T-GROW) model

The GROW model was originally developed by Graham Alexander, and was later popularized by Sir John Whitmore (Whitmore, 2002). The different stages of the model can be summarized as follows:

- **Goal**   What do you want to achieve?
- **Reality**   What is happening now?
- **Options**   What might you do?
- **Will** (or **Wrap-up**)   What will you do?

The model has since been expanded to involve an initial stage which represents either the **T**opic for discussion (T-GROW – see Downey, 2003) or the **I**ssues the coachee wants to focus on in the conversation or engagement (I-GROW – see Greene & Grant, 2003). The latter will be outlined in detail below.

Issues

The first stage of the model enables the coachee to talk about the general issues or themes that they would like to explore (e.g. managing low-level disruption in the classroom, improving the quality of student engagement, tackling staff underperformance). This is an opportunity for the coach to attend to the coachee's experience, and to try to clarify the central topic for coaching:

- 'What would you like to focus on?'
- 'What would you say are the themes emerging here?'
- 'In what way is this a problem?'

If coachees are facing complex situations then there may be a number of strands to consider, and the coach can be of help in clarifying and summarizing the key points. Where there are a number of issues, *collapsing* and *prioritizing* questions can be helpful:

- 'So let me summarize, it sounds like some of the key issues are . . .'
- 'Of all the themes you've mentioned, which would you most like us to work on?'
- 'Given that we may not be able to work on them all, where would be a good place to start?'
- 'What would you like to work on in the hour we have?'

Goals

Goals are a key feature of coaching conversations, and at various points in the conversation the coach can help the coachee to clarify the goals they have for the immediate session, the engagement and the future. Questions that the coach might ask at this stage include:

- 'What would you like to get out of this session?'
- 'When our hour is up, how will you know if this session has been useful to you?'
- 'We have x sessions together . . . what would you like to achieve?'
- 'How would you like things to be different?'

Whitmore (2002) notes that it can be useful to differentiate between *end goals* (those that describe the final objective, e.g. 'To feel more confident about speaking in public') and *performance goals* (those which define the specific performance required to enable movement towards the end goal, e.g. 'To share a piece of information with a group of staff during morning briefing'). Beere & Broughton (2013) suggest that 'If an end [goal] is where you want to get to, then performance [goals] are the milestones along the way' (p. 118). While that may be the case, a key distinction to remember is that performance goals are usually more under the coachee's direct control (Whitmore, 2002).

The coach needs to be alert at this stage to some of the potential pitfalls associated with establishing goals, such as *other-focused* goals (goals which require someone else to change and which are therefore outside the coachee's control); *woolly* goals (for example, a goal such as 'To improve my performance' is unlikely to provide the necessary focus and direction for coaching); *over-ambitious* or *under-ambitious* goals (both of which can undermine motivation and commitment); and goals which are *avoidance-focused* rather than *approach-focused* (i.e. those which are phrased in terms of something *not* happening – e.g. 'Stop saying "shush" to get attention' – which do not provide a focus on desired outcomes and which can be less motivating; see Elliot & Harackiewicz, 1996). Harris (2008) describes the latter as a 'dead person's goals' – i.e. a goal that a dead person can do more effectively than you. To counteract these difficulties, coachees can be helped to transform their vague or general goals into SMART objectives. Different authors explain this acronym using different terms (see e.g. Whitmore, 2002) but my own preference is to consider whether goals are 'specific, measurable, achievable, relevant, and timed'. To help a coachee transform a vague or general goal into a SMART objective, a coach can use a number of questions, such as:

- 'When you have achieved that, how will you know?'
- 'Imagine it is [time frame] from now and you have made progress in this area . . . What will that look like?'
- 'How will others know that this change has happened?'
- 'What will others see you doing instead of [behaviour the coachee wants to stop doing]?'
- 'What would I see if I was watching on a video? What would I hear?'

- 'How much control do you have over that?'
- 'Will this help you to achieve your overall goal?'
- 'By when?'

It is also important to remember that goals can be revisited, reshaped and revised as the session or engagement continues.

Reality

Once goals have been established, the focus can shift to an exploration of the coachee's present reality to establish what is going on in the present and the distance between the coachee's current situation and their goal. Whitmore (2002) suggests that the interrogatives What?, When?, Where?, Who? and How much? are most helpful in terms of examining the coachee's reality, as they are more likely to bypass subjective interpretations:

- 'What's the present situation?'
- 'What's happening?'
- 'Can you give me an example?'
- 'In what way does it impact on you?'
- 'What have you done already?'
- 'What's working?'
- 'Who is involved?'
- 'What resources do you have to draw on?'
- 'What other factors might we need to consider?'
- 'What? When? Where? Who? How much?'

Options

Having explored the client's reality, the conversation can move on to a consideration of options available to the client, generating a range of possible courses of action. This could be done through the use of general open questions (e.g. 'What options do you have?'), steered questions (e.g. 'What has worked for you previously in similar situations?') or, with permission, with the coach also making suggestions for the client to consider.

- 'What options do you have?'
- 'What else might you try?'
- 'What have you done before in other situations?'
- 'What has worked for you in other contexts?'
- 'What have you seen others do that might help?'
- 'What have you thought about doing but not tried yet?'
- 'Would you like some suggestions?'

Will/Wrap-up

The final phase of coaching involves diverging on one or more of the possibilities that have been considered and eliciting a commitment to action. Questions the coach might ask at this stage include:

- 'What are you going to do?'
- 'When will you do it?'
- 'What might you try in the next few days/the next lesson?'
- 'How will you know if this is helping?'
- 'What barriers might you encounter?'
- 'Who could help you to achieve this?'
- 'On a scale of 0–10, how committed are you to taking this action?'

Throughout, it is important for the coach to attend carefully to the coachee's responses, using the core coaching skills that were outlined in Chapter 3 (e.g. reflecting, clarifying, summarizing, paraphrasing, etc.). This ensures that the coachee feels heard and that the coach has understood the coachee correctly.

I-GROW in action

The following is an example of the I-GROW model being applied in practice, with the stages of the framework emphasized using parentheses.

A coach is working with a teacher and Learning Support Assistant (LSA) who are concerned that a child has not made progress in his spelling (clarifying the **I**ssue). In the coaching session, the team state that they would like to develop a plan for supporting the child to move forward with his spelling skills (**G**oal for the session). Further questioning clarifies that, while the boy can spell some common high frequency words, there are particular spelling patterns that he seems to struggle with (exploring the present **R**eality). When asked what progress would look like, the team respond that they would like the boy to be able to spell eighteen new words by the end of term (**G**oal for the future). The coach asks the team to think about where the child is now in relation to that goal, and what would constitute a step forward. They suggest that they would like the boy to learn six new spellings each week, a goal which is then shaped further through the coach's questioning ('Which words?', 'How will you know he can spell them?'). This generates a specific, measurable achievable goal that the team (and, indeed, the child) can work towards. The team also decide that they will use pieces of the boy's writing to identify particular target words to focus on each day. The discussion then turns to exploring possibilities as to how this might be achieved (generating **O**ptions). The teacher and LSA suggest that the child could spend a short amount of time each morning practising how to spell particular words using a particular computer program. Another option considered is to provide the child with a 'word fan' which he can refer to throughout the day. This is translated into an action plan (**W**ill/**W**rap-up), and it is agreed to experiment and monitor the boy's progress.

Structures: pros and cons

Having outlined a possible structure that the coach can call on, and having emphasized its benefits, it is also important to acknowledge its limitations. First, it should be stated that coaching sessions are not always this neat and tidy. True enough, in some sessions there is a clear progression that could be represented by these stages, and there is certainly something satisfying about it when that happens. However, coaching is a non-linear and dynamic process, and more often it is the case that coach and coachee will fluidly move around the different components of these (or other) models.

Second, the downside of structures is that, by having the structure in mind, one can pay too much attention to the framework instead of being sensitive to where the coachee is at and what their needs are at that moment. A head teacher whose school has just received a negative inspection evaluation – an experience with a potentially significant emotional impact – may not necessarily be ready to immediately start talking about their goals for the session or the future. Obviously, there is a judgement call to be made here, and the coach needs to pay attention to where the coachee may be 'at' and what their needs are. Sometimes, people just need to talk, to express their feelings and to be heard by an understanding listener, and efforts to force the conversation in other directions before the coachee is ready would be both insensitive and unhelpful. If that is the case, the coach can give proper attention to the immediate needs of the coachee, knowing that the structures are always there to call upon later in the session if it seems appropriate to do so. In fact, the greatest value of structures – in my view – is that they paradoxically enable the coach to give their full attention to where the coachee might need to take the conversation at any particular moment, with the security of a framework behind them. Structures provide a helpful anchor that enable coach and coachee to go off-piste without ending up lost and wondering how to get back to the path. With a framework to guide, the coach is able to follow the coachee's lead and attentively pursue whatever line of exploration seems helpful, always knowing that the structure is there to return to if and when it feels necessary. In this way, departing from structure is not an indication of the conversation going nowhere, but a conscious, informed choice that one makes in order to be responsive to the needs of the coachee.

Summary

- Structures are overarching frameworks that can guide the coach's questioning in the course of a coaching session.
- Structures can add direction, progression and momentum to a conversation.

- The most well-known generic coaching model is the GROW or I-GROW model (**I**ssues, **G**oals, **R**eality, **O**ptions, **W**ill/**W**rap-up).
- Other coaching structures will be outlined later in this book.
- A structure is a guide that should not prevent the coach from attending to the needs of the coachee or exploring other areas of conversation.

The structure described here, along with the principles and core skills covered in Chapters 2 and 3, represent the fundamental foundation skills in the coach's toolbox. Some might be critical of the I-GROW model as being an oversimplification, but in my view that is, in fact, its primary strength: that it can be readily learned, recalled and applied in a broad range of situations. Moreover, as we shall see later, the model is flexible enough to allow for the incorporation of other principles and practices. The model is therefore as elegant or comprehensive as one wants it to be, making it an essential foundation tool for both the novice and experienced coach alike. Now, with the foundations in place, we can further enrich and enhance the practice of coaching by incorporating a range of principles and methods that are drawn from across the domains of theoretical and applied psychology.

Suggested reading

Whitmore, J. ([1992] 2002). *Coaching for Performance: GROWing People, Performance and Purpose*. London: Nicholas Brealey Publishing.

Chapter 5

Psychology in coaching

> The people at large will have to be their own psychologists and make their own applications of the principles we establish . . . Our responsibility is less to assume the role of experts and try to apply psychology ourselves than to give it away to the people who really need it . . .
>
> (Miller, 1969, p. 1071)

Psychology has a rich, hundred-year history of research, literature and practice that can inform our understanding of how we can support others to change and develop (Grant & Cavanagh, 2007; Palmer & Whybrow, 2007). Of course, there is a vast body of knowledge to navigate, and not all of it is specifically relevant to the coaching relationship, nor readily applicable to the practice of coaching in schools. There has therefore been a process of sifting in determining the approaches that will be described in this chapter. That process has inevitably been influenced by my own experience, biases and preferences, and there will be other methods relevant to coaching that are not covered here (see, for example, Allan & Whybrow, 2007; Harris, 2008; Law, 2013; Spinelli & Horner, 2007). My intention is not to provide a comprehensive overview of relevant theories, principles and techniques, but to give you a whistle-stop tour of some of those that I have found useful in practice and that inform the applications explored in Part 2. In order of presentation, those are:

1   The person-centred approach (Rogers, [1951] 2003, 1961).
2   Solution-Focused Brief Therapy (de Shazer, 1985, 1988; Berg & De Jong, 2002).
3   Cognitive-behavioural psychology (Beck, 1967, 1976; Ellis, 1962).
4   Albert Bandura's Self-Efficacy Theory (Bandura, 1977, 1997).
5   The 'stages of change' model (DiClemente & Prochaska, 1998).
6   Self-Determination Theory (Deci & Ryan, 1985; Ryan & Deci, 2000).
7   Motivational Interviewing (Miller & Rollnick, 2002).
8   Positive psychology (Seligman, 2003, 2011; Snyder & Lopez, 2005).
9   Research into the common factors of change, i.e. the factors that contribute to the effectiveness of helping relationships (Bordin, 1979; Murphy & Duncan, 2007).

These nine influences will be described below, with clarification of how each specifically applies to the practice of coaching. You will also notice how some of these influences provide a theoretical or research-based rationale for some of the coaching principles and techniques described in Chapters 2–4. References are included should you wish to explore any of the approaches in greater depth – indeed, whole books have been written about all of these topics, so it is important to remember that this section is an overview only. Please note that models and techniques will only be introduced here, and their application will not be described in detail in this chapter; however, where applicable, you will be signposted to parts of the book where further explanation, description or illustration can be found.

The spirit of this chapter is one of *giving psychology away*, reflecting George Miller's long-standing call for psychology to be widely shared for the benefit of people and society. Therefore, as you read, you might like to reflect on the following questions:

- To what extent does this speak to me about my experience?
- How could I make use of this in my role/work as a coach?

Psychological principles and approaches

I The person-centred approach

> If I can provide a certain type of relationship, the other person will discover within himself the capacity to use that relationship for growth, and change and personal development will occur.
>
> (Rogers, 1961, p. 33)

The person-centred approach to psychotherapy was famously pioneered by Carl Rogers ([1951] 2003, 1961). At its heart was a fundamental philosophical belief in the worth and significance of other people, a belief that clients should be respected and treated with dignity as separate, equal individuals who have the right to self-determination (Rogers, [1951] 2003). A core assumption of the person-centred approach is that people have an inherent tendency towards growth and development (what Rogers called the 'actualizing tendency'), and that this potential is released in a social environment where the person feels unthreatened, understood, valued and accepted. In coaching, the coach seeks to create this climate through the expression of what Rogers argued are the 'core conditions' that are necessary for change to occur:

- The coach demonstrates regard for the coachee as a person, and values their experience and perspectives. Suspending the tendency to judge or evaluate, the coach endeavours to listen to and interact with the coachee from a position of non-judgemental acceptance, demonstrating regard for their feelings and perspectives and acting with sensitivity and care. It is important to note that this does not imply agreeing with or colluding with the coachee, but instead accepting their right to be as they are and to see things as they do.

- There is a desire on the part of the coach to enter into the coachee's private world, to attempt to sense their meaning and to see things from their perspective. Furthermore, the coach then attempts to communicate understanding and empathy to the coachee so that the coachee feels heard and is able to correct any miscommunication or misinterpretation. The skill of reflective listening, described in Chapter 3, is central to this process.
- The coach behaves with genuineness and transparency so that the coachee trusts that nothing is hidden, and – hopefully – regards the coach as trustworthy, dependable and consistent, a person who behaves and communicates with sincerity and can be relied upon to be real in the relationship.

The principles of person-centred coaching run throughout each of the engagements described, and provide the 'frame' for all other approaches described in this book.

2 Solution-Focused Brief Therapy

> There's nothing wrong with you that what's right with you couldn't fix.
> (Baruch Shalem, cited in O'Connell, 2002, p. 19)

In the 1980s, a radical new approach to therapy emerged from the work of the team at the Brief Family Therapy Centre in Milwaukee, led by Steve de Shazer and Insoo Kim Berg (de Shazer, 1985, 1988; Berg & De Jong, 2002). De Shazer, Berg and their team revolutionized therapy by, for example, emphasizing talk about the client's preferred future instead of their problems; abandoning the notion of the therapist as 'expert', and spending time exploring what was *right* with their clients instead of focusing on their alleged deficiencies. With its emphasis on people's strengths, their imagined preferred futures, and how they can unlock and harness their resources to take small steps forward, the relevance of SFBT to coaching is clear. It is therefore not surprising that the two have been directly linked in a number of publications that explicitly incorporate the principles and techniques of SFBT into coaching practice (see e.g. Greene & Grant, 2003; Iveson *et al.*, 2012; Jackson & McKergow, 2002; O'Connell & Palmer, 2007; O'Connell *et al.*, 2012). In the context of solution-focused coaching (SFC), key tenets and principles include:

- It is not necessary to explore and understand the origin of a 'problem' in order to be able to begin constructing a solution; instead, the coach can support the coachee to obtain clarity about the preferred future they would like to see happening. This then provides the focus and direction for the engagement.
- Coachees are resourceful people who bring strengths, skills and qualities to the engagement. The coach can attempt to elicit these and support the coachee

to harness their resources as they attempt to move towards their preferred future.

- There are always exceptions in the coachee's life or experience – that is, times when the preferred future is already happening (even if only in part) or times when 'the problem' isn't quite as bad. These represent valuable sources of learning, and the coach can actively guide a search for such exceptions.
- Small changes can lead to bigger changes. Therefore, the coach can focus on helping the coachee to plan a small step forward that will constitute a meaningful sign of improvement.

The principles and practices of SFC inform each of the engagements presented in Part 2, while a number of solution-focused techniques are detailed in Chapters 8, 10 and 12.

3 Cognitive-behavioural psychology

> People are not disturbed by things, but by the views they take of them.
>
> (Epictetus, 1st century AD)

> There's nothing either good or bad but thinking makes it so.
>
> (William Shakespeare, *Hamlet*)

Cognitive-behavioural psychology rests on the fundamental assumption that our feelings are not determined by events themselves, but rather the meaning we make of those events through our thoughts and interpretations (Beck, 1967, 1976; Ellis, 1962). The central role that cognitions (thoughts and images) play in determining our feelings and behaviour is neatly encapsulated in Albert Ellis's ABC model of emotional disturbance (Ellis, 1962, 1988, 2001). In Ellis's model, emotional and behavioural **C**onsequences ('C') are not caused directly by the **A**ctivating event itself ('A'), but are instead the product of **B**eliefs ('B') the individual holds about the event in question. The key distinction is that A contributes to but does not itself cause C; rather, it is the beliefs at B that determine the person's emotional and behavioural reaction. For example:

Activating event	Beliefs about the event	Consequences
Get challenging performance feedback	'That's it, I'm a useless practitioner!'	Anxiety, despondency

At (B), people can experience *thinking errors* that can distort their interpretation of reality and impact negatively on both their feelings and behaviour. These include, for example, *all or nothing thinking* (things are either 'excellent' or 'terrible' with no shades of grey), *personalization* ('This is all my fault' or 'It must be because of me'), *catastrophizing/awfulizing* ('It's a disaster!' or 'That would be awful!'), or *demands* (rigid or inflexible demands of self or others articulated as 'shoulds' or 'musts').

Applied to coaching, this means:

- Sometimes, the way in which a coachee is thinking about a situation may interfere with their performance, development or wellbeing.
- When coachees think about events in extreme, negative, distorted, rigid, or overgeneralized ways, they may be more likely to experience emotional disturbance and self-limiting/goal-defeating behaviours as a result (Dryden, 2011).
- Conversely, if coachees can learn to think in a more balanced, realistic, flexible and adaptive way, they may experience improvement in their feelings and behaviour (Palmer & Szymanska, 2007).
- Crucially, thinking errors can be transformed into more adaptive thoughts through the process of *disputation* (whereby the validity of thinking errors is challenged) and the application of *thinking skills* – flexible and adaptive ways of construing experience that facilitate healthy functioning and goal-achievement (Beck, 2011; Curwen *et al.*, 2000).
- A coach can work with a coachee to support them in recognizing the link between their thoughts, feelings and behaviour; identifying self-limiting thoughts that might be interfering with their performance, development and/ or wellbeing; applying strategies to challenge and transform their self-limiting thoughts; and developing more adaptive ways of thinking and behaving.

The principles and practices of cognitive-behavioural coaching (CBC) are illustrated in Chapters 9, 10 and 13.

4 Self-Efficacy Theory

> [Self-efficacy beliefs] are the most important determinants of the behaviours people choose to engage in and how much they persevere in their efforts in the face of obstacles and challenges.
>
> (Maddux, 2005, p. 277)

The extent to which we will persevere towards our goals and experience a sense of confidence is strongly influenced by our self-efficacy beliefs – that is, the extent to which we believe that we are capable of producing desired results from our own actions (Bandura, 1977, 1997; Maddux, 2005). The important detail here is that this is about our beliefs rather than objective reality; it is therefore possible for people to have skills in a particular domain but at the same time to tell themselves that they do not. Self-efficacy beliefs are domain-specific – that is, we can have high self-efficacy in some areas of our lives and low self-efficacy in others. Furthermore, our sense of efficacy in one area may not automatically generalize to a new context, even if the skills we have are applicable. Instead, we may need to work to bridge between our previous successes and new challenges. Even then, success experiences alone are not sufficient to support the formation of efficacy beliefs; instead, it is how success experiences are processed that matters. Individuals who discount or minimize their successes, or attribute them to external factors (e.g. luck), are unlikely to develop an enhanced sense of self-efficacy.

Applied in the context of coaching, we can:

- Be attentive for signs that self-efficacy beliefs may be relevant to a coachee's situation.
- Ask the coachee about how confident they feel in their ability to make a particular change (a 0–10 scale can be a helpful tool here). Low levels of confidence may be associated with negative self-efficacy beliefs.
- Trawl the coachee's experience for their past successes.
- Support the coachee to transfer their existing skills to new challenges or contexts.
- Facilitate efficacy-supportive processing of success experiences, drawing the coachee's attention to the role they played in events and supporting reflection on what the experience tells them about their capabilities.

Self-efficacy beliefs play a crucial role in the coaching engagement described in Chapter 8.

5 The 'stages of change' model

> Behaviour change [is] a process that occurs in increments and that involves specific and varied tasks . . .
>
> (DiClemente & Velasquez, 2002)

The 'stages of change' model developed by DiClemente & Prochaska (1998) describes a series of stages that people pass through as they change a behaviour. Those stages are:

Precontemplation	The individual is not considering change.
Contemplation	The individual begins to think about making a change.
Preparation	The individual has made a decision to act, and is getting ready for change.
Action	The individual works to implement the change.
Maintenance	The individual works to maintain and consolidate the change.
Relapse	The individual reverts to earlier behaviour and/or a previous stage of the change process.

The aforementioned sequence of stages has been shown to apply across a variety of behaviours, ranging from exercise adoption to gambling to cessation of smoking – see DiClemente & Velasquez (2002) for a summary. Whatever the behaviour, people seem to progress through the same sequence of stages, and the stages appear to be applicable whether the change occurs naturally or with the intervention of a therapist. The crucial point of this is that people moving through the stages may require different tasks at different times. A person at the precontemplation stage is, by definition, not aware of a need to change, and so strategies that can gently bring the possibility of change into their awareness may be a necessary first step. For example, a deputy head once told me how being asked the question 'What impact would you say you're having on the senior leadership team?' drew her attention to the fact that her outspoken style had disrupted the team dynamics and cut short some of the team's valued reflection opportunities. This immediately moved her from the *precontemplation* stage to either *contemplation* or *preparation*, and thereafter prompted further consideration about a change of approach. Working with someone who is at the precontemplation stage as if they are ready to commit to making a change is a mismatch that may lead to dissonance in the relationship and hinder the change effort (see section 7, below).

Applied to coaching, the key messages are as follows:

- When changing behaviour, individuals progress through a common sequence of stages.
- A coachee may enter a coaching engagement in any one of the stages of change cycle.
- Coachees at different stages may need to undertake different tasks. We therefore cannot have a one-size-fits-all approach to supporting others to change their behaviour.
- Careful preparations prior to coaching and at the contracting stage can, if necessary, begin the process of the person moving through the change cycle (see Appendix 1).
- We need to be sensitive to where the coachee is 'at' in the change cycle, and adjust our approach accordingly.
- If there is a mismatch between our approach and the coachee's position in the change cycle, we can obstruct their journey through the change process.

When approaching a coaching engagement, we can have regard to a number of factors that might influence a coachee's readiness for change and that can facilitate or interfere with their journey through the change cycle, as follows (Box 5.1).

Box 5.1 Factors influencing coachee readiness for change

To what extent is the coachee *aware* of a need to change?

To what extent does the coachee *want* to change? *Why* do they want to make this change?

To what extent does the coachee *know how* to change?

To what extent does the coachee feel *confident* in their ability to make the change?

To what extent does the coachee have the *capacity* to change at this time?

To what extent does the coachee have the *support* they need to change?

These factors can then guide our thinking as to how to most appropriately help the coachee to move forward.

6 Self-Determination Theory

> Human beings can be proactive and engaged or, alternatively, passive and alienated, largely as a function of the social conditions in which they develop and function.
>
> (Ryan & Deci, 2000, p. 68)

We cannot approach a coaching engagement – or, indeed, any endeavour in which we seek to support another person to change their behaviour – without an understanding of motivation. Motivation is the driving force behind behaviour, the reason for engaging in (and pursuing) a particular course of action or otherwise, and an understanding of it is essential if we are to be effective agents of change. Motivation is commonly understood as being either *intrinsic* (we do something for its own inherent interest and enjoyment value) or *extrinsic* (we do something in order to attain or avoid a particular outcome). However, this is an oversimplification that fails to capture some crucial subtleties that can helpfully inform the practice of coaching. Thankfully, our understanding of motivation can be further enriched by an awareness of Richard Ryan and Edward Deci's Self-Determination Theory (SDT). Some of the key tenets of SDT, and their applicability to coaching, will be outlined below.

Intrinsic motivation

Intrinsic motivation arises and is sustained in a context where the individual's core psychological needs are satisfied. According to SDT, the core psychological needs are:

* *Competence* – the individual experiences that they are capable.
* *Autonomy* – the individual experiences a sense of volition over their behaviour.
* *Relatedness* – the individual feels secure and connected to others.

A coach can seek to provide the coachee with an experience that satisfies their core psychological needs so as to facilitate the emergence of their intrinsic motivation to change. This principle runs throughout the coaching engagements described in this book, and is particularly relevant to Chapters 6 and 7.

Extrinsic motivation

Obviously, not all human behaviours are intrinsically motivated. Sometimes, people engage in behaviours for their instrumental value rather than for the inherent satisfaction of the behaviour itself, and this is known as *extrinsic* motivation. Extrinsic motivation is classically associated with tangible rewards and punishments, and these indeed represent one form of extrinsic motivation. However, what about the student who does not enjoy his/her homework but completes it because of his/her family's valued work ethic? Or the person who detests their early morning visits to the gym but does so in order to maintain their fitness? Or the person who does not really believe in God but keeps going to church because, well, that's what their family has always done? In the absence of tangible rewards and punishments, what leads individuals to initiate and sustain such behaviours? It is here that SDT really adds to our understanding by introducing four different subtypes of extrinsic motivation, each of which has a slightly

Table 5.1 Four different subtypes of extrinsic motivation (adapted from Ryan & Deci, 2000)

The individual is driven by ...	Example	Impact on behavioural quality
1 *Rewards* and *punishments*.	Doing the recycling to avoid a fine.	Behaviour may lack quality. The person may not persist with the behaviour when no one else is watching.
2 *Expectations* from others.	Doing the recycling just because that is what we are told to do.	The person may carry out the behaviour but without genuine commitment or emotional engagement. The behaviour has been 'swallowed whole' without being digested.
3 Understanding of the *value* of the behaviour.	The person has accepted the underlying value of recycling in terms of its impact on the planet.	The person will *want* to carry out the behaviour and will perform it with care.
4 Their own personal *goals*, *values* and *identity*.	The person sees themselves as someone with a strong sense of environmental responsibility, and the behaviour is coherent with that.	The person is likely to be highly motivated towards the behaviour, and to do it with care and passion.

different impact on the quality of the behaviour shown and the extent to which the individual is likely to persist with it (see Table 5.1).

You will notice that the four different sources of motivation vary according to the degree to which the individual is showing the behaviour because they *want* to show it, rather than it being demanded by an external force or entity. We might say that the further down the table you go, the greater the sense of *self-determination* the individual experiences in relation to the behaviour – that is, the more the behaviour is emanating from within them rather than being imposed from without. We might also say that the further down the continuum you go, the more the behaviour has been internalized – i.e. owned by the individual. Why is this important? Well, research has demonstrated that more self-determined forms of extrinsic motivation are, much like intrinsic motivation, associated with greater interest, engagement, effort, persistence, performance and behavioural quality (see Ryan & Deci, 2000, for a summary). In contrast, less self-determined forms of extrinsic motivation are associated with diminished interest, poorer outcomes, and a lack of commitment to the behaviour, *especially when the external 'controls' are removed* (Deci & Ryan, 1985). In other words, the greater the sense of self-determination and ownership the individual experiences in relation to a given behaviour, the more positive the impact on the individual's behaviour and engagement over time.

Applied to the context of coaching this suggests that, if we are attempting to support another person to change their behaviour, we may need to explore and understand their motivations for doing so. Behaviours engaged in purely to obtain rewards or avoid consequences are less likely to stick, whereas behaviour change is likely to be of better quality – and longer lasting – if the coachee experiences a sense of self-determination over the desired behaviour (e.g. if they connect with the underlying value of a behaviour, or they see how it links to their own goals and values).

Enhancing self-determination

The final insight to emerge from SDT is that we can make lasting behaviour change more likely by working in such a way so as to enhance the person's sense of self-determination and ownership in relation to a particular behaviour. This can be achieved by, for example:

- Supporting the person to develop a sense of *competence* in relation to the behaviour ('I can do it').
- Respecting the person's *autonomy* ('I *want* to do it and have made my own choice to do so').
- Supporting the person to reflect on the genuine *value* or *meaning* of a given behaviour in terms of things that matter to them ('I see it as important').
- Supporting the person to reflect on the extent to which a given behaviour relates to their *own* goals, values or identity ('This is important *to me*').

- Involving the person in devising their own change plan or making strategies their own somehow ('I have *collaborated* in developing this solution').

While these principles arguably apply across all coaching engagements, they are especially relevant to coaching where particular behavioural changes are required from an individual – say, where a teacher needs to demonstrate specific behaviours in order to meet identified performance standards. In this context, we can provide an experience that will increase the likelihood of a person taking on and committing to a behaviour by respecting their right to self-determination and supporting them to take on the behaviour as their own. Application of this principle will be illustrated in practice in Chapter 7.

7 Motivational Interviewing

> The way in which one communicates can make it more or less likely that a person will change.
>
> (Miller & Rollnick, 2002, p. 8)

Motivational Interviewing (MI) is a way of being with and communicating with people that seeks to elicit their own motivation and resources for change (Miller & Rollnick, 2002). MI was originally developed by a psychologist and therapist called William Miller (later, in collaboration with Stephen Rollnick) in his role as a substance-abuse counsellor working with sufferers of alcoholism. Given the distinctly clinical context in which MI was developed, you might reasonably wonder about the relevance of the approach to coaching work with classroom practitioners. However, the theory and practice of MI – and, indeed, the research that informed its development – provides three key insights that can inform our understanding about how we can work with others in order to achieve change. Applied to the context of coaching, those are:

1   In a coaching relationship, the style of communication adopted by the coach can directly influence (positively or negatively) the likelihood of change occurring. Being overly confrontive, persuasive or directive can give rise to *resistance* from the coachee, and can actually reduce the likelihood of change occurring. In contrast, methods which demonstrate empathy for the coachee, and which allow the coachee to formulate and voice the arguments for change, will be more likely to result in subsequent changes in their behaviour.

2   People change when they see the change as important and when they believe they can do it. Coaches can seek to arouse a motivation to change by working to develop the coachee's sense of a discrepancy between their current reality and how they want things to be. The coach can also work to enhance the coachee's sense of self-efficacy so that they feel confident in their ability to make the change happen.

3   'Resistance' to the coach's efforts is not an indication of a 'faulty coachee'
     – the sign of a mule too stubborn to be pulled forward or a child too tight-
     lipped to accept the medicine being offered; rather, as previously discussed,
     'resistant' behaviour arises as a direct function of the coach's behaviour (e.g.
     the coach being too directive or getting ahead of where the coachee is 'at').
     'Resistance' indicates that the two parties are no longer on the same page and
     is a symptom of *dissonance* (jarring) in the relationship – i.e. a sign that the
     two parties are in different places, have different agendas, or that the
     coach is pushing too hard for the coachee's comfort. It is, in fact, a valuable
     cue that the coach may need to work to re-establish *consonance* (together-
     ness) in the relationship. It is counter-productive to attempt to overcome
     resistance with force of argument, since this might simply further entrench
     the coachee's position; instead, the task of the coach is to roll with resistance
     by listening, understanding and emphasizing the person's personal choice
     and control.

The principles and practices of MI are illustrated in Chapter 6.

8 Positive psychology

> For the last half-century, psychology has been consumed with a single
> topic only – mental illness – and has done fairly well with it . . . But this
> progress has come at a high cost. Relieving the states that make life miserable,
> it seems, has made building the states that make life worth living less of a
> priority.
>
> (Seligman, 2003, p. xi)

Positive psychology, like coaching psychology, emerged at the turn of the
twenty-first century as the psychological community attempted to find ways of
contributing to society that would offer a counterbalance to the discipline's
historically disproportionate focus on disorder, distress and dysfunction. The
focus of positive psychology can be defined as the development of human
strengths and competences, and the enhancement of optimal functioning, wellbeing and flourishing (Seligman & Csikszentmihalyi, 2000; Seligman, 2011). It is so
closely aligned with coaching psychology in terms of its aims and objectives
that the two could be considered to be sibling disciplines (see Green *et al.*, 2012).
For further information on the relationship between positive psychology and
coaching, see Linley & Harrington (2007).

     As is indicated by the 829-page *Handbook of Positive Psychology* (Snyder &
Lopez, 2005), positive psychology is a huge area of study that it would be
impossible to cover in detail in this section. The following are therefore presented
as some select nuggets that have particular relevance to the applications presented
in this book.

The importance of positive emotion

The so-called 'negative' emotions such as fear and anger have long been recognized as being the product of an evolutionary fight-or-flight response to threat or danger, the body's way of priming itself for action that will enhance its chances of survival. In contrast, positive emotions (e.g. joy and contentment) were thought to be merely a signal of optimal functioning, and received very little empirical attention (see Fredrickson, 2005). Then, in the late 1990s, Barbara Fredrickson proposed a broaden-and-build theory of positive emotion, in which she suggested that positive emotions also have a valuable causal influence on the individual's functioning; specifically, that they broaden people's thinking and behavioural repertoires and build enduring personal and social resources (Fredrickson, 1998). Indeed, research has shown this to be the case; for example, it has been demonstrated that inducing positive emotion can enhance creativity, foster open-mindedness, improve intellectual functioning and increase productivity (see Seligman, 2003; Fredrickson, 2005). The implication of this for coaching is that we can help people to perform more effectively by positively influencing their emotional state. Moreover, positive emotion is not just a nice by-product of a coaching engagement, but rather a key variable to attend to if we wish to support the individual's optimal functioning both during and after the coaching session. This is a point that will be returned to in Chapter 9.

A focus on strengths

A strength is defined by Linley (2008) as 'a pre-existing capacity for a particular way of behaving, thinking or feeling that is authentic and energizing to the user, and enables optimal functioning, development and performance' (p. 9). As summarized by Biswas-Diener & Dean (2007), research shows that in many cases building on strengths is more effective than trying to improve weaknesses; furthermore, research has demonstrated that knowledge and use of one's strengths is associated with enhanced wellbeing and vitality (Govindji & Linley, 2007). Therefore, the coach will specifically seek to support an individual to identify and harness their strengths in the pursuit of their goals. This echoes one of the central tenets of SFC and is a principle that runs throughout the engagements described in Part 2 of this book.

Understanding and developing positive traits

Positive psychology informs our understanding about the nature of positive human traits such as confidence, resilience and optimism (Snyder & Lopez, 2005). This enables us to plan interventions to support coachees to further develop such qualities, with corresponding benefits for their performance and wellbeing. In addition, supporting individuals and teams to develop these qualities can enhance the overall capacity of those in the organization to succeed, persevere and maintain high performance in the face of challenge and adversity (Luthans *et al.*, 2007). This will be illustrated in Chapter 13.

For further illustration of the application of positive psychology to coaching relationships, see Biswas-Diener & Dean (2007).

9 Common factors of change

> The most influence that practitioners can exert on outcome is not based on our theoretical acumen or technical proficiency; rather, our impact lies in building a positive alliance with [our clients].
>
> (Murphy & Duncan, 2007, p. 31)

The final piece of psychology we can draw on to inform coaching practice is arguably the most important. It emerges from research into the factors that contribute to the effectiveness of therapy, and the relative importance of each. To cut to the chase, the research has demonstrated that, whatever specific approach is being applied, there are certain *common factors* that will influence the likelihood that a helping relationship will lead to a positive outcome (Murphy & Duncan, 2007). More recently, similar research has indeed indicated that the same common factors apply in the same way to coaching relationships (see, e.g., de Haan & Page, 2013; McKenna & Davis, 2009). The following pie chart summarizes what those factors are and the relative influence of each (Figure 5.1).

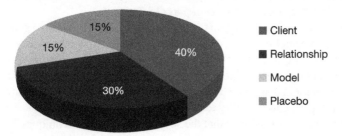

Figure 5.1 Factors contributing to successful outcomes (adapted from Murphy & Duncan, 2007)

Applied to the context of coaching, this means:

Client factors are by far the largest single contributor to successful outcomes, accounting for some 40 per cent of the pie – that is, the internal and external resources that the coachee brings to the engagement (e.g. personal qualities, strengths, motivation, confidence, social supports) have more bearing on the outcome than any of the other contributory factors. It is therefore important for coaches to enter such relationships with a specific intent to elicit and harness the resources that the coachee brings to the engagement. The coachee is not regarded as an empty vessel to be filled with the coach's purported 'expertise', but is recognized as a capable person who brings skills and competences to the relationship.

Relationship factors are the next-biggest contributor to successful outcomes, with 30 per cent of the pie being attributable to the coachee's perception of the quality of the *relationship* that exists between coach and coachee. In professional parlance, this is referred to as the quality of the *alliance*, indicated by the degree to which the client experiences the relationship as a positive, collaborative partnership (Bordin, 1979). A positive alliance is characterized by the following aspects (Bordin, 1979; Murphy & Duncan, 2007):

- *Bonds:* A quality relational bond exists between coach and coachee; the coachee senses that their perspective is listened to and valued; their experience is validated; the coachee trusts the coach, has faith in them as a change-agent, and feels safe in the relationship.
- *Goals:* There is agreement about the goals that are being worked on; the goals are of importance to the coachee.
- *Tasks:* There is agreement about the tasks of coaching, i.e. what activities should be undertaken in and out of sessions in order to achieve change?

It is by attending to these three key components of the alliance (bonds, goals, tasks) that the collaborative partnership that is so crucial for determining the effectiveness of the coaching engagement is established and maintained.

So, *client factors* and *relationship factors* account for 70 per cent of the pie. The remaining 30 per cent is accounted for by two other factors: *placebo/expectancy effects* (15 per cent) and *models and techniques* (15 per cent).

The placebo effect refers to the extent to which change can be influenced simply by the coachee's expectation that some good will come from the endeavour. Coaches can attend to this factor by, for example, presenting as credible and professional; providing the coachee with information that demonstrates the approach or engagement has been well thought through; and communicating genuine belief in the coachee's ability to change.

Perhaps what is most surprising is that the specific models and techniques used by the coach, and the coach's technical proficiency in exercising them, also only account for 15 per cent of the pie. In other words, specific techniques are far less important than we might think, and only account for a relatively small percentage of the variance in outcomes. Of course, this is not to say that models and techniques have *no* impact: they clearly do, but the research suggests that their influence is perhaps less important than might otherwise be anticipated. As noted by Murphy & Duncan (2007), models provide structure and focus to a conversation, and may provide both coach and coachee with new ways of viewing situations; however, there are other factors that seem to take centre stage in accounting for the effectiveness (or otherwise) of the relationship.

In summary, then, the effectiveness or otherwise of a coaching engagement is less attributable to the specific models or techniques used by the coach (although these do play a part) and is more to do with: (1) the resources the coachee brings to the relationship; and (2) the coachee's perception of the quality of the relationship itself. The crucial point to remember is that models and techniques aren't as important as we might intuitively assume them to be, and we must ensure that we attend to the other common factors of change if we want to increase the likelihood of a positive outcome occurring. In other words, if we only have regard to the technical delivery of the approach we are calling upon, we are neglecting other far more important factors and are less likely to be effective. As with the principles of the person-centred approach, an understanding of and attention to the common factors of change permeates the coaching engagements described in Part 2 of this book. This theme is focused on in more detail in Chapter 6 and Appendix 1.

Summary

Psychology has a rich legacy of theory and research that can inform our understanding of how to support others to grow and develop through coaching. The contribution of each of the aforementioned influences can be summarized as follows (Table 5.2).

I hope that you have found it interesting to reflect on how these influences might be relevant to your role. As I have stated, I believe that these methods

Table 5.2 The contribution of psychology to coaching

Influence	Contribution
The person-centred approach	• People have a natural tendency towards growth and development that is released in a facilitative social environment. • A coach can create a suitable climate through the expression of the core conditions of regard, genuineness and empathy.
Solution-Focused Brief Therapy	• We do not need to explore the origin of a problem to arrive at a solution. • We can support the individual to clarify their preferred future and help them to identify where it is already happening or what is already helping them to achieve it. • Planning a small step forward can begin the process of change and lead to larger changes.
Cognitive-behavioural psychology	• Our feelings are not determined by events but by the meaning we make of them. • We can support people to develop flexible, adaptive and realistic ways of appraising situations that impact positively on their performance and wellbeing.
Self-Efficacy Theory	• Our self-efficacy beliefs strongly influence the extent to which we will persevere towards goals. • We can support the coachee to transfer their existing skills to new contexts and facilitate efficacy-supportive processing of success experiences.
The 'stages of change' model	• We may need to differentiate our approach according to where the coachee is 'at' in the stages of change.

(Continued)

Table 5.2 (Continued)

Influence	Contribution
Self-Determination Theory	• Intrinsic motivation arises in a context where the individual's core psychological needs (competence, autonomy, relatedness) are satisfied. • Extrinsic motivation is where the behaviour is engaged in for its instrumental value. • There are four different 'types' of extrinsic motivation that vary in the extent to which the behaviour is experienced as self-determined. • A greater sense of self-determination is associated with enhanced behavioural quality and persistence. • We can work in such a way so as to enhance the coachee's sense of self-determination over their actions, thereby making lasting change more likely.
Motivational Interviewing	• We can make it more or less likely that a person will change according to the way we communicate with them. • People change when they see change as important and believe they can do it. The coach can work in such a way so as to facilitate the emergence of these perceptions. • 'Resistance' is a helpful signal of *dissonance* in the relationship, and a sign that the coach may need to change tack.
Positive psychology	• Inducement of positive emotion can causally influence performance and functioning. • Strengths use is associated with enhanced wellbeing and vitality. Therefore, we attempt to elicit and harness individual (and collective) strengths. • We can support individuals to develop positive traits such as *confidence* and *resilience* that then impact on their performance and wellbeing.
Common factors of change	• We need to ensure we elicit and harness the coachee's resources. • Technique is less important than the development and maintenance of a sound collaborative alliance.

have broad applicability, and are relevant to anyone who has an interest or investment in helping others to move forward. However, the focus of this book is on their application to coaching with the adults in schools and it is now time to see them in action. In the coming chapters we will see how these approaches and principles have been applied in coaching to support the performance, development and wellbeing of education practitioners and teams.

Suggested reading

Palmer, S. & Whybrow, A. (eds) (2007). *Handbook of Coaching Psychology: A Guide for Practitioners*. Hove: Routledge.

Part 2

Applications in education

Chapter 6

Non-judgemental observation

> I have come to feel that the more I can keep a relationship free of judgment and evaluation, the more this will permit the other person to reach the point where he recognizes that the locus of evaluation, the centre of responsibility, lies within himself.
>
> (Rogers, 1961, p. 55)

A central concern for any school is how to support and enhance the performance and development of its classroom teachers. It is for this reason that observations of classroom practice have become such a prominent feature of the landscape in education settings, with observations taking place at junctures throughout the academic year for each individual teaching practitioner. In the present climate, observation processes are linked to and inform, for example, performance management appraisals, school inspections and continuing professional development (CPD) for teachers. Being observed at work can be, in my view, a constructive experience, in that it can bring strengths to one's attention, inform consideration about areas for development and raise awareness about blind spots one might have about one's practice. It stimulates learning and reflection, guards against complacency, and is a helpful vehicle for challenge. Observation is thus a key tool for supporting practitioner learning and development, which in turn supports the ongoing process of school improvement. It is also a valuable component of coaching engagements in schools if the aim is to support the development of classroom practice. Of course, much depends on how the observation is conducted, and how the observer supports the observee in subsequently making use of the information gathered. At its worst, observation has the potential to be a stressful and deskilling experience that can have a negative impact on the practitioner's confidence and wellbeing, especially if the observer is making judgements about the observee's performance. However, as noted, observation can be a powerful developmental tool that can enable the fine-tuning of teaching strategies that are directly relevant to the practitioner's day-to-day context. The question then becomes: How can we minimize the negative aspects of observation while maximizing its potential as a learning opportunity? To this end, the application of coaching psychology can support us in making observation a constructive learning experience that has a positive impact on the teacher's subsequent motivation to change and develop. This chapter sets out a non-judgemental, non-evaluative approach to teacher observation that engages the practitioner in actively reflecting on their practice and collaboratively reviewing the impact of their teaching strategies on pupil learning and engagement. Having clarified the details of the process, its application to supporting the performance and development of a classroom practitioner will be demonstrated.

Principles

The following principles are derived from some of the psychological approaches outlined in Chapter 5, namely:

- the person-centred approach (5.1);
- Solution-Focused Brief Therapy (5.2);
- Self-Efficacy Theory (5.4)
- Self-Determination Theory (5.6);
- Motivational Interviewing (5.7);
- the common factors of change (5.9).

While the principles run throughout the coaching engagements described in this book, they will be detailed here since this represents the first opportunity to clarify how they explicitly apply to practice.

Take a person-centred approach

The approach is person-centred in that the observer provides a non-judgemental space in which the observee feels safe to openly explore the reality of their practice. The emphasis is not on *evaluating* the practitioner, but on engaging them as an equal collaborator and supporting them to reflect on the impact of their teaching strategies. The observer works to create an interpersonal climate that is conducive to change by demonstrating regard for the observee as a person, and valuing their experience and perspectives; communicating empathy for the observee's feelings and views; and behaving with genuineness and transparency so that the observee trusts that nothing is hidden (Carl Rogers referred to these as the 'core conditions' that are necessary for change to occur – see 5.1 for more detail on these points). Observation notes are recorded in a non-judgemental, transcript style to reduce the amount of judgement and evaluation exercised on the part of the observer (see below).

Be solution-focused

Inviting the observee to set goals enables them to begin to articulate their preferred future, i.e. how they would like things to be (see 5.2). The observer can then support the observee to identify the early signs of this preferred future happening, uncovering small green shoots of success that can then be nurtured and developed.

Enhance self-efficacy

People's self-efficacy beliefs – that is, their beliefs about the extent to which they can produce desired results from their own actions – are powerful determinants of the extent to which they will persevere towards a goal (5.4). Reflecting a key principle of Motivational Interviewing, the observer will seek to enhance the observee's sense of self-efficacy by drawing their attention to their successes (see below).

Meet the core needs: respect self-determination

Self-Determination Theory holds that intrinsic motivation arises in an environment where the individual's core needs for competence, autonomy and relatedness are met (5.6). The observer can attempt to meet these needs by, for example, drawing the observee's attention to their successes, emphasizing personal choice and control, and establishing a constructive bond with the observee. Since a sense of self-determination is associated with greater behavioural quality and persistence, the observee is left to decide the actions they will and will not take as a result of the experience.

Foster a motivation to change

The observer approaches the engagement with a particular mindset that is informed by the defining the spirit of Motivational Interviewing (MI) (5.7) – that is:

- *Collaboration* rather than *confrontation.* The observer avoids taking a 'one-up' stance, instead developing a partnership that is very much on a level playing-field and in which the observee's expertise and perspectives are honoured. Through support and exploration, rather than persuasion and exhortation, a positive atmosphere is created that is conducive but not coercive to change.
- *Evocation* rather than *education.* The emphasis is on eliciting from the observee, rather than imparting wisdom or insights to address their perceived deficits. The observer avoids arguing for change as this is thought to provoke resistance, which is in turn associated with a decreased likelihood of subsequent behaviour change. Instead, arguments for change are elicited from the observee through a combination of skilful questioning and reflective listening.
- *Autonomy* rather than *authority.* The observee retains the responsibility for change, and is free to take counsel or otherwise. The observee may be invited to consider new information or perspectives, but with the clear message of 'take what you want and leave the rest'. The observer does not tell the observee what he or she must do.

Informed by this defining spirit, the observer can then attend to the four main tasks of MI:

- Express empathy
- Enhance self-efficacy
- Develop discrepancy
- Roll with resistance.

The detail of these will be unpacked further, below. Throughout, the aim is to create an environment in which the observee feels safe to actively examine and reflect on the reality of their practice, and in which they can discover their own motivation to change and develop.

Attend to the common factors of change

To establish a constructive, collaborative alliance (see 5.9), the observer will work to establish a constructive bond with the observee by adopting a person-centred approach. The observation focuses on goals that the observee wants to achieve, while the observee's view is sought about the tasks that will be undertaken both during and after the session.

Methods

Clarify the focus and goals of the observation

As noted in Chapter 2, adults like to be self-directed and learn best when a learning experience relates to goals that they have chosen or that matter to them. Similarly, Miller & Rollnick (2002) emphasize that motivation to change arises in an accepting atmosphere where the present can be explored in relation to what is wanted and valued (5.7). For these reasons, the observer will seek to agree a focus that is of importance to the observee, since this enhances the likelihood of learning and change occurring. Asking observees to identify what they would like to get from the engagement can enhance their participation in the process, while any feedback given about their practice is more likely to be well received by the observee if it is relevant to a goal that they are invested in pursuing (Schein, 1988). In some circumstances, depending on the nature of the engagement, there may be a need to negotiate over goals so that the needs of both the individual and the organization are addressed (McMahon, 2005; see Appendix 1).

Record in transcript

Judgemental, evaluative or interpretive feedback holds less informational value than specific feedback about the nature of the practice observed, and it is the latter that is the more powerful driver of development. We know this to be true with children – we call it *Assessment for Learning*, and have adapted methods of assessment in schools to reflect this principle – that is, we maximize the *specific informational value* of assessment feedback given to students while decreasing the emphasis on any evaluative component (William & Black, 2006). In the method described in this chapter, the same principle is applied to support adult learning through observation.

The observer takes notes during the observation that will facilitate the observee's reflection on the reality of their practice. It is therefore important to avoid the use of interpretation and evaluation, instead capturing the detail of the strategies used and their impact on the children's learning and engagement. Thus, observation notes are recorded in a transcript style so as to minimize the amount of judgement and evaluation exercised on the part of the observer. Samples of the teacher's language or behaviour are recorded verbatim, while specific information about the student's behaviour and engagement is noted (e.g. numbers of students on-task, noise level, behaviours demonstrated, student contributions to the lesson). For example:

TEACHER: 'Well done, Student X. Well done, Student Y . . . Student Z, I can see you're ready to learn as you've got your books on the table' (two other students immediately get their books out).

In this illustration, the transcript style of recording captures valuable detail that enables there to be a later discussion with the teacher about the difference between *vague* and *specific* praise, and the corresponding impact of both styles on the engagement of students in the classroom. Moreover, recording in this style enables the teacher to read the notes for themself and to examine the detail of their practice without the obscuring lens of the observer's interpretations. In this way, the teacher is able to actively reflect on their practice and draw their own conclusions about what they see. To use the language of Rogers, this puts the teacher at the 'centre of responsibility', and returns the locus of evaluation to them. Judgement and evaluation are squarely removed from the process, and the observer instead focuses on describing the objective detail of the strategies used and the impact they have on, for example, student engagement, the classroom climate, and/or children's learning. The different parts of the lesson structure (e.g. entry, class discussion, activity) can be demarcated on the observation notes with headings and line breaks to facilitate exploration in the coaching session.

Allow the observee to read the transcript

At the beginning of the subsequent reflection session, the observee can be invited to read the observation transcript for themselves. This facilitates their active engagement in processing the information gathered and allows them to 'look in the mirror' without any direction from the observer. Often, this can result in insights that might not otherwise have occurred, while sharing the observation notes in this way emphasizes the open, transparent and collaborative nature of the process.

Express empathy

The expression of empathy is underpinned by an attitude of non-judgemental acceptance (5.1) and is realized in practice through the skill of reflective listening (see Chapter 3). In this context, the observer listens to the observee's views about the lesson and communicates their understanding of the observee's perspective in the form of a statement – e.g. 'You're pleased with the engagement during the task, but noticing that you needed to stop the group a number of times during the discussions.' This is done without judgement, criticism or evaluation, in order to connect with the observee's meaning and to demonstrate that their point of view has been heard, respected and accepted. It also allows the observee to hear back their reflections and thereafter enables them to choose the next avenue of exploration.

Enhance self-efficacy

People are sometimes quick to skip over the things they do well, instead being typically drawn to the aspects of their practice they were less pleased with. It is here that the observer can have a role in encouraging the observee to recognize and value that in their practice which is effective or skilful, thereby promoting a sense of self-efficacy and competence (c.f. Bandura, 1977; Miller & Rollnick, 2002; Ryan & Deci, 2000). However, there are a number of ways in which we can do this, not all of which may have the impact we desire. Table 6.1 illustrates some of the options available to us.

As you can see, each of the strategies varies in the extent to which they involve judgement/evaluation, the amount of information they carry, and the extent to which the practitioner is involved in actively processing the information. Since this approach is non-judgemental and non-evaluative, the judgemental forms of positive feedback are not used. Each of the other strategies may have their place, depending upon the impact we want to have. Why is it important to avoid making even positive judgements? Again, we invoke Carl Rogers (1961) to explain: 'Curiously enough a positive evaluation is as threatening in the long run as a negative one, since to inform someone that he is good implies that you also have the right to tell him he is bad' (p. 55).

Strengths can also be captured and amplified by asking the observee to explain the rationale behind their use of a particular strategy. Often, the things that people do well become such a part of their automatic repertoire that they take them for granted and no longer acknowledge the value of what they do. Asking the observee to explain *why* they did something that was successful can help them to reconnect with the underlying principle(s). This can reinforce a sense of competence and efficacy while also bringing helpful knowledge to the surface of their consciousness so that it can be applied in new situations. If the person is reluctant to recognize

Table 6.1 Drawing attention to positive aspects of practice

Encouraging self-reflection	Observer asking an open question that stimulates deeper reflection – e.g. 'I noticed here that you ...What was your intention and what was the impact of that?'
Drawing attention	Observer drawing an action to the practitioner's attention and then handing the reins over to them – e.g. 'I see that you [action taken] ...Tell me more about that.'
Noticing	Observer describing what happened without imposing judgement – e.g. 'I noticed that you had 100 per cent of the class on-task here.'
Expression of feelings	Observer expressing how they *felt* without giving judgement – e.g. 'I felt excited when I saw that.'
Praise (specific action, non-judgemental)	Observer giving *their perspective* on a particular action without giving judgement – e.g. 'I liked the way you ...'
Praise (specific action, judgemental)	Observer making a judgment about a specific action – e.g. 'Good communication of intended learning outcomes at the start of the lesson.'
Praise (vague, local, judgemental)	Vague praise, observer's judgement, directed at specific action ('Well done').
Praise (vague, global, judgemental)	Vague praise, observer's judgement, directed at global feature ('Great lesson!').

positive features of their practice, another alternative is to hold their practice up against an inferior strategy for comparison. For example: 'I noticed that you gave a countdown before asking for attention, rather than just starting talking. Why did you do that?'

Through recognizing and collecting strengths in this manner, a platform is built from which further development can occur. Moreover, this process of bringing strengths to awareness enables the observee to apply the behaviour or underlying principle in other situations. For example, a teacher who reflects on the value of having 'chunked' a specific teaching activity into smaller sections then has the opportunity to generalize that principle when planning other tasks or lessons. Awakened strengths and successes can also provide a platform for challenging the observee, in that they can be supported to identify the nature of their practice at its best, and then helped to use that learning to address areas of difficulty or lower performance.

Develop discrepancy

For a person to consider change to be important, they need to be aware of a discrepancy between their current reality and how they would like things to be (5.7). Without such a discrepancy, there can be no motivation to change. In this method, an observee may have already become aware of a discrepancy they wish to address in the course of reading the lesson transcript. However, this may not be the case. If that is so, then a key task for the observer is to work to develop such a discrepancy so as to foster the emergence of a motivation to change. Crucially, the observer can support the observee to reflect on the extent to which their current practice is consistent or discrepant with, for example, their goals and values. This can be achieved through application of the range of core coaching skills described in Chapter 3, ranging from those which are more non-directive in nature (e.g. asking open questions) to those which introduce more of the observer's thoughts into the conversation (e.g. drawing attention, noticing, wondering aloud, giving feedback). For example:

- *Open questions:* 'What are your thoughts about aspects you might like to develop?' This gives the observee the freedom to determine their own path of exploration in the conversation.
- *Steered questions:* 'What would you say about your use of feedback to this pupil?' Such questions can be used to steer the conversation down a particular line of enquiry.
- *Drawing attention:* 'Tell me about this part of the lesson … What was happening here?' or 'What was your intention here, and what was the impact of that action?' This enables the observer to draw the observee's attention to key moments during the lesson, while maintaining the observee's active engagement in the discussion.
- *Noticing:* 'I noticed here that the amount of low-level disruption seemed to increase during the class discussion. What did you think?' This brings specific observations to the observee's awareness, enabling both parties to consider and explore its significance.
- *Wondering aloud:* 'I'm wondering what the expectation is for talking during class discussions . . .'. This models the coach's thought process and tentatively introduces particular ideas for the observee to consider.
- *Giving feedback:* 'I noticed here that you started giving the task instructions before ensuring that the group were quiet (specific observation), which seemed to lead to you needing to stop several times to correct behaviour (impact). What do you think?'

At any point in the conversation, the observer has a decision to make about where to operate from on the non-directive/directive continuum. It is impossible to set out hard-and-fast rules to inform such decision-making, although it generally pays to begin with the less directive strategies and then move down the continuum as befits the needs of the observee and the situation. Observers can make the mistake of being too directive too quickly, preventing the observee from thinking for themselves and potentially provoking what might be considered to be 'resistant' responses (see 5.7, and below). Importantly, if strategies are used that introduce some of the observer's thoughts or suggestions into the conversation, this is done in such a way as to demonstrate respect for the observee's view about the contribution being offered. Calling on such a broad range of skills changes the role of the observer from one of 'evaluator' or 'feedback-giver' to one of 'facilitator', and encourages the active engagement of the observee in the process.

Roll with resistance

'Resistance' behaviours are behaviours shown by the observee that indicate that the person may be moving away from the direction of change (Miller & Rollnick, 2002). Of course, an inherent feature of the approach described in this chapter is that resistance is less likely to occur in the conversation, simply due to the way in which the engagement is conducted (e.g. the observee determines the focus for the observation, sets their own goals, offers their view about the lesson and chooses their own development priorities). However, as noted above, the observer is constantly making decisions about where to operate from on the non-directive/ directive continuum of skills, and there may be times when the observer's chosen contribution elicits a response from the coachee that could be considered to be a 'resistance' behaviour. Such behaviours could take the form of, for example:

* *Arguing:* challenging or discounting the observer's contribution, or expressing hostility to the observer.
* *Interrupting*: talking over or cutting off the observer.
* *Negating*: expressing an unwillingness to recognize problems, accept responsibility, or take advice.
* *Ignoring*: not paying attention to the observer's contribution.

The above categories are taken from Miller & Rollnick (2002), who adapted them from Chamberlain *et al.* (1984). Other 'resistance' behaviours might include, for example, arguing against change, talking about the downsides of changing, declaring the intention not to change, or expressing pessimism about change (Miller & Rollnick, ibid.).

Now, the key point to remember here is that 'resistance' is not the sign of a 'faulty client', but is a signal of dissonance in the relationship – that is, a sign that the observer and observee are no longer on the same page for some reason. Most often this is the result of the observer getting ahead of where the observee is 'at' or electing to use a directive strategy when a less directive one would have been preferable. What is happening, in a nutshell, is that the observer has pushed too hard and so the observee pushes back. The sound of this 'pushing back' is captured in observee statements that I am sure will be all-too-familiar to those who try to support others to change – 'That's not a problem', 'That wouldn't work', 'I don't want to change that', 'Yes, but' – other examples come to mind for you, I am sure. So, how do we respond to this signal of dissonance when we encounter it? Well, our lessons in MI (5.7) tell us that we don't want to argue back or try to overcome the 'resistance' with force, since this may further entrench the observee's position, and disrupt the rapport between observer and observee. We want a dance, not a

Table 6.2 Responding to resistance

Shift focus	Acknowledging and validating the observee's concern and then steering the conversation elsewhere ('Sounds like you don't want to explore that ...That's fine. Okay, what would it be helpful to look at next?').
Come alongside	Agreeing with the observee's perspective ('Yes, it's possible that won't work').
Agree with a twist	Agreeing with a slight change of direction, for example: Observee: 'You don't know what it's like to teach this class.' Observer: 'That's right, I don't, and I wouldn't attempt to tell you how to do your job. What do you think is needed?'
Reframe	Accepting the facts of the observee's statement but offering a new interpretation of it that reopens the possibility of change, for example: Observee: 'It's hopeless. They're unteachable.' Observer: 'We haven't found a way forward that would work for you yet.'
Emphasize personal choice and control	Reassuring the person of their right to self-determination ('Of course, it's up to you').

wrestling match! Instead, when encountering 'resistance', we need to remember a key principle: roll with it. So, how *do* we roll with resistance?

First, we need to acknowledge and accept the fact that we might ourselves be wide of the mark, or may have simply jumped too far ahead of the observee's present position. Then, we need ways of responding that demonstrate respect for the observee's position and which do not further develop the argument. One way of doing this is to call on reflective listening to demonstrate that we have listened to the observee ('That's not something that would work for you in this situation'), and to then validate their concern. Other responses to resistance are described by Miller & Rollnick (2002); I have organized them into the acronym 'SCARE' to facilitate recall (see Table 6.2).

Having responded to the 'resistance', we can then treat it is as a valuable indicator of dissonance in the relationship and work to re-establish consonance (togetherness) by, for example, returning the agenda to the observee and reverting to the less-directive coaching skills.

Collaboratively generate ways forward

Elicit the observee's ideas about ways forward

As the conversation continues, the observee may well identify aspects of their practice that they wish to refine or develop further. If so, the observer can make a note of their ideas so as to develop a pool of possibilities that the observee can choose from later. The observer can also explicitly ask the observee to consider options for development – e.g. 'Having reflected on your lesson, what are your thoughts about how to move forward from here?' Options could include continuing with something that is working, building on existing successes, or making changes to practice to address areas for development that may have emerged.

Invite the observee to consider alternative perspectives/ideas

There may be occasions where the observer has a particular opinion or suggestion that it might be helpful for the observee to consider. In such situations the observer can ask the observee if they would like to hear an observation or thought and, if this is desired, introduce the idea, thereby allowing the incorporation of the observer's skills and experience into the session. This can be done using tentative rather than authoritative language (e.g. 'I was wondering what might happen if . . .', or 'Something I have seen work sometimes for others in similar situations is . . .') with the observee then being asked their opinion ('What do you think?'). This again reinforces the collaborative nature of the process, while respecting the observee's autonomy and emphasizing the equal status of observer and observee in the dialogue.

Formalize a written action plan

At the end of the session, the observee is given time to write an action plan in which they commit to pursuing some of the alternatives from the collaboratively generated pool of ideas. The observee's right to self-determination is respected, and it is left to them to decide from the pool of options the ideas they would like to pursue. This is important for increasing the likelihood that the observee will be motivated and committed to carrying out the identified actions (5.6). The observer can contribute ideas or suggestions to this process, but the observee remains free to accept or reject them. The key point is that the observee chooses the next steps for their development, and pursues them with a sense of self-determination.

Evaluate the session

In the course of a reflection session, the observer has to make multiple decisions about where to operate from on the continuum of coaching skills – i.e. whether to listen, reflect, question, give feedback, or make a suggestion. While the observee's initial response to such actions is one form of feedback regarding the helpfulness of the observer's interventions, it can also help if the observer later asks the observee for feedback about the session in relation to the key components of the collaborative alliance (5.9), namely:

* The quality of the rapport between observer and observee.
* The extent to which there was agreement and alignment about the goals being worked on.

Table 6.3 Evaluating the collaborative alliance

	Strongly agree (1)	Agree (2)	Disagree (3)	Strongly disagree (4)
We had a good rapport.				
We were working on goals I wanted to work towards.				
I got the sense we were on the same page.				
The things we did were helpful.				

• The extent to which the observee experienced the two parties as being on the same page.
• The extent to which the observee perceived that the things done in the session were helpful.

I have sometimes used questions to verbally check in with observees about these points at the end of sessions; however, inspired by the work of Scott Miller, John Murphy and Barry Duncan, I have more recently begun to use a brief questionnaire to explore these points, as shown in Table 6.3.

Asking the observee to consider such questions opens a discussion about the degree to which there has been a fit between the observee's needs and the observer's approach, and enables the observer-coach to modify their way of working in subsequent sessions if necessary. By rating sessions in this way, the collaborative alliance that is so essential for achieving change is developed in response to the individual's preferences (Murphy & Duncan, 2007). Coaching thus becomes a feedback-driven endeavour, thereby enhancing the likelihood that it will prove to be effective and supporting the ongoing professional development of the coach.

Case study

A case study will now be presented in which this approach was applied within the context of a coaching engagement to support a secondary school practitioner to develop a particular aspect of her practice. Italics are used to indicate the different components of the approach.

Jasmine was a secondary school teacher who taught in the languages department of a comprehensive school. Discussions with her line manager had led to the suggestion that Jasmine might benefit from additional support in order to develop her approach to the management of low-level disruption in some of her classes. Rather than send Jasmine on an external course that may not have addressed the specific realities of her classroom practice, the school's Leader of Professional Learning (LPL) suggested coaching as an intervention. Having discussed this with

Jasmine and obtained her agreement to participate, the LPL arranged for coaching to take place.

Contracting

A tripartite contracting meeting took place involving Jasmine, the LPL and the external coach so that the focus of the work could be clarified and the goals of the engagement agreed. It emerged that Jasmine wished to target the work on addressing low-level disruption in one of her Year 9 classes (average age approximately 13 years). This was a group where the majority of the class were engaged in learning, but a certain core of 'irrepressible' students would regularly demonstrate low-level disruption (e.g. calling out, bickering, or speaking to each other across the classroom) that would interrupt the flow of the lesson, disrupt the climate, and interfere with the learning of others. The aim was to develop strategies for addressing low-level disruption (LLD) in the class so that more of the students would be engaged for more of the time. Jasmine's hoped-for outcome was for greater engagement from the 'irrepressible core'.

Observation I

In the lesson observed, Jasmine was teaching the identified Year 9 group. At the beginning of the lesson, the students walked in a few at a time and began chatting to each other as they entered the classroom. There was consequently a higher level of noise and disruption at this point, which meant that the later-arriving students were walking into a noisy classroom. The noise level reduced when the students were given a task to do. LLD increased further during class discussions, with the students calling out answers and talking across the classroom to each other. During the lesson, Jasmine made use of a number of strategies that seemed to have a positive impact on LLD (e.g. moving a student within the classroom, putting a student's name on the board as a warning, and giving encouragement to the group).

Coaching session I

At the beginning of the coaching session, the coach handed the transcript to Jasmine and gave her time and space to read through the observation notes. This enabled her to review the lesson for herself, and to begin thinking about aspects she was pleased with or less pleased with. As she spoke, the coach listened to and reflected understanding of her perceptions and feelings (*express empathy*). Thereafter, the coach facilitated Jasmine's active reflection on the lesson, supporting her to identify aspects that had gone well or strategies that seemed to have a positive impact (*enhance self-efficacy*). In so doing, it was noted that near the beginning of the lesson the students quietened down when they were given an activity to do. Drawing on this principle, the coach 'wondered aloud' if having something for the students to do on entry to the classroom (a starter activity) might help Jasmine to reduce the levels of LLD. Jasmine did not think this would help, suggesting that the students would still be talking to each other even if there was an activity for them to do. Although this was a strategy that many teachers make use of to good effect, the coach did not try to force the point and instead *rolled with resistance*, respecting Jasmine's view and reflecting understanding of her perspective before moving the conversation on to another area ('You're thinking that's not the way forward with this group. Okay, let's move on.'). The coach then drew Jasmine's attention to parts of the lesson where LLD was higher to *develop discrepancy* ('I noticed that LLD seemed to increase at this point . . .'). This helped Jasmine to clarify that class discussions were a potential hot-spot for disruption, and that reducing calling out during class discussions was a goal that she wanted to work towards. Having identified this, she decided that she would like to try to elicit the students' buy-in for not calling out during discussions by having a class conference to revisit the classroom expectations and the rationale behind them (*collaboratively generating ways forward*).

After the session, the coach asked Jasmine to give feedback about the different components of the collaborative alliance. In this case, Jasmine noted that, while there was a good rapport between her and the coach and that the two parties were mostly on the same page, in Jasmine's view the coach had relied too much on *eliciting* observations from her. Instead, she would have preferred a greater degree of feedback and opinion from the coach with regard to factors that were potentially contributing to positive engagement or disruptive behaviour. With this on the table, it was possible for the coach to adjust his approach in the next round of coaching.

Observation 2

Jasmine had taken the step of having a class conference with the group, and there was a clear improvement in terms of the amount of LLD during class discussions. To respond to Jasmine's request for more feedback and opinion, the coach used a 0–10 scale to indicate his perception of the amount of LLD at different parts of the lesson. Again, the students' entry to the classroom was a particular hot-spot in this respect.

Coaching session 2

During the coaching session, the coach was able to refer to the scales to draw Jasmine's attention to the parts of the lesson where LLD was at its highest and lowest. Responding to Jasmine's request for more feedback about possible contributory factors, the coach elected to *develop discrepancy* by putting himself in the mindset of a student and talking through the student's experience of the classroom from the moment of entry ('When I come into the classroom I'm thinking "How strict is it in here? Where is the line?" I can see and hear others talking which makes me think it's less strict than other classrooms.'). In this way, Jasmine saw that the point of the students' entry to the classroom was a key part of the lesson that needed tightening up. She determined to reboot the classroom entry procedures to communicate tighter boundaries from the start. This would involve greeting the students outside, asking them to line up, and only allowing them to enter the classroom when quiet. She was motivated to make these adjustments to her practice, and confident that she could move forward in this respect.

Review

A tripartite review meeting was arranged involving Jasmine, the LPL and the coach. This represented an opportunity for all parties to reflect on the impact of the coaching and to consider the aspects of engagement that had been helpful and less helpful. It was agreed that Jasmine had made progress towards her goal of reducing LLD in the classroom, and that the strategies implemented as a result of coaching had begun to move her practice in the desired direction. Jasmine also reported that the experience had positively impacted on her confidence about dealing with other classes, although there would be further work to do to transfer the gains experienced in coaching to other groups. She reflected on the emotional impact of this approach, noting that it had been 'less stressful' than some of her previous experiences of observation (where her performance had been subjected to an evaluative process).

Evaluation

Jasmine's self-report feedback indicated that the coaching had had a positive impact on her performance, development and ability to help herself in future. She also valued how the coaching engagement had been tailored to her needs in response to her feedback:

> The coach and I had an honest discussion about what aspects of the coaching were/were not so helpful after the initial session. This second session was consequently exactly tailored so that discussion was extremely interesting and helpful. It was very valuable to have feedback from a 'second pair of eyes' in the room, and for the coach to put himself into the 'mindset' of the students. This has provided several points for me to bear in mind in future.

Reflections and conclusions

How was coaching applied to support improvement of performance, development and/or wellbeing?

This chapter has presented a non-judgemental approach to teacher observation that can be applied in schools to support the self-directed learning and development of education practitioners. The approach puts the observee at the heart of the exercise, freeing them from the lens of evaluative judgement and enabling them to 'look in the mirror' for themselves. The result is an approach to teacher observation that demonstrates *respect* for the observee's views, skills and experience, *engages* them as an equal, active partner in the process, and *enables* them to determine for themselves the ways in which they would like to develop as a result. The coach's role is to guide the coachee's exploration in such a way so as to facilitate the emergence of an intrinsic motivation to change and develop.

In this case the method was applied to supporting a secondary school languages teacher to develop strategies for reducing LLD in her classes. This resulted in the development of concrete, practical strategies that the teacher was committed to implementing, and corresponding benefits for the students in her class. The fact that the approach was non-judgemental and non-evaluative meant that the teacher experienced less stress as part of the observation process, thereby improving her capacity to engage with and learn from the exercise. We can see, therefore, that coaching psychology has much to offer to schools in terms of supporting the development of classroom practitioners.

What coaching models, skills or techniques have we covered?

This chapter has illustrated how the principles of the person-centred approach can be applied in coaching to support the creation of a non-judgemental climate in which the practitioner feels safe to openly and honestly reflect on the reality of their practice. This means:

- Demonstrating *regard* for the practitioner's worth, experience, perspectives, skills and ideas.
- *Accepting* the practitioner's right to see things as they do, and their right to choose their own path; not making or communicating *evaluative judgements* about them or their practice.
- Communicating *empathy* for the practitioner's feelings and perspectives.
- Behaving *genuinely*, *authentically* and *transparently.*

The approach is also informed by the four main tasks of MI:

- *Express empathy*: demonstrating attention to, understanding of and regard for the coachee's perspective.
- *Enhance self-efficacy*: using non-judgemental strategies to draw the practitioner's attention to the aspects of their practice that had a positive impact.
- *Develop discrepancy*: heightening the coachee's awareness of a discrepancy between their current reality and how they want things to be.

- *Roll with resistance*: not attempting to overcome 'resistance' through force of argument, but rather demonstrating regard for the coachee's perspective and treating it as a cue to slow down, stop, or change direction.

How else could this approach be applied?

The approach can, of course, be used by coaches or coaching psychologists in the course of their work with classroom practitioners and could focus on any one of a number of themes – for example:

- Supporting individual practitioners to improve the quality of teaching and learning and/or develop the use of strategies for managing behaviour.
- Supporting practitioners to develop approaches to questioning and providing feedback in lessons.
- Supporting Early Years Practitioners to develop the quality of their inter-actions with children during free play.

However, while the above are all worthwhile coaching applications, perhaps the greatest value of the approach described here is that it can be readily utilized by school practitioners themselves. Specifically, the method described in this chapter could be used by teachers in schools (or across schools) where peer coaching is used to support practitioner development. Indeed, peer coaching has become increasingly prevalent in schools with the emergence of collaborative learning approaches such as the Lesson Study model (DCSF, 2008) and the 'Teacher2Teacher' continuing professional development programme advocated by the National Union of Teachers (NUT, 2008). Both are approaches which aim to support professional development through informed professional dialogue between peers, and the principles and practices of the psychology-informed approach described in this chapter could complement both of these methodologies. Teachers could be trained in these principles and methods, and then perhaps provided with supervision or coaching to further embed the learning in their practice. If this were done, then this would enhance the quality of the support that teachers provide to each other, thereby reducing dependency on external coaches and building the school's capacity for sustainable self-improvement. When you think about the numbers of children that would benefit as a result, it is really quite exciting and enlivening.

At this point there is an important caveat to consider about the use of this method in relation to performance management processes in schools. As noted, a key feature of the approach is the removal of judgement and evaluation from the observation process so as to enhance the quality of the exercise as a learning experience. However, the fact remains that schools need to ensure standards of practice, and must have in place policies and associated mechanisms for appraising the performance of teachers against identified competences. Thus, it is not suggested that this approach could replace existing performance management observations, since these serve a different function. Nonetheless, it can be seen how this approach could be used to complement existing processes or structures by providing the practitioner with a constructive learning experience to support them in the process of moving towards identified performance standards. In this way the evaluative appraisal process would first determine the performance areas that need to be addressed, while the approach described in this chapter could thereafter be applied to help the practitioner find the necessary motivation, confidence and clarity to move forward. Indeed, we will see this evidenced in practice in the next chapter.

The four main tasks of MI (express empathy, enhance self-efficacy, develop discrepancy, roll with resistance) could also be applied in a range of other 'helping' engagements or conversations, for example:

- A teacher meeting with a parent to discuss ways in which to further support their child's learning at home.
- A senior leader working with a teacher to support them in further developing their practice.
- A coach working with a senior leader to support them in planning how to achieve their organizational vision.
- A psychologist working with a teacher to support them in planning how to provide for a child with emotional and behavioural difficulties.

What can we learn about how to help others to change?

- The coaching engagement described demonstrates the value of adopting a *non-judgemental* approach, thereby creating a climate of *acceptance* in which the person feels safe enough to express themselves openly and explore the possibility of change.
- The importance of forming, developing and maintaining a sound interpersonal *connection* is illustrated.
- A person will not have a motivation to change unless they are aware of a *discrepancy* between how things are and how they want them to be. If we are to support others to change, then we may first need to develop their awareness of such a discrepancy through, for example, questions, observations and feedback. Failing to attend to this principle can cause change efforts to fail – that is, if we try to encourage the person to consider how they might move forward without first attending to this crucial step. Since developing discrepancy involves bringing information to the coachee's attention that highlights how their behaviour may be discrepant with their goals, we might consider this to reflect a principle of *challenging*.
- In response to Jasmine's feedback, the coach adjusted his approach to take account of Jasmine's own particular learning preferences and recognized that what worked for others may not work for her. This reflects a principle of *individuation*.

- The coach focused on *engaging* Jasmine as an active partner in learning, creating an atmosphere of *collaboration* rather than leaving her with the sense of feeling 'done to'. This enabled her to engage deeply in the conversation, resulting in a more powerful learning experience than might have been achieved through her being a passive recipient of feedback.
- Rather than criticize or make judgements about Jasmine on the basis of the observed disruption in the classroom, the coach supported her in learning from her experience and then using that learning to inform her future practice.

How could you apply these skills or principles in your own practice?

Reflection questions

1   How could you use the non-judgemental approach to observation in your practice? Who in your school would benefit from this sort of learning experience? Who would benefit from being trained in this approach?

2   In what contexts could you apply the four main tasks of Motivational Interviewing in order to support another person to change and/or develop?

3   To what extent can you:
    a   Communicate empathy for another person's feelings or perspective?
    b   Use a range of methods to enhance the person's sense of self-efficacy?
    c   Use the range of coaching skills to develop the individual's sense of a discrepancy between how things are and how they want things to be?
    d   'Roll with resistance' when you encounter it?

Which of these skills are you strong on? Which might you wish to develop further?

Suggested reading

Miller, W. & Rollnick, S. (2002). *Motivational Interviewing: Preparing People for Change*. New York: The Guilford Press.

Rogers, C. (1961). *On Becoming a Person: A Therapist's View of Psychotherapy*. London: Constable & Robinson.

Chapter 7

Coaching for performance

Coaching is the essential management style or tool for optimizing people's potential and performance. Commanding, demanding, instructing, persuading with threats, overt or covert, cannot produce sustainable optimum performance, even though they may get the job done.

(Whitmore, 2002, p. 97)

In the last chapter, we saw how a coaching approach can be used to support the self-directed learning of education practitioners. However, there may be occasions in schools where the organization has particular views about the ways in which a practitioner needs to develop in order to improve standards, as a result of, for example, performance management appraisals. Certainly, this is a key priority for schools for a number of reasons. First, there is the impact on student attainment: a number of studies in the US have shown that, unsurprisingly, pupils taught by very effective teachers stand to make significantly greater gains in their learning over the course of a year – as much as 40 per cent more than those taught by teachers who are judged to be performing poorly (Sutton Trust, 2011). Remarkably, the effect of moving a teacher's performance up the quality distribution by one standard deviation has a larger impact on student achievement than a costly ten-student reduction in class size (Rivkin *et al.*, 2005). Then, there is the implication for the school as a whole, since a low-performing teacher will limit the overall effectiveness of the setting. Finally, there is the impact on the teaching practitioner themselves: teachers who are performing well (and who know they are performing well) will experience greater satisfaction and wellbeing and this, in turn, will again impact on the educational experience of the children under their care. For all these reasons, the improvement of teacher performance in a way that also meets the needs of the organization is a necessity for schools, and the availability of effective support mechanisms for achieving such an aim is crucial. So, when particular performance standards are required of an individual, how can schools support that person to realize them?

The psychology of performance improvement

Let's assume for the purposes of this exploration that the person isn't intrinsically motivated to carry out the behaviour required. How do you encourage the individual to perform (i.e. behave) in the desired fashion? Well, one option would be to adopt a highly directive, top-down, controlling style, in which you spell out exactly what is required, effectively commanding the person to carry out a particular behaviour. This could even be backed up with offers of rewards for demonstrating the behaviour or threats of punishment for failing to behave as desired (as long as you are prepared to accept and repair the potential damage to the relationship associated with the latter). But what would be the outcome of this? To address this question, we can call upon research associated with Self-Determination Theory (5.6). This shows that less autonomous forms of extrinsic motivation (e.g. rewards and punishments) can be associated with diminished interest and a lack of commitment to the behaviour when the external controls are removed. In other words, commands, rewards and punishments could well obtain *compliance*, at least in the short term, and if that is all that is needed then such methods could well be an option – for a while. However, if we want to see a higher standard of behavioural quality and a lasting *commitment* to the behaviour in the long term, then – as Sir John Whitmore notes – we need to think beyond external controls. In fact, what we want, ideally, is for the individual to 'take on' the behaviour and internalize it so they perform to a higher standard and we don't have to monitor and put effort into maintaining contingencies. So how do we increase the likelihood that an individual will take on and genuinely commit to an externally prompted, non-intrinsically motivated behaviour? This is where Self-Determination Theory (SDT) comes to our rescue.

According to SDT, behaviour change is likely to be of better quality – and longer lasting – if the individual experiences a sense of self-determination over the behaviour. Remembering the learning from Chapter 5, we can work in such a way so as to achieve this by:

- Supporting the person's sense of *competence* in relation to the behaviour ('I can do it').
- Respecting the person's *autonomy* ('I *want* to do it and have made my own choice to do so').
- Supporting the person to reflect on the genuine value or *meaning* of a given behaviour in terms of things that matter to them ('I see it as important').
- Supporting the person to reflect on the extent to which a given behaviour relates to their *own* goals, values or identity ('This is important *to me*').
- Involving the person in devising their own change plan or making strategies their own somehow ('I have *collaborated* in developing this solution').

So, to support internalization of behaviour, can we provide the person with an experience that will address the above factors and meet their needs in this respect? This is where performance coaching can help.

Performance coaching

In performance coaching, a coach works with a coachee to support them to move towards particular performance standards, described in terms of specific behaviours the coachee needs to show. If the standard is one that has been identified by a third party, then the engagement may involve an attempt to increase the likelihood that the coachee will 'take on' the behaviour (or behaviours) desired. Of course, the key part of that phrase is *attempt to increase the likelihood*, and that is literally all we can do. There are no guarantees that the coachee will change their behaviour, since a key principle of the engagement is respect for the coachee's right to self-determination. We cannot force them to change, and they retain the right to take or leave as much or as little from the coaching relationship as they desire. There is no hidden agenda, no manipulation and no coercion. Instead, we approach the coaching engagement with full respect for the practitioner's right to make their own decisions about what they do next, and a determination to provide them with a quality experience that will enable them to make such decisions with added clarity and insight. Our aim is to help them to experience a sense of competence in relation to a particular behaviour, to reflect on the potential value and meaning of a behaviour, and for them to then make their own choices about what to do next. The remainder of this chapter will illustrate a psychology-informed approach that can be used to this end, and will demonstrate its real-life application in a school context.

A method for performance coaching

The following sequence of steps provides a method for performance coaching that is informed by the psychological approaches described in Chapter 5 of this book:

1   Clarify what the desired performance looks like.
2   Observe the practitioner at work; look for the existing signs of the desired performance already happening, even if only in part.
3   Allow the coachee to evaluate their progress towards their goals.
4   Draw the coachee's attention to signs of them moving towards their goals.
5   Develop the coachee's awareness of any discrepancy that exists between current status and goal.
6   Collaboratively consider ways to close the gap.
7   Develop an action plan.
8   Review progress; refine the plan, address any obstacles to change.
9   Final review and evaluation.

Throughout this process, the coach has regard to the coachee's motivation for engaging in the desired behaviour or otherwise. If the coachee is able to experience a sense of self-determination in relation to the behaviour (e.g. they can make the required behaviour their own, or can see how it relates to goals or values that are important to them), then meaningful change is more likely to occur. All this takes place in the context of a relationship that, it is hoped, the coachee will experience as safe, supportive and constructive (5.1). This meets the core need for *relatedness* and increases the likelihood that the coachee will engage openly and honestly with the process.

Each of the aforementioned aspects will now be unpacked further, with a real-life practice example used to illustrate.

Case study

In this case the coaching engagement focused on supporting a secondary school science teacher (Richard) who was undergoing performance improvement procedures. In reality, a number of performance goals were worked on in the coaching engagement, which followed the full structure described in Appendix 1 and incorporated the use of the non-judgemental approach to teacher observation described in Chapter 6. However, for clarity of illustration, Richard's progression towards one particular performance goal is focused on and summarized here.

I Clarify what the desired performance looks like

It is a well-worn fact that if you don't know where you are headed, the chances are that you could end up somewhere else. Therefore, the first step is to get a the clear picture of what the desired performance looks like so all parties know what is being aimed for. This exploration can be informed by solution-focused questioning, generating a description of the preferred future that is desired (5.2). For example: 'Let's say that the desired performance has been achieved . . . What would that look like?' But to whom do we ask that question? Well, in the first instance, the coachee may well have views about what needs to be different, and if so then involving them in setting the goals for the engagement demonstrates respect for their views and their need for autonomy. Of course, in performance coaching it may well be that another member of the organization has views about the desired outcome, in which case they will also need to be present and contribute as the vision is collaboratively co-constructed and negotiated. The conversation may also be informed by other information that is available about the practitioner's performance (e.g. information from performance appraisals or classroom observations).

In this case a tripartite meeting took place between the teacher, the school's Leader of Professional Learning (LPL) (who had arranged to provide coaching to support the teacher in moving forward as a result of concerns raised about his performance) and the coach. The LPL needed to be at the meeting to ensure that the goals agreed would meet the needs of organization as well as the coachee; however, the coachee was fully involved in the goal-setting process. The overall aim was to improve student engagement in Richard's lessons, and for there to be evidence of a clearer progression in student learning across his lessons over time. However, this would require movement towards a number of goals which would be targeted through a range of support mechanisms. It was collaboratively agreed that, within this broader plan, coaching would focus on the following performance goal: 'Pupils will understand the intended learning outcomes and the extent to which they have achieved them.'

It is worth just clarifying what is meant by this. The school wanted to see Richard delivering lessons where he communicated clear learning outcomes for the students to aim for – that is, explicit success criteria that would clarify what the students should be able to do at the end of each lesson; then, at the end of the lesson, the pupils would be able to review the extent to which they had been successful. The hypothesis was that this would have a positive impact on student engagement and progression in and across lessons. This provided a clear, discrete focus that Richard was willing to work towards; he was motivated to try to improve the levels of student engagement in his lessons and was keen for the coaching to happen.

2 Observe the practitioner at work; look for signs of the desired performance already happening, even if only in part

Observation of the practitioner at work is a way of gathering evidence about the practitioner's performance that can be used to support their reflection on their practice. The non-judgemental approach to observation described in Chapter 6 can be used for this purpose. In the course of the observation, the coach can specifically look for signs of the desired performance already happening, since these represent small green shoots of success that can be nurtured and grown. The coach can also look for examples of where the practitioner might adjust their practice in order to close the gap between their current performance and the goal.

Richard was observed teaching a Year 9 class (average age approximately 13 years). The lesson was one in which the group would be asked to apply previously-learned scientific knowledge in a new context. The main task was a worksheet activity that required the students to apply their knowledge and understanding of concepts about speed and forces (including equations such as speed = distance/time); specifically, they would use this knowledge to solve scientific word problems about objects moving through the solar system. The lesson structure comprised: a starter activity in which the students would recall the order of the planets in the solar system, a video about the solar system and then the main worksheet activity. Richard had also prepared an additional hint sheet that would provide students with the necessary equations if they desired it.

Sure enough, Richard shared some intended learning outcomes with the class at the beginning of the lesson. However, the outcomes he communicated did not specify exactly what the students should be able to do by the end of the lesson, meaning that the students were not clear about the success criteria they were aiming for. This represented a way in which Richard's practice might be further shaped in order for him to move closer towards his goal.

As the observation progressed, the coach looked for any signs of resources or strengths that might be harnessed in order to help Richard to move forward. In this case, Richard's approach to the lesson, and his interactions with the students within it, suggested that he was capable of thinking in terms of specific learning outcomes. His behaviour suggested that he was looking for:

- *All* the students to be able to solve some basic scientific word problems.
- *Most* of the students to be able to solve more complex problems using provided equations.
- *Some* of the students (i.e. those working at higher skill levels) to be able to solve problems that would require them to retrieve the equations from memory.

These were not the outcomes he had communicated, but the fact that this was evidently present in his thinking was a resource to draw upon.

It was notable that Richard didn't refer back to the stated learning outcomes during the lesson, nor did he revisit them at the end to support the students in evaluating the extent to which they had achieved them. As a result, the students weren't clear about what they were aiming for and found it difficult to judge if they had been successful. So, while some learning outcomes were present and visible at the start of the lesson, that was about it. Richard was carrying out the required practice, but there was something tokenistic about it. Something suggested that his heart wasn't in it.

3 Allow the coachee to evaluate their performance

At the beginning of the coaching session, the coach hands the observation transcript to the coachee to enable them to review the extent to which they are on track to achieving their goals. This encourages self-evaluation, engages the practitioner in actively reflecting on their practice, and allows them to form their own views without interference from the observer – thereby respecting their need for autonomy.

In this case, Richard noted that he had communicated some learning outcomes to the students, but acknowledged that the students had found it hard to judge if they were achieving them.

4 Draw the coachee's attention to signs of them moving towards their goals

A key principle of the solution-focused approach is the assumption that there will always be exceptions, times when either 'the problem' is not as bad or aspects of the preferred future are already happening. We can approach the coachee determined to draw their attention to these exceptions for a number of reasons: first, doing so may enhance the coachee's sense of self-efficacy in relation to the desired behaviour (thereby increasing their sense of competence); second, such exceptions could represent a platform on which to build; and, finally, they might be a source of valuable learning to inform future action-planning.

In this case, Richard's behaviour during the lesson had suggested that he *was* very capable of planning a clear, specific set of learning outcomes. In fact, the tacit outcomes that he seemed to be looking for constituted a clearer, more specific set of learning outcomes than those he had referred to at the beginning of the lesson, and this was brought to his attention.

5 Develop the coachee's awareness of any discrepancy that exists between current status and goal

Having clarified what the coachee is already doing that serves in the direction of the desired performance standard, the next step is to develop their awareness of any discrepancy that exists between their current status and the goal (5.7). Remember, without awareness of such a discrepancy there can be no motivation for change. Strategies for achieving this are described in detail in Chapter 6.

It is worth reminding ourselves at this stage that Richard's goal was for the intended learning outcomes to be understood by the pupils, and for them to know if they had achieved them. However, the outcomes Richard originally presented were not specific enough, making it harder for the students to understand what he was looking for. Furthermore, Richard had told the students that he was looking for one set of outcomes while his behaviour in the lesson had communicated that he was measuring success differently (as previously described). This left the students (and, indeed, the observer) confused about what the intended learning outcomes were. There was therefore a discrepancy between Richard's current performance and his goal. To raise Richard's awareness of this discrepancy, the coach could have drawn upon the range of strategies described in Chapter 3 (e.g. open questions, steered questions, drawing attention). In this case, the coach elected to give Richard feedback about his own confusion ('I felt confused here. I wasn't sure if the outcomes you originally presented were *really* what you were looking for . . . It seemed to me that you were looking for [the outcomes described in section 2 of this chapter] . . . What do you think?'). This provided Richard with the opportunity to reflect on the apparent discrepancy and to recognize it for himself.

Richard acknowledged that there was an inconsistency between his stated lesson outcomes and the reality of what he was looking for during the main activity. He also noted that, had he been more specific in how he phrased his learning outcomes, the students would have been more likely to understand them and clearer about what they were aiming for. He was therefore now aware of a discrepancy between his current reality and his goal.

6 Collaboratively consider ways to close the gap

With the coachee aware of a discrepancy between their current reality and how they want things to be, we can then facilitate their reflection on how to close the gap. Actively engaging the coachee in problem-solving in this way demonstrates respect for their opinions and can further enhance their sense of competence. If the coach has ideas to contribute to the pot, and the coachee wants to hear them, then they can do so. This makes problem-solving a collaborative process in which the ideas of both parties can be considered, and in which the coach's experience and expertise (if they have any) can also inform the discussion. However, the coachee's right to self-determination is respected, and it is left to them to choose the ways forward that they do or do not wish to pursue. This further satisfies the core need for *autonomy*.

In this case, the coach asked Richard to consider what might have happened in the lesson had he shared the more specific learning outcomes his behaviour had suggested he was looking for. Richard reflected that it would have helped the students to better understand what they were aiming for (i.e. what he had wanted from them), which could have had a positive impact on their motivation and engagement. It would also mean that at the end of the lesson he and the students would be able to collectively evaluate the extent to which they had made progress towards the intended learning outcomes.

Richard's realization that the learning outcomes could be phrased much more specifically in terms of what the students would be able to do seemed to be a light-bulb moment for him. He was excited by the awareness that this practice could have a positive impact on student motivation and engagement in the classroom, and saw that it was possible to use learning outcomes in a more meaningful way than he had done previously. The awareness that this practice was already present in his behaviour to some extent seemed to also boost his confidence.

At this point Richard confided that, when planning and delivering his lessons, he had not previously seen the value of using learning outcomes and had been recording and sharing them simply because that was what the school's management expected. This accounted for his somewhat tokenistic use of them during the observation, and the lack of quality in his use of the strategy. However, he had now imagined the impact that the use of more specific learning outcomes could have, and seemed genuinely motivated to develop his practice in this respect. Already, you can see the difference it can make when a person genuinely buys in to the rationale for a particular behaviour, sees how it can make a difference to them, and can thereafter make a choice to pursue it (as opposed to swallowing whole what they are told).

7 Develop an action plan

Having considered a range of possibilities as to how to close the performance gap, the coachee is supported to develop a specific action plan that will translate the possibilities into reality. Depending on the engagement, this may well sit outside the confidentiality parameters so that members of the organization are aware of what is being worked on. This introduces an element of accountability (for both the coach and coachee) and enables others to take actions that might further facilitate transfer of gains to the workplace, e.g. checking in with the coachee and/ or providing the coachee with constructive feedback. The coachee is then given time to implement the planned changes.

In this case, Richard determined to make the learning outcomes much more specific so that he and the students would be easily able to evaluate their progress towards them.

8 Review progress; refine the plan; address any obstacles to change

An agreed time later, the coach can return to support the coachee in reflecting on their progress. It may be that the coachee has made progress at the first attempt, in which case this can be celebrated, consolidated and learned from. However, change doesn't always happen at the first time of asking, and there may be both practical and psychological obstacles to address in order to support the person in moving forward. At the same time, the plan may need to be reviewed and refined following the initial change attempt.

At the time of the second observation, Richard had clearly made progress towards his goal:

- At the beginning of the lesson, Richard shared the intended learning outcomes with the class. The outcomes were much more specific, and clarified what success would look like for children performing at different skill levels. He now had clear success criteria for the students to work towards and measure their progress against. The impact of this was tangible in terms of the improvement in student engagement.
- Richard referred back to the learning outcomes during the lesson, reminding the students of the link between what they were doing and their targets.
- At the end of the lesson, Richard revisited the intended learning outcomes and asked the students to self-evaluate the level of performance that they had managed to achieve.

Richard read the transcript of the lesson, and was given space to notice any differences across the two observations. This enabled him to actively process any observed changes and to formulate his own view about the impact of the changes he had made – again, respecting his autonomy, rather than judging and evaluating him. He noted that things were 'miles better' and that he had moved closer towards his goal. The coach was able to further emphasize the impact of Richard's change of approach by drawing attention to the high levels of engagement during the lesson ('Did you notice that at this point 100 per cent of the group were engaged?'). It was also possible for the coach to affirm the changes in Richard's practice by giving specific feedback from an observer's perspective (e.g. 'It was really clear to me what you were looking for').

9 Final review and evaluation

The final review meeting took place with Richard, the school's LPL and the coach so that the needs and views of the three key parties could be represented. The respective parties' views on the progress Richard had made towards his goals were shared, with reference to supporting evidence. In addition, it emerged that Richard had recently been observed at work by another colleague who had also noted his progress. All were agreed that Richard had taken steps towards achieving his goal, and this had been corroborated by a third-party observer.

Crucially, as well as developing the quality of his practice in terms of use of specific learning outcomes, Richard reported a change in his commitment to such an approach. He said that previously he had 'gone through the motions' of setting and displaying learning outcomes, but had not properly connected with the meaningful purpose and value of having done so. In his words: 'There can be a tick-box approach to the criteria for what makes a good lesson, and you don't necessarily feel the worth or the value. *You don't own it.*' (Emphasis added.)

Now, having seen the genuine value of using learning outcomes, and having seen the difference it could make to his daily experience, he was more committed to the use of the strategy. The result was a noticeable improvement in Richard's execution of the approach, with corresponding benefits for the students.

In terms of what had helped to achieve this progress, Richard emphasized a number of principles of the coaching engagement. He attributed progress to the process being positive, starting from what he was doing well and building from there. Richard also noted that his ownership of the *process* was important, and that this had been achieved by involving him in determining the areas of focus and identifying the goal for coaching.

Evaluation

Both Richard and the LPL reported a positive impact of coaching on Richard's performance, development and wellbeing. In terms of qualitative feedback, Richard stated:

> This was the most positive experience of my teaching career so far. I felt that the coaching was focused completely on what I already did well and how this can be developed or used more so that I improve further . . . As the goals came from a very collaborative discussion and so were specific to me I felt they were not only something that I wanted to achieve, but something that I could achieve. For the first time I felt I really understood how to use learning outcomes.

Reflections and conclusions

How was coaching applied to support improvement of performance, development and/or wellbeing?

In this chapter we have seen how a performance coaching approach was applied to support a secondary school science teacher to improve the quality of teaching and learning in his classroom. In terms of the impact of this approach, Richard demonstrated:

- *Behavioural changes* related to the specific performance area (making learning outcomes more specific, and using them more meaningfully in his lessons).
- Enhanced *commitment* to the use of a particular teaching strategy (use of intended learning outcomes).
- Greater *self-awareness* about practical and psychological obstacles that were interfering with his performance (the practicalities of his approach, and his commitment to the use of learning outcomes).
- Improved *confidence* and *self-belief* in his capacity to perform to the desired standard.

Prior to coaching, Richard had begun each lesson with learning outcomes because that was what he had been directed to do, without properly connecting with the purpose and *value* of that strategy. Yes, this had led to his compliance, but it did not help to secure his commitment nor maximize the potential benefit of the approach. Through coaching, Richard had discovered that he could use learning outcomes to good effect, had found a meaningful rationale for their use and thereafter made his own choice to use them. The result of this was, across the duration of two coaching sessions, a significant improvement in his application of this strategy and a change in his commitment to using it. The strategy was now his, and this was evident in his behaviour. As predicted by SDT, Richard's motivation to change was enhanced by the sense that he was making his own decision to move forward in this respect as a result of seeing how the change would be of meaningful benefit to him and his students.

The case example suggests implications for the potential value of coaching as a robust school improvement strategy. Coaching is often described as being a mechanism for supporting self-directed learning (see, for example, Lofthouse *et al.*, 2010; van Nieuwerburgh, 2012), and this is certainly the case for most engagements one encounters. However, it is important to note that in this case the need for improvement was identified by other practitioners in the organization in which Richard worked, who also had a say in determining the parameters of the coaching engagement in terms of the goals that could be worked towards. While it was essential to take measures to secure Richard's willing participation in the process, the case study has demonstrated that, if set up and facilitated correctly, coaching can in fact meet the needs of the broader organization as well as the individual. As such, it represents a valuable strategy available to schools for supporting the ongoing process of school improvement. At the same time, the principles of the approach mean that it provides the teacher with a more positive experience than otherwise might be expected from a 'poor performance' intervention.

What coaching models, skills or techniques have we covered?

In this case, we have seen how a nine-step coaching model can be applied to support practitioners to move towards particular performance standards. This comprises a sequence of steps through which the practitioner is supported to envisage a desired outcome; identify what they are already doing to take them towards that outcome; look for ways to further close the gap between their present reality and the desired outcome; develop a concrete action plan as to how to move forward; and to then review, evaluate and refine their approach.

We have also seen how we can increase the likelihood that a person will demonstrate improved performance and commitment in relation to a particular target behaviour, namely:

- Supporting the person's sense of *competence* in relation to the behaviour ('I can do it').
- Respecting the person's *autonomy* ('I *want* to do it and have made my own choice to do so').
- Supporting the person to reflect on the genuine value or *meaning* of a given behaviour in terms of things that matter to them ('I see it as important').
- Supporting the person to reflect on the extent to which a given behaviour relates to their *own* goals, values or identity ('This is important *to me*').
- Involving the person in devising their own change plan or making strategies their own somehow ('I have *collaborated* in developing this solution').

All these strategies increase the extent to which the person experiences a sense of self-determination in relation to the behaviour.

How else could this approach be applied?

In this case, the engagement focused on supporting the performance and development of a science teacher who was undergoing performance improvement procedures; however, the approach could readily be applied to support high-performing practitioners to move towards 'stretch' goals. It could also be of use in situations where organizations may wish to develop individuals' commitment to particular behaviours, such as those associated with a new initiative or an organizational vision. The approach represents a valuable tool for school staff who have a responsibility to support practitioners in similar roles in their own or other settings, while the principles could be applied by school leaders in their work with members of their teams.

What can we learn about how to help others to change?

This approach demonstrates the benefit of the following principles:

- *Envisaging:* determining what the preferred future or outcome looks like and then working towards that.
- *Appreciation:* recognizing the positives and then building from there.
- *Utilization:* drawing on what is available, including the practitioner's own resources.
- *Challenging:* drawing the practitioner's attention to ways in which their behaviour may be discrepant with their goals.
- *Collaboration:* working *with* the practitioner, rather than *doing to* them.

The case study also tells us something about motivation and commitment – that is, individuals are more likely to initiate and sustain a higher quality of performance if they experience a greater degree of self-determination in relation to the desired behaviour. In other words, if the person has a sense of ownership over the behaviour, can see a genuine meaning or value in the behaviour, and/or has connected it to a goal or value that is important to them, then behaviour change is more likely. Indeed, this is one of the fundamental reasons why coaching – done well – is an effective intervention.

Finally, the case study demonstrates the role that core needs play in influencing our performance and wellbeing. In this case, it was when Richard's core needs for competence, autonomy and relatedness were satisfied that he experienced enhanced motivation and commitment, and if we are working with another person to support them in achieving behaviour change, attention to these needs is of paramount importance. However, these are just the core needs described by SDT, and there are other human needs described by other psychological approaches that we might also have regard to. Consider the following, for example:

- *Contribution*: the individual has a sense that they are contributing to others or making a difference in some way.
- *Purpose* and/or *meaning*: the person is contributing to the realization of a larger cause or vision.
- *Engagement:* the person is able to exercise their strengths in pursuit of the goal.
- *Learning* and/or *challenge*: the person experiences growth and development.
- *Stimulation:* the person experiences either variety or challenge.
- *Creativity/self-expression*: the person is able to exercise a drive to be original or to do things in a different way.

- *To be valued*: the person has the sense that they are valued and cared for, or that they matter.

Stop to reflect for a moment: how do *you* feel when those needs are satisfied versus not satisfied? What impact does this have on your performance and wellbeing? I suspect that you will notice a relationship between satisfaction of some of these needs and those variables. Different needs may take more of a priority for different individuals at different times, but if we can learn to pay attention to these core drivers, it enhances our ability to create relationships and environments which enable people to unlock and express their potential.

How could you apply these skills or principles in your own practice?

Reflection questions

1   In what circumstances could you use the nine-step performance coaching method described in this chapter? Who might benefit?
2   Think of some situations where you would like another person (or other people) to 'take on' (internalize) a particular behaviour. How can you support them to experience an enhanced sense of self-determination in relation to the behaviour?
   a   How will you help them to own the behaviour?
   b   What can you do to influence their perception of the importance of the behaviour?
   c   How can you help them to consider how the behaviour relates to their own goals and values?
3   Which of your needs are satisfied at present? Which ones would you like to be satisfied that are not?
4   If you lead an organization, how do you satisfy the core needs of the people who work in it? How can you further develop a need-satisfying environment?

Suggested reading

Ryan, R. M. & Deci, E. L. (2000). Self-determination theory and the facilitation of intrinsic motivation, social development, and wellbeing. *American Psychologist*, *55*: 68–78.

Chapter 8

Coaching for development

> Inherent in developmental coaching is an assumption of movement from where the client is now to where he or she wants to be, whether that is in relation to making practical changes in the work environment, making changes in response to emotional pressure, or making changes in levels of understanding and responses to the world around them.
>
> (Cox & Jackson, 2014, p. 215)

In Chapter 7 we saw how coaching can be applied to support education practitioners to move towards identified performance standards. However, coaching is far more than just a remedial intervention to be adopted in perceived deficit scenarios, representing an individualized form of continuing professional development (CPD) available to potentially any practitioner. The benefit of coaching as opposed to some other forms of CPD is that the support can be precisely tailored to the needs of the coachee, focusing on matters that are specifically relevant to their day-to-day reality. In this chapter we will see how coaching psychology can be applied to enhance practitioner development, in this case supporting a senior leader to develop her proficiency at 'people management'.

A method for development coaching

The following points are a guide to development coaching:

1 Determine the focus area and the hoped-for outcome (the latter may, of course, be reshaped as the engagement continues and new information comes to light).
2 Consider which approaches or models might be relevant to supporting the coachee's development.
3 Work with the coachee to support reflection on the identified development area, drawing on the desired approach.
4 Develop an action plan.
5 Review progress; refine the plan; address any obstacles to change.
6 Final review and evaluation.

With regard to point 2, the specific approach drawn on will vary according to the situation and the coachee. For example, the following might be attempted:

- Using the GROW model to generate practical options as to how the coachee might face particular situations.
- Taking a solution-focused approach, asking the coachee to imagine their preferred future, looking for signs of that preferred future already happening, and helping them to plan a small step forward that draws on their strengths and resources (5.2).
- Using a cognitive-behavioural approach to identify, dispute and transform self-limiting beliefs that may be impacting on the practitioner's development, while also supporting them to plan new behaviours (5.3).

The specific technique used is less important than the extent to which the coachee experiences the relationship as a positive, collaborative alliance (see 5.9). In other words, we need to ensure that we establish a constructive bond with the coachee, that we are on the same page about the goals being worked on, and that there is agreement about the tasks that will be engaged in both in and out of the sessions. To this end, the coach can transparently share the rationale for using a particular tool or exploring a specific line of enquiry, enabling the coachee to make an informed decision about whether or not they wish to pursue it.

The remainder of this chapter will demonstrate the application of development coaching in a school context, drawing on the principles and practices of Solution-Focused Coaching (SFC – see 5.2) and Self-Efficacy Theory (5.4). At each stage, italicized headings will identify the specific techniques or principles being applied.

Case study

Background

Rosanna was a senior leader in a secondary school who had been in post for just over a year. While a highly effective practitioner, she had no previous experience of management or leadership, and was encountering some difficulties in the role. The head teacher sought coaching for Rosanna to support her in addressing some of these difficulties and to consolidate her transition from practitioner to leader. A series of coaching sessions was arranged, beginning with a contracting meeting.

Contracting

In this case, a tripartite meeting was arranged involving the head teacher (as the person who both commissioned and requested the coaching engagement), the coachee and the coach. At the meeting, the rationale for seeking coaching was transparently discussed, and the focus of the engagement was identified. The head teacher was keen for Rosanna to find her own effective style of leadership and management that would enable her to feel confident in her ability to secure the co-operation and engagement of the members of their team. Rosanna was also of the view that this was the necessary focus, and so with both parties in agreement the conversation could continue.

Eliciting the preferred future

A preferred future is the coachee's vision of life without the problem, an imagined time when the goals of the engagement have been achieved and the benefits of doing so have been realized. To elicit a vision of the future, the coach can ask the coachee a variation of one or more of the following questions:

- 'Imagine it's the end of the academic year and some changes have happened that you are pleased with . . . What is happening?'
- 'Imagine that our work is concluded and has been successful . . . How do you know?
- 'Let's say things are happening as you would like them to . . . What would that look like?'
- 'Imagine watching one video showing the problem being enacted . . . Now imagine another video showing your preferred future being enacted . . . What's different?'
- 'How would you like things to be different?'

The coach asked Rosanna to imagine that their work had concluded successfully and that she was experiencing the benefits of a successful engagement. When asked how she would know that this had happened, Rosanna's initial reply was that she would have a 'toolbox of strategies' that she could use for managing what she referred to as 'people situations'. This could have been interpreted in different ways, and the specific meaning Rosanna intended was somewhat ambiguous. Some further shaping of her response was required in order for it to provide a useful focus for coaching.

Shaping the preferred future

On many occasions the preferred future descriptions initially offered by coachees will require further shaping in order to provide the necessary clarity, direction and motivation for the engagement. Table 8.1 shows some of the problems that can be commonly encountered when eliciting preferred future descriptions, and offers some questions/prompts to support the process of shaping the response into a more helpful description (see also Berg & De Jong, 2000; Iveson *et al.*, 2012):

While Rosanna's initial response was a useful starting point for discussion, it was not sufficiently detailed and some further clarification of her wishes was needed. The coach proceeded to ask shaping questions in order to elaborate and clarify the description (e.g. 'If you were doing that successfully, what would be different?', 'How would you feel?'), while reflecting back his understanding of

Table 8.1 Shaping preferred futures

If the preferred future is ...	Prompts like these can be used ...	To shape a description that is ...
Vague and general	'What would that look like?' 'What would that sound like?' 'In what circumstances?' 'What specifically is happening?'	Detailed and specific
Negative (i.e. about something not happening)	'What will be happening instead?' 'When you aren't doing that, what will you be doing differently?'	Phrased in positive terms
All about others changing	'How will things be different for you?' 'What will you be doing differently?' 'What will people see you doing?'	One that involves the person
Unrealistic	'What would be the first sign of that happening?' 'How likely is that, do you think?'	Realistic
A strategy or process for achieving an aim, rather than an outcome in itself	'Assuming we did that in a way that worked for you, what would the outcome be?' 'Let's say that's successful ... How will you know?'	A description of a specific outcome

Rosanna's meaning to ensure that they were on the same page. The resultant description was much more detailed and unambiguous. It transpired that, if Rosanna was managing 'people situations' as she wanted to, the members of her team would be engaged in achieving the goals of the school and would be responsive to her attempts to motivate them. Furthermore, she would feel confident about approaching the members of staff with requests in her management role. The head teacher agreed that this would be a worthwhile endeavour, and would address the need that had led her to seek coaching in the first place.

At this point it was important for the coach to clarify that he had not previously occupied a leadership position and so would not be able to provide mentoring-type advice. Instead, the emphasis would be on providing Rosanna with a safe and confidential space in which she could reflect on her experience and the different options available to her. With all parties clear about the direction for coaching and what the coach could and could not offer, the conversation continued. Having elicited a description of the coachee's preferred future, it was now important to determine the distance that needed to be travelled to achieve it.

Scaling

Scaling questions can be used to give an indication of where things are currently 'at' in relation to the coachee's preferred future. The coach can ask the coachee to imagine a scale from 0 to 10, with 10 being that the preferred future is happening and 0 being the opposite of that (i.e. as bad as things could get). The coachee can then be asked to indicate the point on the scale that represents where things are currently. Depending on the coachee's response, the coach might follow up with any one of a number of questions in order to understand the reason for their rating and, as long as the coachee has not indicated that things are at zero, to elicit helpful details about the existing signs of success that might be built upon. Follow-up questions might include:

* 'Tell me more about the reason for your rating.'
* 'What tells you things are there and not any lower?'
* 'What's helped you to get there?'
* 'What's stopping it from getting any lower?'

Later in the conversation or engagement, the scale can be returned to in order to identify goals, to set small-step targets towards them, and to measure progress. For example:

* 'Where would you like to get to?'
* 'What would a next step look like?'
* 'Last time things were at a [x] . . . Where have we got to?'

A deceptively simple strategy, scaling questions can be a powerful means of challenging all-or-nothing thinking (see Chapter 9) and introducing/emphasizing the idea of graduated approximations towards a desired outcome. They also have value in supporting the identification of small, manageable changes that are perceived as being within reach and which, if achieved, can lead to added hope and momentum.

The coach enquired about Rosanna's confidence in the 'people situations' she had referred to, and asked her to indicate her rating on a 0–10 scale. Rosanna said that it varied from person-to-person, and gave a number of responses ranging from 0 to 10 which were recorded on a visual scale and annotated with each team member's initials. The scale is reproduced here, but with the initials removed and replaced with alphabetic labels (team members A–F) for the purposes of anonymity (Figure 8.1).

Evidently, Rosanna felt very capable of managing some members of her team (E and F), but was less confident with others (A and B). The scale provided a platform for a discussion around reasons for the variation in her ratings, while her

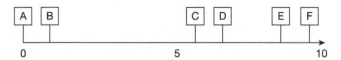

Figure 8.1 Rosanna's confidence ratings

higher ratings suggested possible areas of exploration in a search for her strengths and resources. However, there was insufficient time to explore this latter point in detail in the contracting meeting, so this discussion was deferred until the first coaching session.

Summarizing the session

The session was closed with the coach providing a summary of the ground covered in the meeting, which gave all participants another opportunity to check they had understood each other correctly and/or whether any key information had been omitted. This also enabled the coach to point out the fact that Rosanna's ratings clearly indicated that there were successes to build on, and to propose that this should become an early focus of the first coaching session proper. Importantly, the coach sought Rosanna's agreement about this, since her preference may have been to instead focus on 'problem' areas. As previously discussed, coaching engagements are more likely to result in positive outcomes if there is agreement between coach and coachee about the tasks undertaken within and between sessions. Pressing ahead with a particular line of enquiry without first obtaining the coachee's buy-in is less likely to be successful.

Coaching session I

Setting the direction

At the beginning of the session it was important to check in with Rosanna to see if she was still willing to explore her successes as previously suggested. Having confirmed that she was happy to do this, it was agreed to proceed as planned.

Exploring what is already going well

The solution-focused coach maintains an explicit interest in what is going well for the coachee, rather than focusing purely on problematic elements of their situation. As well as influencing the climate of the session, this can bring successes and strengths to the coachee's attention, and can inform the construction of solutions:

- 'What's going well at the moment?'
- 'What helped you to achieve that?'
- 'How did you do that?'
- 'What is already helping, even if only a bit?'

With Rosanna's agreement, the first session began with an exploration of the situations in which her confidence was higher. This allowed Rosanna and the coach to clarify some of her skills and strengths, and to think about whether they might be drawn on in the pursuit of her goal. In Rosanna's view, her strengths in relation to people management were mainly relationship-focused (i.e. her ratings were higher where she had good or better interpersonal relationships with the team members), and she believed that she had little to draw on when she did not have an existing good relationship with the practitioner in question. This, understandably, impacted on her confidence when dealing with certain members of staff. She succinctly summarized the issue as: 'When I don't have a really good personal relationship with them, I've got nothing. How can I get them to do the things I ask?' In expressing this view, Rosanna was indicating a lack of belief in her capacity to achieve desired results with some members of her team – i.e. a low level of self-efficacy (5.4). Whether or not this was the objective reality, her subjective perception was that she had no tools in her toolbox to aid her. This was despite a background of performing very successfully in other domains of her life, and despite achieving good successes with some of the practitioners in the school. The question was how to support her to move on from this. Notably, Rosanna's belief that she had nothing to call upon was an example of self-limiting extreme thinking (see Chapter 9), and the coach acknowledged the possibility that this perception may not, in fact, reflect the reality. To test this idea further, the coach invoked the solution-focused practice of exception-seeking.

Exception-seeking

In the parlance of SFC, exceptions are times when either 'the problem' is not as bad or when aspects of the coachee's preferred future are already happening. There is an assumption that, whatever the nature of the problem or goal being worked on, there are always times when things are better, even if only fractionally. These may have occurred outside the coachee's awareness, been dismissed as flukes, or seen as irrelevant, but they can be a valuable source of information and ideas. The search for exceptions can also involve an exploration of the coachee's successful functioning at other times or in other domains:

- 'When are there signs of that already happening?'
- 'When have you been able to do that more successfully?'
- 'What has worked for you in the past?'
- 'What has worked for you in other situations?'

In this case, the coach hypothesized that the skill of 'getting others to do things that are asked of them' was something that Rosanna would already have considerable experience of, given that she was a highly competent classroom practitioner. The rationale was shared with Rosanna, who agreed to experiment with exploration of this theme. Having sought Rosanna's agreement to explore this area (again ensuring agreement about the tasks undertaken), the coach asked Rosanna to trawl her experience to identify strategies she used to get students to do things that she asked of them. This generated a long list of strategies encompassing relationship-building strategies, attunement and empathy, motivational strategies, supportive strategies (e.g. removing barriers to work completion), and assertiveness. With a bank of resources generated, it was now time to see if they could be applied to Rosanna's current situation to take her in the direction of her preferred future.

Identifying a next step forward

Sometimes, there may be a large gap between the coachee's present situation and their preferred future. If this is the case, it is unlikely (although not impossible) that the gap will be closed quickly. Furthermore, the impression of a large distance to travel can be demotivating for some coachees, who may become disheartened at the sight of a large chasm to leap. To address this problem, and to make the prospect of achieving change seem more manageable, the solution-focused coach can support the coachee to identify a small, achievable change that will constitute a meaningful step forward. This also further focuses the work and increases the likelihood of change occurring. To achieve this, the coach can ask questions such as:

- 'What would a sign of progress be?'
- 'What would a step forward on the scale look like?'

The emphasis is on planning a clear, small step forward that will make a difference to the coachee but is perceived to be within their reach. In Rosanna's case, given that her scale included multiple ratings, it was necessary to identify a particular starting point from which to work. Rosanna considered two of the areas in which she was less confident (team member A = 0/10; team member B = 1/10), and picked one of these as a focus. Importantly, Rosanna did not immediately target her attention on the most difficult challenge, instead choosing one that seemed more achievable to her. When asked what a sign of progress would look like, Rosanna articulated that a good sign would be getting team member B to meet a deadline for submitting children's exam papers to the exam board, something which had not been achieved previously. This had led to Rosanna making embarrassing telephone calls to the exam board to request extensions, and paying for packages of papers to be separately couriered. The coach and Rosanna explored the benefits of attaining this goal for her, for the students, and for the organization. Thereafter, it was agreed to make this goal the immediate focus.

Bridging from success to problem

Bridging is a strategy in which the coach supports the coachee to apply existing strengths and successes to new challenges or domains. Sometimes, people can dismiss their existing skills as being irrelevant to something that seems new and unfamiliar, but further scrutiny might highlight opportunities for transferability and generalization that have been hitherto overlooked.

The coach drew Rosanna's attention to the long list of strategies that she had previously used successfully with both adults and students, and asked her to reflect on whether any of them could be brought to bear on the situation under discussion. This was an exercise of open exploration, considering different possibilities, their applicability, and their possible impact. Rosanna began to consider options in this respect, but the session was coming to a close, so there was insufficient time to explore this in detail.

Between-session tasks

At the end of each session the solution-focused coach can support the coachee to identify actions that will take them in the direction of their preferred future. This could be doing more of what is working, doing something different, or simply noticing things that are happening that they would like to see continue (O'Connell & Palmer, 2007). In this case, given that the session had come to an end before the bridging exercise could be completed, Rosanna agreed to reflect further outside the session about the ways in which her skills and strengths might be applied in the pursuit of her goal.

Coaching sessions 2–3

Setting the direction

At the beginning of subsequent sessions the coachee is again asked to indicate their best hopes for the hour. This facilitates the construction of a rough agenda for the session which ensures the coachee's priority needs are addressed. With Rosanna, it was agreed to review the progress from the previous session before coming on to discuss a new problem situation.

Reviewing progress since the last session

Second and subsequent coaching sessions represent an opportunity to review progress; consolidate and celebrate successes; develop new strategies for change; and to consider whether to identify new goals or to bring the coaching engagement to a close (O'Connell, 2002). If scaling questions have been asked in earlier sessions, then these can be revisited as a platform for exploring the extent to which change has occurred.

When considering her progress on the between-session task, Rosanna reported that she had, in fact, gone further than simply reflecting on the ways in which she might apply her strengths. Instead, she had actually taken action to move towards the identified goal, and had experienced some considerable progress in the situation with team member B. Whereas previously no students' work had been submitted to the exam board in time for the original deadline, this time *twenty* students' work had been entered. To achieve this, Rosanna had implemented a number of strategies, including:

- Trying to tap into shared values with team member B.
- Explaining the impact of not meeting the deadline on all involved.
- Putting supportive strategies in place.
- Using humour.

These were all strategies that had been identified in the previous session as those that had worked for her at times in other situations or domains. To achieve this result through the application of her existing skills was a very pleasing success that had a range of benefits for the school, the students and Rosanna herself. The coach asked Rosanna to review her confidence rating on the previously constructed scale, and she indicated that her overall confidence in dealing with team member B had moved from a '1' to a '7'. This represented a significant change in a short space of time.

Facilitating efficacy-supportive processing

Self-Efficacy Theory holds that success experiences alone are not enough to strengthen an individual's self-efficacy beliefs; instead, it is how those experiences are processed that is the key (5.4). Therefore, when individuals experience success as a result of their own efforts, it can be important to ensure that they acknowledge this and derive whatever learning they can from the experience in order to strengthen their belief in their capabilities. With this aim in mind, the coach asked Rosanna to reflect on what she had learned from the situation, to which she replied:

> I've realized that I am good at leading people in my life, and that the only barrier was in me – a lack of confidence. I've realized that I do have strategies that I can call on to lead others, and it was stupid of me to think I couldn't do it.

In expressing this view, Rosanna demonstrated that her self-limiting belief about her ability to lead had been significantly challenged, and that she had reconnected with a bank of skills and resources that had previously been inaccessible to her. She seemed energized by this realization, and had noticeably grown in confidence.

Planning further small steps forward

Thereafter, the focus of the engagement shifted to the next short-term goal, which for the sake of brevity will not be detailed here. Suffice to say that Rosanna's positive trajectory continued and all parties agreed that further coaching was no longer necessary.

Efficacy-supportive feedback

Towards the end of the coaching session or engagement, the coachee can be provided with specific feedback about, for example, strengths they have demonstrated, qualities they have shown or successes they have experienced. This concludes the session positively, while aiming to further strengthen the coachee's sense of self-efficacy. Throughout the conversation, the coach listens for strengths and competences so that these can be brought to the coachee's attention – for example, 'I noticed that you are values driven and conscientious, and are determined to give your all for the benefit of the students.' Of course, it is important for such feedback to be both genuine and sincere.

Evaluation

At the time of evaluation, Rosanna reported that the coaching had had a positive impact on her performance, development, wellbeing and her ability to help herself in future. She concluded:

> I feel confident in my ability to use my skills in new situations. I feel happier and more effective in my role as a leader. I feel that I can meet new challenges and come up with strategies to help in my personal and professional life.

The tangible impact of the engagement was also noted by the commissioning head teacher, who similarly reported a noticeable impact on all dimensions measured. She observed that:

> [The] work with Rosanna has substantially increased her confidence as a leader. It has also given her the tools she needs to become an outstanding one. [It] enabled her to see the resources and strength she had inside herself and the strategies to use them effectively.

Reflections and conclusions

How was coaching applied to support improvement of performance, development and/or wellbeing?

This chapter has demonstrated how coaching was applied to support the continuing professional development of an education practitioner, in this case enabling a senior leader to discover that the capacity to lead and manage others effectively was something that already existed within her own resources. This resulted in professional growth, increased performance and enhanced confidence on the part of the coachee, with corresponding benefits for the setting.

What coaching models, skills or techniques have we covered?

The case study illustrates the application of the principles and practices of SFC and Self-Efficacy Theory. This included:

- Eliciting and shaping a description of the coachee's *preferred future*.
- Using *scaling* questions to determine where things were 'at' in relation to the preferred future and to support planning of a small step forward.
- Exploring *what was already going well* in the coachee's life and practice.
- Searching for *exceptions* – times when the preferred future was already happening, even if only in part.
- *Bridging* strategies from an area of success to an area of challenge or difficulty.
- *Facilitating efficacy-supportive processing* of success experiences by asking the practitioner to draw conclusions from their experience.
- Providing *efficacy-supportive feedback* about strengths the practitioner had demonstrated or qualities they had shown.

The 'preferred future' description – once shaped – provided a focus and direction for the work while ensuring that both coach and coachee were clear about the changes desired. This also enabled both parties to recognize and value success when it was achieved. Scaling questions were helpful for exploring the coachee's present reality and stimulating discussion about what was working well; they were also called upon later in the engagement to support the identification of target areas for change and to provide a means of measuring progress in the review session. Finally, the classic solution-focused search for successes, strengths, resources and exceptions led to the discovery of a range of strategies that were later applied to support the coachee to achieve her goal.

How else could this approach or these principles be applied?

In this engagement, coaching psychology was applied to support a senior leader to develop her confidence and proficiency at engaging and motivating other members of her team; however, the methods described in this book have broad applicability and could be utilized to good effect in a range of contexts and situations. For example:

- Supporting a classroom practitioner to further develop proficiency at, for example, facilitating learning, managing behaviour, motivating the children, or creating a positive classroom environment.
- Supporting a learning mentor to develop their skills for coaching children.
- Supporting a middle or senior leader to develop their skills for managing difficult conversations with parents.
- Supporting a specialist leader of education to develop their proficiency at coaching other adults.

In all these cases, the psychological approaches described in Chapter 5 can be applied to provide the practitioner with a safe, confidential space in which they can reflect on aspects of their professional and personal development. As Cox & Jackson (2014) summarize, the emphasis is on supporting the person to move from where they are to where they would like to be, whatever their starting point and whatever internal or external factors may be relevant. Given that coaching can be tailored to the exact needs of the professional in their specific context, it therefore represents a valuable, versatile option available to schools for supporting the ongoing development of their staff.

What can we learn about how to help others to change?

A key theme that emerged in the course of this engagement was that of the coachee's sense of self-efficacy – that is, their belief in their ability to produce desired results from their own actions (Bandura, 1977, 1997; see 5.4). At first, Rosanna was unable to recognize and value some of her own skills, and there was a psychological gap between her previous experience and the new challenges she was encountering. Consistent with Self-Efficacy Theory, her efficacy beliefs were domain-specific, and did not automatically generalize from one situation or context to another. It is likely that the efficacy-reducing belief of 'When I don't have a personal relationship with them, I've got nothing' was a key factor in this case; this self-told story seemed to prevent Rosanna from recognizing and harnessing her existing skills, effectively nailing them shut in a closed box and thereafter resulting in her sense of feeling deskilled. An important part of the coaching intervention was supporting Rosanna to recognize the value of her existing experience, and then to bridge the gap from her previous successes to her new situation. Continuing the metaphor, this prised the nails from the closed box and enabled Rosanna to see the relevance of her existing skills to achieving her goal. Her subsequent processing of this success experience then challenged her self-limiting belief about her capabilities and resulted in improved confidence. Had Rosanna not made progress by tapping into her own resources, then other approaches to support her in developing her proficiency and confidence may have been required (e.g. skills training, mentoring, modelling). For other ways to support coachees to develop self-efficacy beliefs, see Maddux (2005) or Luthans et al. (2007). However, the key point is that working to enhance the individual's sense of self-efficacy is a key goal for anyone attempting to support others to change. Clearly, the methods of SFC have much to offer in this respect, reflecting the principles of *utilization* and *appreciation* described in previous chapters.

It is important to note that a constructive alliance characterized by collaboration between coach and coachee was a core feature of the work, and the techniques alone would most likely not have survived without this key ingredient. In sessions themselves, the alliance was maintained by e.g. listening to the coachee, respecting her as an equal partner, sharing the rationale for different strategies used, and seeking her opinion about possible avenues of exploration before embarking down a given path. As emphasized by O'Connell (2002):

> It needs to be reiterated that how we relate to clients as human beings is more significant than any techniques or theories. Technique is no substitute for a relationship built on respectful and attentive listening, reflective silences, empathy, genuineness, immediacy and acceptance.
>
> (O'Connell, 2002, p. 41)

As well as illustrating the value of specific techniques, the case study has also demonstrated the value of solution-focused *principles* about how to effectively help others to change. The benefits of a future-focused orientation have already been discussed, but there are also some other points of note to acknowledge. Importantly, the case shows us the potential impact of planning and achieving a small change, which can then lead to a ripple effect in terms of escalating confidence and gradually increasing returns. We might refer to this as reflecting the principle of *developing*, in that growth is stimulated by initially encouraging a small forward movement. The point is well encapsulated by Milton Erickson, who observed that 'Therapy is often a matter of tipping the first domino' (cited in O'Connell, 2002, p. 41). In the context of coaching, this means supporting the coachee to plan small, realistic steps towards their preferred future, thereby increasing the likelihood of change occurring and closing the gap between the present reality and their desired outcome. As this happens, we see them begin to move forward and gather momentum as they realize that change *is* within their grasp. The focus on planning small steps forward means that, as de Shazer (1985, 1988) and Berg (Berg & De Jong, 2002) argued, meaningful change can sometimes be achieved in very few sessions; if this is the case, then prolonged, resource-intensive coaching engagements may not be necessary for some individuals.

How could you apply these skills or principles in your own practice?

Reflection questions

1   In what circumstances could you use the six-step development coaching method described in this chapter? Who might benefit?
2   How could you use solution-focused techniques in your own life or practice? In what circumstances might you be able to support people to envisage a preferred future and then to draw on their successes and strengths to respond to the challenges they are facing?
3   What can you do in the coming days and weeks to support another person to develop an enhanced sense of self-efficacy?
4   How can you bring your own strengths and successes to bear on a challenge that you may be facing?

Suggested reading

Iveson, C., George, E. & Ratner, H. (2012). *Brief Coaching: A Solution-Focused Approach.* Hove: Routledge.

Maddux, J. (2005). Self-efficacy: The power of believing you can. In C. Snyder & S. Lopez (eds), *Handbook of Positive Psychology.* New York: Oxford University Press.

O'Connell, B., Palmer, S. & Williams, H. (2012). *Solution-Focused Coaching in Practice.* Hove: Routledge.

Chapter 9

Coaching for wellbeing

> If we want to improve school performance, we also need to start paying attention to teacher wellbeing. How teachers feel on an everyday basis is likely to affect their performance and so, in turn, the performance of the pupils they teach.
>
> (Briner & Dewberry, 2007, p. 4).

So far, the applications described in this book have focused on supporting the performance and/or development of education practitioners. However, coaching can also focus on the enhancement of *wellbeing*. Is this important, you might wonder? Shouldn't teachers just get on with the job of providing for the pupils? Actually, there is some research to suggest that attending to staff wellbeing can help them to do just that. A study by Briner & Dewberry (2007) found a positive correlation between staff wellbeing and pupil performance, even after controlling for other factors that may also have influenced the outcomes. Of course, a correlation does not imply a causal relationship, so we need to consider that pupil performance may be the variable that influences wellbeing rather than the other way around. However, research associated with positive psychology can also inform our understanding here. In the late 1990s, Barbara Fredrickson proposed a theory that positive emotions actually broaden people's thinking and behavioural repertoires and build enduring personal and social resources (5.8). Indeed, research carried out to test this hypothesis has shown that inducing positive emotion can enhance creativity, foster open-mindedness, improve intellectual functioning, and increase productivity (see Seligman, 2003; Fredrickson, 2005). Thus, the research does seem to suggest that there is a direct relationship between wellbeing and performance – that is, if we intervene to enhance a practitioner's wellbeing, we can predict that there will be a corresponding impact on their functioning. Thereafter, this may lead to increasing returns from upward spirals as wellbeing feeds performance which feeds wellbeing, and so on. Therefore, interventions that focus on enhancing staff wellbeing can be valuable to schools who wish to have a positive influence on the performance of their staff. This chapter will illustrate how psychological principles and approaches can be applied in the context of coaching in order to enhance practitioner wellbeing and performance.

A method for coaching for wellbeing

1   Determine the focus area and the hoped-for outcome (the latter may, of course, be reshaped as the engagement continues and new information comes to light).
2   Consider which approaches or models might be relevant to supporting the coachee's wellbeing.
3   Work with the coachee to support them in applying the relevant approach, ideally leaving them equipped with tools that enable them to continue to self-coach.
4   Develop an action plan.
5   Review progress; refine the plan; address any obstacles to change.
6   Final review and evaluation.

Case study

Background

Michael was a primary school practitioner who was becoming concerned that he was developing anxiety relating to a 'public speaking phobia' (his description). The head teacher of the school arranged for Michael to have coaching to support him in addressing the problem.

Contracting

Prior to the first session taking place, Michael was provided with information about the nature of coaching, the coach's role and experience, the confidentiality parameters of the sessions, and the number of sessions that had been contracted. This degree of transparency is important for building trust while also providing the coachee with a sense of clarity, direction and safety. It also ensures that both parties are on the same page in terms of their expectations and their understanding about their respective roles and responsibilities. The head teacher was willing for Michael to self-select the goals of the engagement, and so in this instance there was no need for a tripartite contracting meeting to take place (see Appendix 1). Michael was asked to start thinking in advance of the first coaching session about his preferred focus for discussion and the outcomes he would like to achieve from the coaching engagement.

First coaching session

Clarifying the focus and goals of the engagement; forming a collaborative alliance

At the beginning of the first session the coach briefly set the scene as to how the two parties had come together, and checked in with Michael to see if he had understood and/or had questions about the confidentiality parameters. After that, the preparatory questions about the focus of the work and Michael's best hopes for the engagement were revisited. As Michael talked through his situation and provided relevant background information, the coach listened attentively and attempted to elicit, understand and summarize the key issues.

Michael had been a teacher at the school for seven years. Having a number of years of experience under his belt, and having worked in the same school for that period of time, the expectation was that he would now begin to 'step up' and take on more leadership responsibilities in the school. This meant, among other things, having a more prominent role in staff meetings and speaking to the team of staff as a whole group. Michael was experiencing increasing anxiety about speaking in public to groups of adults and saw this as being something he was 'no good' at. This was becoming a problem for him in terms of the impact it was having; each time such a situation loomed in the calendar, he would become stressed and preoccupied, dreading the approaching event (to the point of experiencing physical reactions) and spending disproportionate amounts of time and energy either worrying about it or preparing for it. As such, it would completely take over, and this was having a deleterious impact on both his performance and wellbeing. It was also beginning to have a knock-on impact in other domains of his life, in that he was finding himself becoming less confident when talking to new people outside work. In terms of the outcome he wanted to achieve, Michael wanted to be able to speak to a group of staff without getting as nervous. This was important to him, as he did not want to be an 'invisible practitioner' in the school.

So how can we support a person who is experiencing such issues with their emotional wellbeing? Of course, we have options that we can call upon, and there is no 'right' or 'wrong' approach; however, the principles of cognitive-behavioural coaching (CBC) can be particularly relevant to such explorations.

The central premise of CBC is that people's feelings are not caused directly by events, but rather what they make of those events through their interpretations – that is, the way in which a person *thinks* about an experience will influence their feelings and behaviour. Applied to this case, this led to the hypothesis that Michael's anxiety may be in some way related to the way he was thinking about speaking to groups of staff. To explore this hypothesis, the coach suggested that they work together to develop a diagram to map out a situation Michael had encountered and his reactions to it. For this purpose, the cognitive-behavioural SPACE coaching model was introduced.

Using the SPACE model to understand a person's reactions

The SPACE model (Edgerton & Palmer, 2005) is a CBC framework that can be used to develop insight into a person's reactions to a situation. The basic framework is shown in Figure 9.1.

The *Social context* is the environment the person is in when they experience their reaction. The different components of the person's reaction are then represented in the four different PACE domains: their *Physical* reaction, their

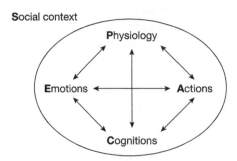

Figure 9.1 The SPACE model

Actions (behaviours), their *Cognitions* (thoughts) and their *Emotions*. To populate the framework, the coach asks the coachee to talk through their situation and annotates the diagram as relevant information emerges.

In this case, the first step was to ask Michael to think of a particular situation he had experienced when his anxiety had occurred. He elected to focus the exploration on a situation in which he had wanted to share a piece of information with the group of staff during the morning briefing. The coach drew a blank SPACE diagram, and asked Michael to begin talking through what had happened. As Michael talked about the situation and his reactions to it, the coach annotated the diagram with key pieces of information from Michael's account. In addition, the coach also asked further prompting questions about what was happening for him in each of the PACE domains.

Michael began by describing his physical reaction to the situation, since this was the thing that was most concerning to him (NB: different coachees may have different preferences as to the point in the model at which they begin). He described that, when getting ready to speak, his heart had been racing and he was shaking; then, when he did speak, he spoke quickly without taking a breath and his voice 'bubbled up' in his throat (his description). This was accompanied by emotions of anxiety, embarrassment and frustration. In terms of the impact on his actions, this led him to rush his contribution and cut it short in an attempt to get it over and done with. The coach was also able to enquire about any cognitions (e.g. thoughts or images) that Michael may have experienced by asking: 'What was going through your mind?' (Beck, 2011). This resulted in the identification of some cognitions that may well have been a contributory factor to Michael's feelings, including:

- 'Everyone's thinking "Why is he nervous?"'
- 'It shouldn't be this difficult!'
- 'It will make out I'm not very good at my job!'
- 'I'm going to be found out for being a bad teacher and they will all think I'm rubbish!'

Figure 9.2 illustrates the completed SPACE diagram.

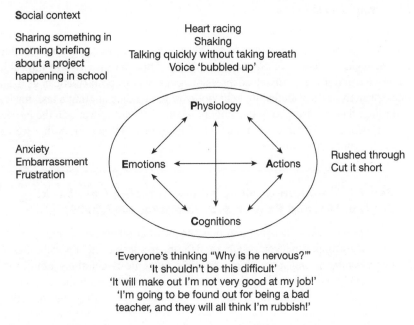

Social context

Sharing something in
morning briefing
about a project
happening in school

Heart racing
Shaking
Talking quickly without taking breath
Voice 'bubbled up'

Physiology

Anxiety
Embarrassment
Frustration

Emotions

Actions

Rushed through
Cut it short

Cognitions

'Everyone's thinking "Why is he nervous?"'
'It shouldn't be this difficult'
'It will make out I'm not very good at my job!'
'I'm going to be found out for being a bad
teacher, and they will all think I'm rubbish!'

Figure 9.2 A SPACE diagram representing one of Michael's anxious reactions

The coach was able to draw Michael's attention to the interactive relationship between his thoughts, feelings and behaviour, and the particular role that some of his thoughts may have had in contributing to his reactions. This was achieved by asking questions such as 'How did that thought impact on your feelings?', 'What did that do to your body?' and 'When you felt that, what did you do?' This highlighted a link between some of Michael's thought patterns and his feelings of anxiety, embarrassment and frustration. Already, Michael was developing some insight into the role that his thinking may have played in determining his emotional and physical reaction; however, the session was coming to a close, so it was agreed to return to this theme in the second coaching session.

Second coaching session

Recap from previous session

To begin, the coach and Michael referred back to the SPACE diagram that had been completed in the first session. Having refreshed their memories of the work completed, the discussion turned to identifying ways in which Michael's thinking might be contributing to his anxiety. Such explorations can be guided by a search for possible *thinking errors* in the coachee's interpretations that might be contributing to their unwanted feelings.

Identifying thinking errors

Thinking errors are extreme or illogical ways of thinking about events that can distort the person's interpretation of reality and impact negatively on both feelings and behaviour (Palmer & Szymanska, 2007). This can give rise to unhealthy negative emotions (e.g. anxiety, depression, guilt, shame, problematic anger), and unconstructive or self-defeating behaviours (e.g. avoiding starting a task for fear of failing, thereby decreasing the amount of time one has to work on the project; see Dryden, 2011). There are a number of common thinking errors that we can make, as summarized in Box 9.1.

Box 9.1 Common thinking errors (adapted from Beck, 2011, p. 181, and Palmer & Szymanska, 2007, p. 99)

- *Mind reading*: insisting that one knows what others are thinking (e.g. 'They think I'm incompetent') and failing to consider other possibilities.
- *Fortune-telling*: assuming a possible outcome is definitely going to happen without having the necessary evidence to reach that decision (e.g. 'It's all going to go badly', 'I just know this isn't going to work out').
- *All-or-nothing thinking*: evaluating experiences on the basis of extremes; things are either 'excellent' or 'terrible', 'perfection' or 'failure', with no shades of grey. Also called *black-and-white thinking*.
- *Catastrophizing*: predicting that the worst case scenario will happen without considering other more likely outcomes – e.g. 'If I challenge her about that aspect of her work it will be the end of our relationship and she will never speak to me again.'
- *Awfulizing*: exaggerating how unpleasant or uncomfortable something has been – e.g. 'That was a totally awful experience!'
- *Magnification/minimization*: disproportionately emphasizing the negative or downplaying the positive aspects of oneself, another person, or a situation – e.g. 'That negative feedback proves I'm incompetent', 'They're only giving me positive feedback because we get on.'
- *Personalization* or *blame*: entirely blaming oneself or others for the unwanted outcome of events, overlooking the contribution of the broader range of factors – e.g. 'The school going into special measures was all my fault.' Personalization can also mean believing others' behaviour is because of us – e.g. 'They look unhappy, it must be something I've done.'
- *Emotional reasoning*: because you feel something strongly, thinking that it *must* be true, perhaps ignoring or discounting other evidence ('I feel anxious . . . I just know this performance management meeting is going to go badly').

- *Labelling*: using global labels to describe oneself or others – e.g. 'idiot', 'failure', 'incompetent' – rather than focusing on specific behaviours or considering other contradictory evidence.
- *Demands*: rigid and inflexible demands made of oneself or others, usually expressed in the form of *musts*, *shoulds*, *have-tos* and *ought-tos*, e.g. 'I must always perform perfectly', 'She should be more motivated than she is'). Often followed by overestimation of how bad it is that such expectations are not met – e.g. 'I shouldn't have behaved that way, and because I did it's terrible and I'm a terrible person.' Demands can also involve denial of reality rather than accepting that things are the way they are ('This shouldn't be happening!'; 'I should be able to do this easily!').
- *Low frustration tolerance*: telling oneself that any discomfort or unpleasantness experienced in the pursuit of one's goals is simply too much to bear or not worth it (also known as I-can't-stand-it-itis).
- *Phoney-ism*: holding the belief that one is a phoney, fraud or impostor who is sooner or later going to be found out by others. This is also known as *impostor syndrome* (see later this chapter).

Often, thinking errors are not the product of conscious, deliberate reasoning, but are instead automatic thoughts that seem to spring up quickly and spontaneously in the stream of consciousness (Beck, 2011). Frequently, such automatic thoughts can occur outside people's awareness, and learning to recognize and catch them is a skill that develops with practice.

Reflection question

Refer back to Michael's SPACE diagram. Can you identify any possible thinking errors?

To support this exploration, the coach asked Michael to identify if any of the thoughts were particularly 'hot' – that is, thoughts that could have a significant impact on his feelings and which could therefore be a key target for intervention (Beck, 2011). Michael quickly indicated that a particularly hot thought was 'It shouldn't be this difficult!' This was an example of a *demand* that things be different to the way they were. Through questioning, the coach prompted Michael to consider the impact that this belief was having on his feelings and behaviour. Of course, this thought did not take his anxiety away; rather, he could see on reflection that it led to frustration, which in turn led to further changes in his physiology (e.g. higher temperature, further increased heart rate). Michael noted that, as well as compounding his physical symptoms, this would also make him more inclined to think 'I can't be bothered', and then rush what he was saying to try to get the whole thing over and done with as quickly as possible. With a particularly problematic thought having been identified, the focus turned to supporting Michael to transform his self-limiting thought into more adaptive alternatives. To this end, the coach introduced Michael to the cognitive-behavioural method of *disputation.*

Disputing self-limiting thoughts

Disputation is a process in which questioning is used to challenge and evaluate the validity and utility of thinking errors. The coach draws the individual's attention to the evidence for and against their conclusions, encourages consideration of alternative interpretations, and supports the coachee in developing a more rational and balanced appraisal of themselves and/or the situation they are facing (Ellis, 1988). The starting point is an assumption that the unhelpful thought may not necessarily be true, no matter how strongly it is believed, with the coach and coachee then working collaboratively to try to view the problem or situation differently (Palmer & Szymanksa, 2007). This process of guided discovery typically involves exploring one or more of the following avenues (see e.g. Beck, 2011; Dryden, 2011; Seligman, 2003):

- Where is the evidence for your belief? Is there any evidence on the other side?
- How logical is it to conclude that from your experience?
- What is the impact of thinking that? How helpful is that thought?
- What alternative ways of thinking about it are there?

In this way, the coachee can be supported to examine their thoughts and beliefs, and to begin to generate new ways of perceiving themselves, the world and other people that will support them in achieving their goals. In this case, the coach elected to challenge Michael's belief that 'It shouldn't be this difficult' by drawing his attention to the fact that this was a self-imposed demand rather than a reflection of any objective reality. This was achieved by asking him: 'Where is that written?' This began the process of developing Michael's insight into the fact that his belief was just something in his mind and, therefore, something he could change.

Thinking skills

The search for alternative ways of thinking can also be guided by an awareness of more adaptive thinking skills that coachees can be supported to develop (Dryden, 2011; Palmer & Cooper, 2000; Palmer & Szymanska, 2007; Gyllensten & Palmer, 2012). These are summarized in Box 9.2.

Box 9.2 Thinking skills

- *De-awfulizing/De-catastrophizing:* is it really as bad as it could be? Is it 100 per cent awful? Might some good come from this? Will it pass? (e.g. 'It could be worse, and it's certainly taught me something').
- *Broadening the picture:* considering the range of factors influencing a situation, or considering the broader context in which an event has occurred ('That was a bad lesson, but it's one part of a bigger picture').
- *High frustration tolerance:* accepting frustration or discomfort as a necessary part of the route to achieving one's goals ('I might not like it, but I can stand it, and it will be worth it to do so').
- *Contingency planning:* What's the worst that can happen? If that happens, how will I handle it? Will I still be able to experience some happiness? Having prepared for that, how likely is it that the worst will happen? (We might call this 'facing your dragons', since the scary thought or image is faced and challenged rather than avoided).
- *Delabelling:* focusing on specific behaviours or events rather than using broad labels about ourselves or other people ('I don't like what he did, but that doesn't make him a total ***').
- *Compassion (to self or others):* accepting ourselves/others as fallible people who will inevitably have flaws or make mistakes, rather than damning them.
- *Changing demands to preferences:* replacing dogmatic, absolutist demands with more flexible preferences, often usefully followed by *de-awfulizing* the consequences of the preference not being satisfied, for example: 'I would prefer to always achieve high standards but if I don't on some occasions it's not awful and it doesn't make me an inadequate person.'
- *Acceptance:* instead of demanding that reality/the universe be different, accepting that it is as it is and then planning what to do from there. NB: This does not necessarily mean liking the way things are, colluding, or passively doing nothing. However, approaching a problem situation from a place of acceptance changes the quality and intensity of one's emotions and can lead to more effective problem-solving.
- *Gratitude/appreciation:* keeping sight of and in touch with the positive aspects of a situation and one's life more broadly.
- *Befriending yourself:* what would I say to a friend if they were in this position? Would I be so harsh and critical?
- *Relative thinking:* am I thinking in all-or-nothing terms? Are there some graduated steps in between?

Through the process of disputation and the application of thinking skills, Michael was supported to challenge and transform the self-limiting thought he had uncovered. This included changing his rigid demand to a more flexible *preference* ('I would prefer it if I wasn't nervous, but this is the way it is and I can do something about it'); and demonstrating more acceptance of reality, rather than trying to deny it ('I don't like it, but it's the way it is for now'). All of this would increase the extent to which he was willing to *accept* the anxiety, rather than getting frustrated about it and making matters worse. Michael noted that he would remind himself: 'I'd like it if I wasn't nervous, but I *am*, and I won't be so hard on myself.' With this belief in mind, he would try to take a bit more time over what he wanted to say, and would also work on controlling his breathing.

Michael seemed energized by the discovery that he could exert control over his thinking in order to influence his feelings and behaviour, and wanted to apply the same principles and skills to another 'hot' self-limiting belief – that he was going to be 'found out' for being a 'bad teacher' and everyone would think he was 'rubbish'. This was an example of *phoney-ism*, in which the individual fears that they are a phoney or a fraud whose true nature is soon to be discovered by significant others. The result of this belief was understandable anxiety when Michael encountered a public-speaking situation, and it seemed that this belief was potentially key to his situation. Would it be possible to dispute and transform this belief in a similar way?

Disputation (2)

To reiterate, Michael's self-limiting thought was: 'I'm going to be found out for being a bad teacher and they will all think I'm rubbish!' Implicit in this statement was a belief that Michael actually *was* a bad teacher, which understandably led him to feel anxious in situations in which he might be exposed. To explore this belief, it was first important to understand what Michael meant by the term 'bad teacher', so he was asked to elaborate on this. The coach used questioning to help him to paint the picture. He identified:

- Someone whose knowledge about their subject isn't very good.
- Can't explain things clearly.
- Can't respond to questions.
- Lacking in confidence.
- Disorganized.
- Doesn't listen to advice.
- Doesn't follow school policies.
- Stressed and shouting.
- Not managing the children.
- Speaking to the children in an unpleasant way.
- Children don't make progress.

- Poor quality of teaching.
- Boring lessons.

This was quite a character! Michael was then asked to identify the evidence that *he* was a bad teacher – the evidence for the prosecution. Indeed, in his view, there *was* some evidence of this, as follows:

- I can't always explain things clearly to adults.
- If I'm put on the spot, I can't respond to questions.
- I'm not as overtly confident as other teachers.

The coach then asked if there was any evidence for the defence – i.e. any evidence *against* the idea that Michael was a bad teacher. He identified:

- The children make progress.
- I've got good relationships with the children.
- The children enjoy coming to school.
- I'm organized.
- I follow school policies.
- I don't raise my voice very often.
- I'm good at behaviour management and the in-class stuff.
- I've had quite a few 'good' and a couple of 'outstanding' lesson observation ratings.
- I respond to feedback and correct things if needed.

With both lists populated, the coach asked Michael to justify the conclusion that *he* was a bad teacher from the available evidence. Michael reflected on the lists and realized that his conclusion was perhaps faulty. The coach drew Michael's attention to the fact that he was drawing overgeneralized conclusions about his overall quality or worth as a practitioner on the basis of several specific difficulties, and suggested that this might be a key thinking error to target in his intervention plan. Instead of thinking of his difficulties as an indication that he was a bad teacher, Michael could acknowledge his many positive features and keep his difficulties in perspective as a specific skill issue ('I'm not a bad teacher, I just find this particular thing difficult').

Having taken steps to address two of his self-limiting beliefs, it was now time to develop strategies to help Michael to achieve his goal of speaking to a group of adults.

Developing a multimodal intervention plan

To develop an intervention plan, the SPACE diagram can be used as a platform for generating and considering alternatives. The intervention plan is multimodal in that it enables both coach and coachee to consider interventions across the SPACE modalities that may support goal-achievement. This is achieved by asking questions such as:

- 'What changes might you make to your social context?'
- 'What physical strategies can you use?'
- 'What can you do differently?'
- 'What alternative ways of thinking about it are there?'
- 'How might this impact on your feelings?'

In this case, the coach supported Michael to develop a new SPACE diagram which captured the strategies he had generated earlier in the session, while also stimulating consideration of other practical ideas as to how he might increase his chances of achieving his goal successfully. Michael had previously reported that he had used imagery of things going well to try to prepare for a staff meeting, and the coach suggested that he might instead try *coping imagery* as an alternative approach (Beck, 2011; Palmer & Dryden, 1995); rather than imagining a picture of total success – an image that can be quickly punctured in reality – this would involve imagining a scene in which he could see that mistakes were happening but that he was dealing with them effectively. This can be a more realistic and confidence-boosting strategy than asking coachees to imagine mastery of the situation. This included an element of contingency-planning, in which Michael was asked to imagine things that might go wrong and how he might handle the situation if they did (e.g. 'Have some notes to check if I forget what I want to say'; 'Have some water in case my throat goes tight'). The new and final SPACE diagram is illustrated in Figure 9.3.

A lot of ground had been covered in one session, and it was agreed that some reflection time to further process some of the ideas would be helpful before definitely committing to action. Michael was also keen to explore further the concepts of thinking errors, disputation and thinking skills, and so was provided with materials to support him in doing this between sessions.

Coaching sessions 3–4

Follow-up sessions provide an opportunity to review progress, celebrate successes, refine and revise action plans, engage in problem-solving, and to further explore the relevance of the cognitive-behavioural model to the coachee's situation. Each session usually commences with a process of agenda-setting, in which the coach and coachee collaboratively agree the priority areas of discussion (Beck, 2011). This ensures that the coachee's needs are met, while increasing the likelihood of the time being used effectively.

In the next two coaching sessions, Michael reported a number of significant changes in his feelings and behaviour at work. He had done more work of his own with the lists of thinking errors, disputation strategies and thinking skills, and this had led to some additional insights that served to further decrease his anxiety and increase his confidence. In the first instance, he had realized that his overall sense

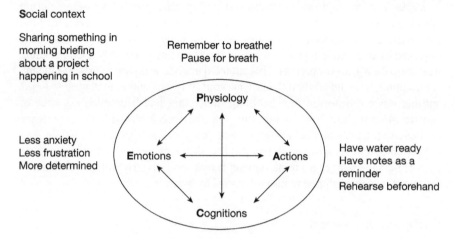

Social context

Sharing something in morning briefing about a project happening in school

Remember to breathe!
Pause for breath

Less anxiety
Less frustration
More determined

Physiology

Emotions ←→ **Actions**

Cognitions

Have water ready
Have notes as a reminder
Rehearse beforehand

'I'd prefer it if I wasn't nervous, but this is the way it is
and I can do something about it.'
'I'm not a bad teacher, it's just that I find this
particular thing difficult.'
Use **coping imagery** to imagine dealing with difficulties

Figure 9.3 A SPACE diagram representing Michael's new approach

of wellbeing at work had been affected by a number of discrete experiences that he had interpreted in a way that had eroded his confidence (e.g. being given critical feedback by an external professional without the positives of his practice being acknowledged). Specifically, his reasoning was 'Because they only gave me criticism, I must be a bad teacher' – an example of him *personalizing* experiences and *labelling* himself as a result. This was an erroneous overgeneralization that had now been challenged, and he was able to identify alternative ways of explaining some of his previous experiences (*broadening the picture*). Crucially, this had enabled him to rediscover his confidence in himself as a practitioner. Michael was no longer putting his self-worth at the mercy of external events (e.g. how other people give feedback) but was focusing on factors that were more under his control (the meaning he made of the feedback through his interpretations).

Michael had also developed a number of strategies which helped him to make any work difficulties less of a 'big thing'. These included:

- 'I keep saying to myself: "Whatever happens will happen. After today's done, it's over and I won't remember it next week"' (*acceptance* and *keeping perspective*).
- 'If something does go wrong at work, it's not the end of the world. It doesn't mean I've lost a family member' (*de-awfulizing*).
- 'I'm not the only teacher who struggles with something. Other people struggle with things too' (*normalizing*).

While Michael had not yet achieved the specific goal of speaking during morning briefing, he reported that he had, in fact, overcome what were, for him, two even more significant challenges: he had managed his anxiety while being observed by two external professionals at the same time; and he had led a reading workshop for a group of parents. This latter experience was particularly significant, since although he did admit to feeling nervous, this was within manageable limits and his voice did not do the 'bubbling thing' that had been such a source of consternation for him. In his words, this 'felt like a breakthrough'. The experience challenged his previous belief that he was 'no good' at speaking in public, and suggested that developing proficiency at this skill was more about work, practice and the management of his thinking than it was about fixed qualities/deficiencies. He therefore felt equipped to move forward by himself.

Closing the engagement

The coach and Michael were in agreement that it did not seem like a further session was necessary, so the coach's attention turned to closing the coaching relationship. This involved spending some time reviewing the distance Michael had travelled since the onset of the work and supporting him to trawl the learning that had taken place in the course of the engagement. In so doing, Michael was able to bank the tools he had learned (e.g. SPACE, recognizing thinking errors, disputation, thinking skills) so that he could call upon them in future situations. The session ended with Michael completing an evaluation of the coaching process, in which he indicated that the engagement had positively impacted on his performance, development, wellbeing and also his ability to help himself in future. Specifically, he stated:

> I have benefited greatly from talking things through in detail and getting to the root of my concerns. I have had several breakthrough moments where I have realized how out of proportion some of my worries and fears about work had become. I have learnt strategies to minimize my reaction to certain situations that I find hard to deal with at times . . . I now feel more confident at approaching different situations that may arise in my career and I will continue to work on this as an important part of my professional development.

Reflections and conclusions

How was coaching applied to support improvement of performance, development and/or wellbeing?

In this case, coaching was applied to support a classroom practitioner to address some emotional difficulties he was experiencing in relation to a commonly encountered workplace problem (anxiety about speaking in public). In sessions, Michael learned to apply cognitive-behavioural concepts and tools, and in so doing was able to address both the particular emotional difficulty he was experiencing and some broader underlying confidence issues that had emerged during his explorations. Perhaps what is most notable is that, by the end of the engagement, Michael had 'taken on' the methods and principles shared and continued to reflect on and apply them outside of coaching. Indeed, one of the key aims of CBC is to support the coachee to learn cognitive-behavioural concepts and skills so that they develop the capacity to solve future problems themselves and can effectively become their own coach (Palmer & Szymanska, 2007). In this case, there was evidence of Michael doing just that across coaching sessions 3–4, which enabled him to make (in his words) 'rapid and pleasing progress'. While the specific goal he set himself was not achieved during the course of the engagement, Michael had experienced success in the face of what he perceived to be even more significant challenges. This contradicted one of the limiting beliefs he held about himself – that he was 'no good' at speaking in public – and left him with renewed confidence to face other similar situations in future. Throughout the course of the engagement, Michael became more aware of his self-limiting thinking and, moreover, acquired the strategies needed to dispute and transform it.

What coaching models, skills or techniques have we covered?

In this chapter we have seen how the principles and practices of CBC were applied to support a coachee with issues related to wellbeing, including:

- The SPACE model for developing insight into reactions to situations and supporting development of a multimodal intervention plan.
- Identification of common thinking errors.
- Strategies for disputing self-limiting thoughts.
- Thinking skills that can replace self-limiting thoughts with more balanced, realistic and adaptive alternatives.

It is important to reiterate that, while the CBC approach was used to good effect in this case study for supporting the emotional wellbeing of a practitioner, some of the other methods described previously in this book could equally be used to this end (e.g. a solution-focused approach). CBC represents one method among others, rather than a panacea, and cannot be assumed to be something that will work for all coachees. Equally, there are other approaches not covered in this book that would suggest a different approach to dealing with difficult thoughts and feelings (e.g. Acceptance and Commitment Therapy – see Harris, 2008).

How else could this approach or these principles be applied?

CBC is relevant to a range of other situations where there may be both practical and psychological barriers to goal-achievement, including the following.

Confidence

As demonstrated in Chapter 8, a key component of confidence is our self-efficacy beliefs – i.e. the extent to which we believe we can produce desired results with our own actions (Bandura, 1977). However, individuals may hold extreme, rigid beliefs about their capabilities that impact negatively on their feelings and behaviour (e.g. 'I've got no skills for dealing with this situation'; 'I'll never be able to do this'). The SPACE model could be applied to supporting individuals to recognize, dispute and transform confidence-undermining beliefs and to plan new ways of approaching situations in which confidence has previously been a barrier.

Resilience

Resilience comprises a set of flexible, adaptive behavioural, cognitive and emotional responses to change, challenge or adversity (Neenan, 2009). The methods of CBC can be applied to support individuals to develop their capacity to respond to such circumstances, through identifying and disputing resilience-undermining thoughts (e.g. 'This shouldn't be happening!', 'This situation is totally awful!'); developing alternative resilience-enhancing thoughts (e.g. 'It's not 100 per cent awful, and some good may come from this'); and planning new, adaptive behaviours (see Neenan, 2009; Palmer, 2013). This is illustrated further in Chapter 13.

Impostor syndrome

Impostor syndrome refers to a state of mind in which the individual believes they are a fraud, an undeserving impostor who has managed to bluff their way into a position of responsibility and is sooner or later going to be found out. Impostor syndrome can be underpinned by self-limiting thinking – for example, holding unrealistically negative beliefs about one's own capabilities; holding unrealistically exaggerated beliefs about the capabilities of others, against which one cannot measure up; taking an all-or-nothing view about role competence (e.g. 'If I'm not perfect, I'm worthless at it'); and attributing one's achievements to luck or other factors while discounting or minimizing the role of one's own efforts and competences. CBC frameworks and principles could be used to challenge the self-limiting thinking underpinning impostor syndrome, and to support the individual to develop a less self-critical mind-set.

Other applications for CBC include perfectionism; procrastination; other emotional difficulties (e.g. depression, shame, anger); stress management; assertiveness; career transitions; and performance improvement (see e.g. Dryden, 2011; Neenan, 2009; Neenan & Dryden, 2002; Neenan & Palmer, 2012; Williams *et al.*, 2014). Thus, the frameworks of CBC are highly versatile tools that can potentially be applied across a broad range of themes or situations.

What can we learn about how to help others to change?

In the first instance, the case illustrates the importance of the coachee doing *work* between sessions in order to achieve their goals. Michael engaged with the concepts explored and committed to spending time outside coaching (and, indeed, time outside work) reflecting on his situation and the ways in which he might make changes in order to move forward. This led to additional insights that had not been covered in the sessions themselves, and no doubt increased the likelihood of the engagement having a positive impact. Achieving change can take work, effort and persistence, and Michael's efforts ensured that the return on investment from the time and resources put into coaching was maximized. This reflects the importance of *engaging* the coachee as an active participant in the change process, *enabling* them by drawing their attention to tools that will help them to move forward, and supporting their *application* of the approaches to their own unique situation. The value of *structuring* is also illustrated – i.e. the provision of flexible structures that can provide shape and momentum to an exploration or conversation.

What is notable about Michael's journey is how his attention shifted away from external factors that were influencing his feelings (e.g. the demand to speak in public or the way in which other people provided feedback) and instead turned to factors that were more under his control – i.e. his thoughts, interpretations and behaviours. In this way, Michael was empowered to take responsibility for his own reactions and to try to exert a measure of influence over them (again, reflecting a principle of enabling). Thus, when working with others to help them to change, we can be alert to a focus on external factors and can instead seek to draw their attention back to the factors that are under their control ('Okay, so there's a lot of stuff happening that's outside your control . . . What is under your control here?'). Indeed, this is a lesson to all of us. Do we spend our time and energy complaining about external factors (e.g. other people's behaviour, what they have done, what they will and will not do, random life events)? Or do we instead shift our focus to that which we can influence? Only one of these options is the route to liberation.

A key insight in this case was the fact that Michael had drawn negative conclusions about his overall competence/worth as a practitioner on the basis of some specific experiences. This reflected a thinking error of *overgeneralization* that underpinned his confidence issues and subsequent anxiety about speaking in public. However, this is where the methods of CBC can be helpful for bringing such thoughts to our attention, for challenging their veracity, and for suggesting alternative ways of construing our experience. From the CBC perspective, the key mind-set to develop is one in which we only ever rate our specific behaviours or attributes, rather than equating these to the totality of the self – that is, we accept that we may sometimes act poorly, have a bad experience, or have aspects of ourselves that we would like to improve, but refuse to extrapolate this to making judgements about the larger self, which is simply too complex to be rated or rejected. Neenan & Dryden (2002) refer to the 'Big-I/little-i' technique (originally

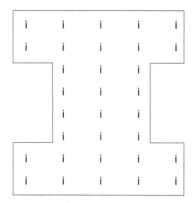

Figure 9.4 Big 'I' and little 'i'

developed by Arnold Lazarus, 1977) to illustrate this principle, in which the self (the Big 'I') is made up of lots of smaller 'i's which represent e.g. your behaviours and experiences.

Using this lens, the key is to accept that we are all fallible people who will have aspects of our behaviour or circumstances that we wish to improve, without this leading to condemnation of the self. Such a mind-set is at the root of self-acceptance and is one of the cornerstones of healthy and optimal functioning. Of course, the degree to which we are all capable of achieving this may vary considerably on a day-to-day basis. Furthermore, this was not the only shift of note in Michael's thinking, and of similar importance was his progress in de-catastrophizing and de-awfulizing the consequences of experiencing difficulties at work.

Above all, this case example illustrates the crucial role that our cognitions can have in shaping our reactions and influencing our performance and wellbeing. It shows how our thoughts and beliefs can either enable or disable us and how, if we work at it, and are prepared to persist over time, we can change our interpretations in order to feel and behave differently. This can be an empowering realization, in that we do not need to allow ourselves to be merely passive victims of our circumstances. While we may not be able to determine all the events of our lives, we can certainly exert a measure of control over our thoughts and reactions in response to them (Neenan, 2012). This, indeed, is what Viktor Frankl described as 'the last of the human freedoms – to choose one's attitude in any given set of circumstances, to choose one's own way' (Frankl, [1959] 2004, p. 75). Frankl developed his thesis and philosophy while he was a prisoner-of-war in Auschwitz, and if this principle holds true in an environment of such unimaginable horror then it is surely one we can aspire to live up to in our day-to-day existences. However, if Frankl's exhortation gives us the inspiration to 'choose our attitude', then cognitive-behavioural psychology is one approach that provides us with the tools to do so. If we can learn to use these tools to recognize our self-limiting beliefs, and to develop skills to challenge and transform them, we can all experience greater wellbeing in life and enhance the likelihood that we will unlock and maximize our true potential.

How could you apply these skills or principles in your own practice?

If you are not already familiar with the principles and practices of CBC, then my suggestion is that you begin by using them in the context of self-coaching to develop familiarity with them and to see if you buy in to their value.

Reflection questions

1   Can you use the SPACE model to map out your reaction to a particular event?
2   What 'thinking errors' can you identify in your thinking?
3   How might you dispute those thinking errors?
4   How might you replace them with more adaptive thinking skills?
5   How could you incorporate the principles and practices of CBC in your own work with others?
6   Think of a situation or challenge you are facing at the moment. What factors are relevant that are outside your control? What can you influence?

A word of caution is required at this stage. If you are going to work with others to support them in identifying thinking errors they experience, then you need to be aware that this could lead to the discovery of *core beliefs* that the individual holds about themselves (Curwen *et al.*, 2000). To understand what these are, consider thinking errors to be the tip of an iceberg with *core beliefs* at its base. These are globalized, rigid and overgeneralized beliefs that the individual may hold about the world, other people or themselves (e.g. 'People are cruel', 'I'm incompetent', 'The world is dangerous'). They are the internalized statements that underpin negative automatic thoughts, encoded as a result of experience (often in childhood) as the individual tries to make sense of themselves and the world. It is therefore important for the aspiring cognitive-behavioural coach to seek additional training in dealing with such eventualities, to know when to refer on to another form of support if something appears outside their competence, and to access ongoing supervision if this is an aspect of their practice they wish to develop.

Suggested reading

Beck, J. S. (2011). *Cognitive Therapy: Basics and Beyond* (2nd edn). New York: Guilford Press.
Neenan, M. & Palmer, S. (eds) (2012). *Cognitive Behavioural Coaching in Practice: An Evidence Based Approach.* Hove: Routledge.

Chapter 10

Coaching for new-to-role practitioners

> [An] induction programme may tick all the boxes in terms of systems, policies and procedures . . . but does little by way of helping the new arrival achieve a socialization within the organization. There is typically a focus on the nuts and bolts rather than on the 'softer' side of the equation.
>
> (Young & Anderson, 2011, p. 19)

As classroom practitioners become increasingly proficient at their roles, sooner or later the opportunity may arise for them to be promoted into a position of increased responsibility either in their own or another organization (e.g. Deputy Head, Curriculum Leader, Special Educational Needs Co-ordinator, Specialist Leader of Education). While promotion to a new role presents exciting opportunities, the practitioner is also likely to encounter a number of challenges. First, there are the practical demands of the new role to get to grips with, such as the need to develop knowledge of relevant systems and processes while learning to prioritize the new range of responsibilities that are encountered. In addition, the practitioner may well be exposed to a number of unfamiliar scenarios that will test their practical and interpersonal problem-solving capabilities. The support provided by the practitioner's line manager, or indeed another colleague in the organization, may well address many of these issues. However, the process of finding one's feet in a new role goes beyond the acquisition of practical knowledge, requiring the practitioner to develop a new role identity and to manage some of the psychological challenges the transition can present (Young & Anderson, 2011). Issues faced by practitioners who are new-to-roles can include the emotional demand of moving from a position of high competence to one of perceived low competence; self-doubt; impostor syndrome (see Chapter 9); and losing touch with existing skills and competences. While some may be comfortable discussing such matters with their line manager, it is often the case that the practitioner will instead elect to suffer in silence for fear of presenting as not adjusting to the role. Indeed, as noted by Young & Anderson (ibid.), people who have been promoted by virtue of the standard of their performance may well be reluctant to acknowledge difficulties or self-doubt in their line-management relationship. If such difficulties and doubts are left unaddressed, then this can place the practitioner under added stress and can impact on their performance and wellbeing. Obviously, the more quickly the practitioner adjusts to the demands of the new role, and finds their confidence within it, the better for them and the better for the organization. In such circumstances, a coaching relationship can be a valuable source of support for the new-to-role practitioner, providing them with a confidential space in which they can reflect on their successes, plan new strategies and openly talk through any doubts and uncertainties. Psychology can inform such practice by providing the coach with tools for addressing both the practical and psychological challenges of role change. This chapter illustrates the successful application of a combination of cognitive-behavioural coaching (CBC) and solution-focused coaching (SFC) with a new-to-role Special Educational Needs Co-ordinator.

Case study

The details of the engagement are described below, with headings used to identify the specific techniques applied.

Background

The coach was contracted to work with a school's newly appointed Special Educational Needs Co-ordinator (SENCo), the primary aim being to provide the practitioner with emotional support to complement the practical support she would receive from other sources. The practitioner (Lisa) was new to the SENCo role but had worked in the school for several years and had earned a reputation as a capable and confident classroom teacher. However, she was now stepping outside her comfort zone into a demanding role that presented fresh challenges.

Coaching session I

Agenda-setting

After a preliminary meeting with Lisa to clarify the scope of the work and to respond to her queries about the process, the first session began with coach and coachee negotiating an agenda. This provided structure and direction to the session (thereby enhancing the likelihood of the time being well-used) while ensuring that Lisa's needs were covered (Beck, 2011).

Role overview

This involves coach and coachee clarifying the different strands of the coachee's role, in order to support subsequent reflection on aspects that are going well and/ or aspects that may need to be developed. In this case, this enabled Lisa to consider the different aspects of her new SENCo role (e.g. scheduling and managing annual reviews of children's provision, working with parents, liaising with other agencies, supporting classroom teachers) and to prioritize some of the many new demands she was facing. Lisa left the session with an action plan, and the next meeting was arranged.

Coaching session 2

At the beginning of the second session Lisa admitted that she was 'not feeling great' about her new role. Further discussion clarified that this was perhaps something of an understatement, and that she had found herself experiencing some anxiety and a lack of confidence at work. She had previously enjoyed the sense of being good at her job – in fact, she stated 'I like to be good at what I do, and I like others to think I'm good at what I do', and her new role was causing her some discomfort in this respect.

Macro- and micro-analysis

Macro-analysis and micro-analysis are two techniques that can be used to analyse coachees' experiences. Macro-analysis involves coach and coachee noticing recurring patterns in behaviour, while micro-analysis places one particular incident under the microscope to look in detail at the sequence of events, thoughts, feelings and behaviours that occurred (Palmer & Dunkley, 2010).

The first step was to elicit further details about the situations that Lisa had encountered that had contributed to this anxiety. Lisa recounted a number of situations, a common theme being where other practitioners had approached her to ask questions to which she did not know the answers. It seemed that it might be helpful to conduct a micro-analysis of one of these situations. Lisa chose to focus the discussion on a situation in which another practitioner had approached her with a query about a child's reading intervention. In this situation a learning support assistant (LSA) had asked Lisa: 'Should I move this child up a level on the reading scheme?' Feeling on the spot and not knowing 'the answer' to the question, Lisa had responded (somewhat defensively): 'I don't know because I've never worked with that child. If you think they're ready, move them up.' She knew that this was an unhelpful response and worried how the LSA would have perceived her as a result. Lisa, while being an effective classroom teacher, was now learning how to deal with requests from others for support and advice.

Exploring the relationship between thoughts, feelings and behaviour

In Chapter 9 we saw how the relationship between a coachee's thoughts, feelings and behaviours can be explored using the SPACE coaching framework. Another way of achieving this is to use an ABC framework in which the coachee is helped to record the *Activating* event that triggered the emotion; the *Beliefs* that they had about the situation; and the emotional/behavioural *Consequences* of those beliefs (Ellis, 1962). The 'belief' may be, for example, an automatic thought, an intermediate belief, or a deeper, core belief (Curwen *et al.*, 2000). This is often done in a column format, as follows:

Activating event	Beliefs about the event	Consequences
Practitioner approaches to ask a question.	'Will I be able to answer this?' 'What will they think about me?'	Anxiety, worry. Defensive reaction.

In this particular case, a modified version of the ABC framework was used with the terminology changed to the less esoteric language of *observations* (**A**ctivating event), *thoughts* (**B**eliefs), and *feelings and behaviour* (**C**onsequences). Lisa's stated goals (to both 'be competent' and 'be seen as competent') were also incorporated, since these contextualized the encounter (Ellis, 1988). The framework was drawn to help Lisa to understand the model, and was constructed collaboratively. This diagrammatic format also allowed the reciprocal and interactive relationship between thoughts, feelings and behaviours to be represented:

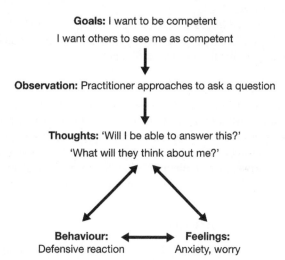

Figure 10.1 Diagrammatic representation of the relationship between Lisa's thoughts, feelings and behaviours in the situation identified

At this stage, the beliefs identified were the surface automatic thoughts Lisa experienced.

Involving the coachee

Having completed this exercise, the coach was conscious of different routes that the conversation might follow. For example, the discussion could focus on further exploring the underlying beliefs that led to the automatic thoughts and anxious feelings, or alternative behavioural responses in such situations could be generated. In such situations it is helpful to involve the coachee in determining the direction of travel, and so the possibilities were presented for Lisa to consider. Lisa chose to focus the remainder of the discussion on generating alternative behavioural responses.

Shifting to a 'future-focus'

When coachees have described a problem situation they would like to address, it can be helpful to ask them to imagine and describe what their preferred outcome would be in similar situations in future. This future-focused approach is underpinned by the principles of solution-focused coaching (see 5.2 and Chapter 8), in that the emphasis is shifted from exploring the problems of the past to talking about imagined successes. Applied to this situation, the coach might have asked one of the following questions:

- 'Imagine the next time you encounter that situation, and it goes as you would like. What happens?'
- 'What are your best hopes for such an encounter in future?'
- 'How would you like that situation to go? What would the outcome be?'
- 'How would you like things to be different?'

When asked what her best hopes would be for such an encounter in future, Lisa identified that she would like the LSA to walk away thinking 'Great, she's answered my question, I know what to do next.' At this point the coach suspected that Lisa was experiencing a pressure common to many practitioners who are new to a 'helping' role, i.e. a perceived need to provide *answers* to the queries one is presented with. This can be driven by an unhelpful belief that 'competence' or 'being helpful' equates to 'knowing the answers' and 'being able to provide the answer'.

Discovery and Socratic questioning

As described by Palmer & Szymanska (2007), guided discovery is a process where the coach and coachee work collaboratively to view the world or particular problem differently. Socratic questioning is a key tool for promoting reflection and challenging thinking in this process, in which the coach asks questions of the coachee to guide their exploration (Padesky, 1993; Neenan & Palmer, 2012). This approach was used throughout the remainder of the dialogue.

Shaping goals: strategy or outcome?

Sometimes the goals that coachees wish to achieve can themselves be barriers to change – e.g. if they are overambitious, unmotivating, woolly, or narrowing. In this case, Lisa's espoused goal was partly focused on one *strategy* – i.e. being able to give the answer to the practitioner's questions. As this would not always be possible, it seemed important to broaden the goal to something more realistically achievable:

COACH: Okay, so you'd like her to walk away thinking 'She's answered my question, I know what to do next.'

LISA: Yes.

COACH: So there are two elements there. You answering her question and her knowing what to do next.

LISA: Yes.

COACH: I'm wondering whether it will always be possible for you to answer their questions?

LISA: Hmmm . . . Well, probably not . . . But I'd still like to be helpful in some way and for her to know what to do next.

COACH: Okay. So, I'm wondering if it might be helpful to revise your best hopes to reflect that . . .?

LISA: Okay, my best hopes would be for her to walk away thinking 'Great, she's helped, I know what to do next.'

This represented a subtle but important change in Lisa's goal. Instead of being focused on one narrow strategy, the goal was now phrased as a desired *outcome*. Lisa wanted to be seen as having been helpful to the person and wanted the person to know what to do next. This opened up other possibilities as to how to achieve this beyond her having the answer herself.

Activating the coachee's strengths and resources; exception-seeking

At this point the coach hypothesized that drawing on the coachee's strengths and resources might prove helpful in finding a way forward (5.2). Since Lisa was a capable classroom teacher it was likely that she had a whole toolbox of strategies that she used with children to help them know what to do next when stuck, and experience of having performed successfully in such situations (*exceptions*). These hitherto untapped resources then became the focus of the conversation:

COACH: I'm thinking it might be useful to further explore what it means 'to be helpful' when someone asks you a question.

LISA: Okay . . .

COACH: Starting from a place where you feel comfortable and confident. So, when you are in the classroom, teaching . . . I don't know, pick a subject.

LISA: Maths.

COACH: Okay, imagine you are in the classroom, teaching maths and a child is stuck on a problem. They put their hand up and ask you a question. How do you help?

LISA: Well . . . I might talk them through what they have to do.

COACH: (Noting down the idea on a mind-map) OK. That's one possibility. What else might you do?

LISA: Give them some praise and encouragement.

COACH: (Adding the idea to the map) OK. What else?

LISA: Tell them what their next step is.

COACH: OK. What else?

LISA: (Thinking)

COACH: Would you tell them the answer to the question?

LISA: (Emphatically) No! That doesn't help them to reach the answer for themselves.

COACH: So what might you do instead?

LISA: Ask them some questions to help them think about it.

The coach could sense that, having drawn upon her experience, the coachee was close to finding a way forward. It was now important to try to help her link her discovery to the problem situation:

COACH: So being helpful can mean asking someone questions to help them think about what to do.

LISA: Yes.

COACH: I'm wondering if that might help you in situations like the one we are focusing on. What questions might you have asked that practitioner in that situation?

LISA: I'm not sure . . . (pause)

COACH: (Realizing the need to 'come back' closer to the coachee's experience having jumped too far ahead) Okay. If you had to make a decision yourself about whether or not to move a child up on their reading scheme, what questions would you ask yourself?

LISA: Do they meet the criteria for the level they are on? Do they feel secure in that level? Are they consistent at that level?

COACH: (Noting L's responses for her to see) Useful questions. What might happen if you asked the LSA those questions, do you think?

LISA: (Smiling) It would give her the confidence to make the decision herself.

COACH: Does that sound like a helpful way forward?

LISA: Yes! Definitely.

Trawling the learning; action-planning

Having guided the coachee to a change of approach, the next action was to review the session so as to trawl the learning that took place. Lisa was asked to think back over the course of the conversation to pick out key learning points and use them to inform an action-plan as to her future approach. She identified that in future situations she would think differently when approached by a practitioner, replacing the thought of 'Am I going to be able to answer this?' with 'I don't need to know the answer, I can help them to think it through.' This reflected a shift in Lisa's underlying beliefs about what it meant 'to be helpful' and 'to be competent' when asked a question by another practitioner. Lisa suggested that this change of mind-set would help her to feel less anxious, while her defensive behaviour would be replaced with the more helpful behaviour of asking the practitioner guiding questions. At this point the coach returned to guided discovery to highlight what was thought to be another key learning point:

COACH: Where did the solution come from?
LISA: (Smiling) Me.
COACH: How?
LISA: I used my experience. The things I know.

This seemed to be an empowering realization for Lisa, who had previously underestimated the value of her past knowledge and experience when faced with a seemingly new problem.

Reflections and conclusions

How was coaching applied to support improvement of performance, development and/or wellbeing?

This case presentation has demonstrated the value of a coaching relationship for supporting a practitioner who is new-to-role. In this situation, a newly appointed SENCo was able to address some of the immediate practical and psychological demands of her new position, while also developing skills and confidence that would leave her better equipped to face other situations in future. The early provision of coaching support facilitated the transition as Lisa developed familiarity with her new role, enabling her to perform better in the short term and possibly preventing later issues from occurring. We can speculate about the ripple-effect benefits from this learning, as represented by Figure 10.2.

What coaching models, skills or techniques have we covered?

The account highlights a number of valuable principles and techniques that can inform future coaching practice, including:

- *Role overview:* supporting a practitioner to take a structured approach to reflecting on the different strands of their role, and the actions they need to attend to in each.
- *Macro- and micro-analysis:* looking for recurring patterns of behaviour and then drilling down to analyse one situation in greater depth.
- The Goals–Observations–Thoughts/Feelings/Behaviours (G–O–TFB) frame-work for supporting a coachee to explore the relationship between their

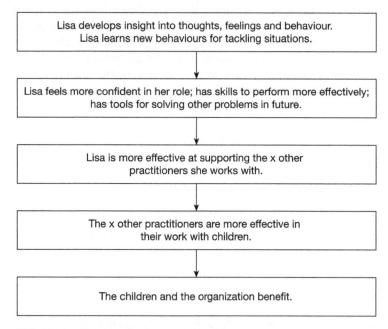

Figure 10.2 Ripple-effect benefits from coaching Lisa

thoughts, feelings and behaviour, and how their observations and interpretations may be framed by their own particular goals or expectations.

• Shifting to a future-focus when coachees are considering problem situations, asking them how they would prefer the encounter to transpire.
• Shaping goals if the coachee's espoused goal reflects a particular strategy rather than a desired outcome.

In this case the classic ABC framework was changed so as to use less esoteric language (observations, thoughts, feelings, behaviours). The disadvantage of this approach is that, given that the elements do not form an acronym, it may be harder for coachees to remember the model in the early stages of subsequent independent application. This is in contrast with the more memorable ABC framework and Edgerton & Palmer's (2005) SPACE framework (Social context, Physiology, Actions, Cognitions, Emotions – see Chapter 9) which some coachees may prefer. Nonetheless, this adds another tool to the coach toolkit that might be drawn upon when guiding such reflection.

How else could this approach be applied?

The case illustrates the broad applicability of psychological principles and practices to supporting the performance and wellbeing of practitioners in school contexts. Lisa was not a struggling practitioner; on the contrary, she was skilled and capable, but even so she experienced anxiety and a lack of confidence in her role. One might speculate how many people this applies to, and how many might benefit from occasional opportunities to reflect on their performance and wellbeing with a coach. Those who are new to roles might particularly benefit from coaching to support them in e.g. overcoming performance obstacles or generalizing and applying previous skills and knowledge (see also Young & Anderson, 2011). This could include, for example, newly qualified teachers, or leaders and managers who have recently been promoted. Coaching psychologists, being external to the organization, are well placed to provide a safe relationship in which the practitioner can openly and honestly reflect on the challenges they are encountering in their new roles; however, the principles and methods applied in this case study could also be used by education practitioners who are themselves coaches or mentors.

What can we learn about how to help others to change?

This case study reiterates themes that have emerged in previous chapters in terms of the value of activating, harnessing and utilizing the person's existing resources in order to achieve change. In this example, the eventual solution was not a new behaviour taught by the coach, but rather an existing strategy that Lisa had used successfully in other circumstances. Reflecting a key principle of the solution-focused approach, Lisa had essentially determined to simply 'do more of what works'. The specific strategy came to light through reflection on experiences where Lisa had been asked a question and had been able to respond helpfully and in a way that she was satisfied with. This further illustrates the value of exception-seeking in problem-solving – i.e. searching for examples when the person has faced a similar problem or situation and experienced a more positive outcome. It was particularly noticeable in this case how Lisa seemed to grow in confidence having realized that she did in fact have strengths that she could draw upon to tackle the challenges of her new role – it was just a case of thinking how they might be applied in unfamiliar situations. Had the coach elected to act as 'expert' and quickly prescribed a solution, the impact may well have been very different in terms of the depth of Lisa's learning and her subsequent confidence in her ability to find solutions herself.

The example also illustrates the importance of being able to recognize whether a coachee has described a particular goal in terms of a *strategy* or an *outcome*. Coaches and other change agents need to be alert to this difference, since focusing on one particular strategy may or may not take the coachee in their desired direction of travel; in contrast, a focus on the desired outcome opens up a range of possibilities as to how the goal might be achieved.

It is also important to note the eclectic nature of the coach's practice in this case, with principles and techniques of both SFC and CBC being drawn on in combination with each other. This illustrates that we can draw on a range of models and principles as befits the needs of the coachee and the situation.

How could you apply these skills or principles in your own practice?

Reflection questions

1   In what circumstances could you use the techniques described in this chapter? Who might benefit from taking a structured approach to reviewing their performance in relation to the different aspects of their role?

2   When someone approaches you with a 'problem' situation they want to discuss, can you support them to think about how they would like things to be different? Can you attempt to help them to phrase their wishes in terms of the desired outcome rather than a strategy for achieving it?

Suggested reading

Berg, I. K. & De Jong, P. (2002). *Interviewing for Solutions.* Pacific Grove, CA: Brooks/ Cole.

Greene, J. & Grant, A. M. (2003). *Solution-Focused Coaching.* Harlow: Pearson Education.

Note

This chapter is adapted from a paper that was first published in *Coaching Psychology International*, August 2012.

Chapter 11

Problem-solving and solution-finding

> The problem-solving approach has been applied to a large range of issues in coaching, training and clinical settings. Its simplicity, when applied appropriately, makes it a powerful tool . . .
>
> (Palmer, 2007, p. 75)

There may be times when an individual, team or organization encounters a problem situation that they wish to think through and resolve. In this circumstance a coaching approach can be of value in that it can give the person space to reflect on their situation and consider the merits of alternative ways forward. Rather than assuming the role of 'fixer' or 'answer-giver', the coach can work in such a way so as to stimulate the person's or team's consideration of alternatives, enabling them to evaluate the options available to them before deciding upon a course of action. For this purpose, structured frameworks that can facilitate problem-solving can be a helpful addition to the coach's toolbox. This chapter provides an example of such an approach, illustrating the successful application of the problem-solving processes outlined in Stephen Palmer's PRACTICE framework to a real-life school-based organizational problem. The aim is to demonstrate the impact that such an approach can have, while leaving you with a simple problem-solving framework that is easy to remember and can be applied in a broad range of situations.

PRACTICE: A framework for problem-solving and solution-finding

PRACTICE is a solution-seeking model developed by Palmer (2007, 2008) as an adaptation of Wasik's (1984) seven-step problem-solving sequence. Using Wasik's structure, Palmer modified the names of the stages to form a memorable acronym that would act as an aide-memoire to those trying to recall the problem-solving steps. In the original model, the steps are:

Problem identification
Realistic, relevant goals developed
Alternative solutions generated

Consideration of consequences
Target most feasible solution
Implementation of
Chosen solution
Evaluation.

Palmer (2011) has since adapted the model so that the 'P' stage could be considered to represent another aspect of the coaching process such as 'Purpose of coaching' or 'Preferred outcome'. Indeed, although PRACTICE is a problem-solving model, it can be argued that it is more solution-focused in nature given the relative proportion of time that is spent on 'solution talk' (e.g. generating goals, considering options, planning actions) in comparison with that spent on 'problem talk' (e.g. describing the problem, gathering information about the problem, discussing possible causes and underlying factors).

Case study

In this particular case, a mainstream primary school found itself facing a crisis as to how it would provide for a number of children with significant Special Educational Needs (SEN) that would be transferring to the school's early years provision as part of their new intake. The coach was asked to work with the school over a number of months to support them in solving the problem.

PRACTICE in action

Step 1: Problem identification

The aim of this stage is to gather relevant factual information about the problem, clarify the nature of the problem (e.g. demands, obstacles and/or conflicts that may be operating), and to identify the hoped-for outcome. See also Palmer (2011) for other options as to how this stage might be conceived.

The problem was identified in a telephone conversation between the school's Inclusion Manager (IM) and the coach, in which the IM expressed considerable concern about the situation the school was facing and queried the school's capacity to cope. The coach listened to the IM's concerns and used questioning techniques to unpack the details of the problem. It emerged that a number of children in the early years Children's Centre would be transferring to the school's large, sixty-capacity nursery room in the September of that year. In addition, the school was aware of other children with needs of similar severity that would be joining the same class from other settings. Two of these children had profound and multiple learning difficulties; three had severe autistic spectrum disorder (including sensory processing difficulties or sensitivities); and three had global developmental delay or significant language needs. All of these children were receiving high levels of additional adult support, but when they transferred to the nursery room the majority of them would need to be provided for from the school's budget and devolved SEN funding. Normally, special provision would have been considered for many of these children, but timescales for processes meant that any such requests would not be resolved in time. The children would all definitely be attending the nursery in September. The coach and IM knew from experience that the main nursery room was overwhelming for some children, as it would most likely be for the children transferring who had sensory sensitivities or emotional needs. In addition, the IM queried how the children would access both the curriculum and the levels of adult support they required. It was hoped that the outcome of the piece of work would be clarity regarding how to provide for the children.

As an initial information-gathering step, it was agreed that it may be helpful for the IM and the school's Special Educational Needs Co-ordinator (SENCo) to visit a special school to learn from their expertise and generate further questions. The next action was to arrange a strategy meeting involving the IM, SENCo, Head Teacher (HT), Nursery Lead Teacher (NLT) and coach.

Step 2: Relevant, realistic goals developed

Like many writers, Palmer advocates the importance of goal-setting in the problem-solving process (see also e.g. Egan, 2002; Greene & Grant, 2003; Whitmore, 2002). Goals help to keep things on track, providing a focus for thought, discussion and action, and representing a useful point of reference when evaluating whether the process is helping to meet the client's needs. They can be associated with mobilization of effort, motivation, persistence, improved performance, achievement, and positive change (see e.g. Locke, 1999; Ryan & Deci, 2000).

It is at this point that practice deviated from the model, in that specific goals were not developed at this stage. Instead, the preference of the group was to generate a series of key questions that would need to be explored to make progress on the problem. The coach took a role in asking questions to facilitate the generation of the list. The final list included:

1   How can we group the children in the nursery room?
2   How can staffing and resources be allocated?
3   What environmental modifications need to be made to the room?

The coach did not pursue the articulation of specific goals, as it seemed that the key questions served a similar purpose in providing a focus for thinking and mobilizing effort into exploring specific themes. This is a point that will be revisited later.

Step 3: Alternative solutions generated

The next step of the PRACTICE framework involves the generation of multiple alternative solutions to the problem in question, with evaluation deferred until a number of possibilities have been generated. This process of *diverging* encourages creativity, prevents a rush to premature decision-making, and can enhance the likelihood of a useful way forward being found (see e.g. Downey, 2003).

At this stage of the process the coach focused on asking questions to stimulate the generation of possibilities; encouraging elaboration of ideas; summarizing; and making suggestions for the client to consider. First, the group explored the questions of how the children could be grouped and how practitioners would be allocated. Working with the details of the number of staff (seven – one teacher and six support staff) and the number of children (sixty-two) in the nursery room, the team considered different possibilities as to how the children might be grouped. The existing model was for the children to be split into four groups, with one or two practitioners working with each group according to need. While also factoring in the team's preference to have a floating member of staff who could flexibly provide support where needed, this resulted in the following alternatives, illustrated in Figures 11.1, 11.2 and 11.3.

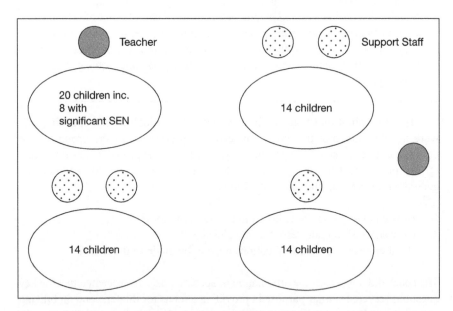

Figure 11.1 Option 1a: four groups, children with SEN placed in the teacher's group

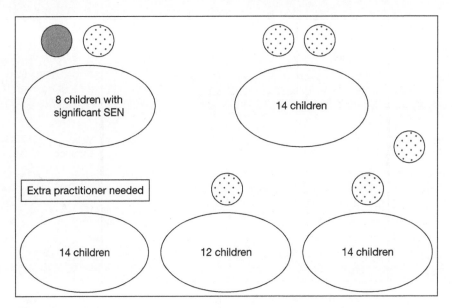

Figure 11.2 Option 1b: operate specific SEN group plus four other groups

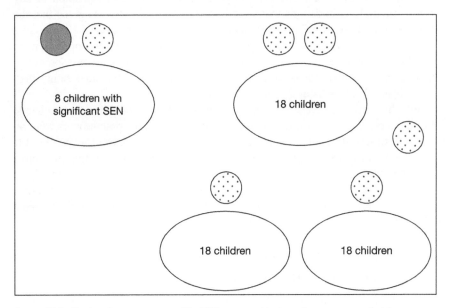

Figure 11.3 Option 1c: operate specific SEN group with three large groups of eighteen
children

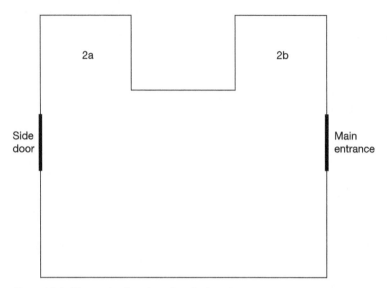

Figure 11.4 Alternative locations for the learning space

Having considered these options, the group then explored the question of any environmental modifications that would need to be made. It was agreed that the children might well find the large open-plan nursery room overwhelming, so a calmer and more manageable space needed to be identified. Two options were considered, these being two corner areas of the main room that were somewhat more contained than others in that they were walled on three sides rather than being open plan (see 2a and 2b in Figure 11.4).

Whichever options were used, it was evident that this would be a major change for the nursery staff, and it was therefore important that the practitioners were on board with any decision. It was agreed that it would be helpful to involve the practitioners in discussing the alternatives since they would be the ones most affected. Also, as they were at the chalk face, they would be able to anticipate obstacles, ask questions and suggest other ideas. Two meetings were arranged involving the members of the Project Group, the school's Speech and Language Therapist, and the Early Years Practitioners themselves.

Step 4: Consideration of consequences

Once a series of options has been generated, it is then important to consider the different alternatives and anticipate the likely consequences of each (D'Zurilla & Nezu, 2006; Palmer, 2007). Each option frequently has its own associated advantages and disadvantages, exploration of which can inform decision-making. As this analysis is conducted, some options are rejected, other ideas may arise and the benefits of some courses of action become clear. Through this process of systematic evaluation and elimination, thinking can start to converge on a plausible way forward.

The group then considered the respective advantages and disadvantages of both the staffing arrangements and the location of the learning space. The coach asked questions to facilitate this process, while using reflective listening and clarifying skills to support participants in expressing and developing their ideas. As this took place within the context of a large group problem-solving session, there was also a role for the coach in bringing quieter participants into the discussion and seeking the views of specific group members. The considerations explored are summarized in Tables 11.1 and 11.2.

With regard to the grouping of the children, Option (1b) was emerging as the option with the most advantages. It would mean the recruitment or redeployment of another member of staff, but it was an efficient use of resources and all the children would then be able to access a quality learning experience. However, the issue of the location of the SEN group had not been resolved. Consideration of the consequences of both options had clarified that, while the two locations would arguably be less overwhelming than other parts of the room, it would not be possible to shield the children from noise. This would most likely present a

Table 11.1 Pros and cons of different staffing arrangements

	Pros	Cons
Option 1a *The children with SEN are allocated to one of the four existing groups*	Fits with some people's idea of 'inclusion' (i.e. the children with SEN are in a group with other children). Allows localization of resources.	Not manageable, given the level of adult support the SEN children would need. Huge demand on the teacher. Difficult for staff to modify their language use to suit all needs and abilities.
Option 1b *A special SEN group is created; the other children are split into four groups*	The SEN children get a higher adult:child ratio. Other groups are of manageable size. Specialist equipment and resources can be targeted at the children who need them. Efficient use of adult support. The children can access a specially modified curriculum.	Leaves one group unstaffed and therefore another practitioner would need to be recruited or redeployed.
Option 1c *A special SEN group is created; the other children are split into three groups*	As above, except other groups are larger. Don't have to recruit or redeploy anyone else.	Groups are too large for meaningful relationships to develop and for learning to be individualized.

Table 11.2 Pros and cons of the two proposed locations

	Pros	Cons
Option 2a	The children could easily access an outside space that could be converted into a safe, quiet play area.	The children would either need to walk through the busy room to get to the space, or would need to come in through a separate entrance. Noise levels in the room could still prove difficult for children with auditory sensitivities.
Option 2b	The children could access the area from the main entrance without having to make their way across the busy room.	The children wouldn't be able to access an outside space easily. Noise levels in the room could still prove difficult for children with auditory sensitivities.

problem for children with auditory sensitivities or those who were particularly distractible. The conversation seemed stuck and it became apparent that a quieter environment would be necessary.

A new alternative

It was at this point that the head teacher suggested a solution, taking one of the diagrams and extending it by drawing an additional room on the model. His proposal was that the children would be grouped as in Option (1b), while the SEN group would be taught in a smaller classroom (2c) next to the nursery room (see Figure 11.5).

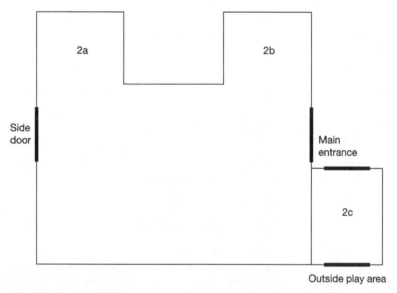

Figure 11.5 A new alternative location

The new alternative would allow the children to access the support levels and resources they needed, while the quieter environment would be more manageable for children with sensory or emotional sensitivities. They would also be able to access a suitable outside play space without difficulty. To address concerns about the children being separated from the others, the head teacher proposed knocking down part of the wall between the nursery room and the classroom, and installing a door so that the children could 'dip in and out' of the main room as they felt comfortable. To resolve the staffing issue, another practitioner would be redeployed. The teacher would oversee the curriculum planning for the group, which would be delivered by two support practitioners. This added another alternative to the pool of options that had previously been considered at Step 3.

Step 5: Target most feasible solution

Having considered a range of alternatives and their associated advantages and disadvantages, the next step of PRACTICE is to target the most feasible way forward.

The consensus in the room was that the new suggestion represented the most feasible way forward. Concerns about the suitability of the learning area had been addressed, and the proposed group sizes seemed manageable. There was a debate about whether this was really 'inclusion', since the children could perhaps spend large parts of their day in a separate room. During this debate the coach asked questions to encourage participants to reflect on their beliefs about the nature of inclusion, and offered some thoughts and observations of his own. As the discussion continued, the view that 'inclusion' was not necessarily 'being in the same room as the others' evolved. Rather, inclusion was considered to be the process of removing barriers to participation so that these children could go to school in their local community. If this meant providing a less overwhelming environment so that the children could succeed, then that was both the school's responsibility and its commitment. Instead of trying to fit the children into the school's box, the school decided to change the box to fit the children.

Step 6: Implementation of the chosen solution

The next step of PRACTICE is the implementation of the chosen solution. This involves breaking actions down into a series of manageable steps, allocating responsibilities and agreeing time frames for action completion.

In most cases this stage of the process would be supported by the coach asking a number of action-oriented questions (e.g. 'What needs to be done first?', 'By when?', or 'By whom?', or 'What needs to happen to make that happen?')

since this seems to encourage a focus on concrete next-step actions rather than vague ambitions. However, in this case time restrictions meant that the meeting needed to come to an end, so the action-planning stage took place at another time without the coach's direct input.

The following months saw an intense level of activity as funds were allocated, resources were purchased, practitioners were redeployed and modifications to the building were made. The staff were also trained in the use of specific approaches that were suitable to the children's needs to both enhance their confidence and broaden their toolboxes. The new classroom was named 'The Pod', and was ready in time for the children to join the provision at the start of the new academic year.

Step 7: Evaluation

The final step of the PRACTICE model is evaluation, in which all parties can review how successful the actions taken have been. This is an opportunity to affirm progress, reflect on learning, and to identify if any modifications to the approach taken are required.

In addition to the ongoing daily evaluation that was taking place in the school, a group meeting was convened later that year to review progress, facilitated by the external coach. The session was underpinned by solution-focused principles and practices (5.2), in that the discussion focused on what had gone well, what could be learned from those successes, and the next steps needed to build on existing progress. The forum was also an opportunity for specific issues or challenges to be problem-solved by the group. The Early Years Practitioners expressed a wish to receive feedback on their practice, so it was decided to provide them with observation-based coaching on the approaches they were using with the children. This would involve the practitioners being observed at work by the external coach, being given feedback on their strengths, and supported to plan their next steps through structured reflection on their practice.

The Pod itself was specifically commented on in the school's subsequent Ofsted inspection, which stated that: 'Those with complex special educational needs and/ or disabilities are well cared for in the specialist children's centre, known as The Pod. In this calm and purposeful learning environment, children make good progress' (Ofsted, 2011, p.10).

Reflections and conclusions

How was coaching applied to support improvement of performance, development and/or wellbeing?

This chapter has demonstrated how a coaching approach can support education practitioners to find solutions to practical problems, in this case supporting a school team to determine how they could provide for a number of children with complex SEN. This led to the creation of a new special educational provision that enabled children with complex needs to be educated in their own community. A collaborative problem-solving approach harnessed the ideas and energy of the team and ensured that they were fully involved in determining the solution they would work towards.

What coaching models, skills or techniques have we covered?

The case study has outlined the PRACTICE framework, which can be applied to support individuals or teams with problem-solving and solution-finding. The case highlights the value that coaching psychology principles and approaches can have when applied to organizational or systemic problems, and indicates the potential applicability of the PRACTICE framework in other such situations.

Two key learning points emerge from this study with regard to the specifics of coaching techniques, the first being in relation to the importance of *goals*. Specific goals were not explicitly stated at Step 2 of this particular project, and instead a series of key questions was generated to begin work on the problem. While these proved helpful in terms of channeling thought and mobilizing action, it became apparent later in the process that they perhaps did not describe the needed elements of the solution in sufficient detail. The options generated at Step 3, while making the environment less overwhelming for the children, did not address the key need for the children to access a *quiet* space, so none of the options generated was satisfactory in this respect. This may have been realized earlier in the process had the coach pursued the articulation of specific goals at Step 2 (e.g. to 'provide the children with a calm, quiet and manageable learning space'). The second learning point with regard to techniques is the value of considering *consequences*, since it was exploration of the pros and cons of each of the options that brought to light the missing detail of the goal. Palmer's problem-solving framework captures this helpful element of the process and explicitly reminds us of its importance.

Although the stages of Palmer's framework are helpfully captured by the acronym PRACTICE, it is worth noting that the problem-solving process did not strictly follow this sequence in this case. Having generated alternatives (Step 3) and considered the consequences of each (Step 4), the group effectively returned to Steps 2 and 3, having realized that none of the initial proposals was satisfactory and that a quieter environment was needed. This emphasizes the non-linear nature of the process and illustrates the fact that a framework is a guide only. Indeed, in your work with other people it is most likely that the conversation will move fluidly between these stages rather than rigidly adhering to the model.

How else could this approach be applied?

The framework could be used by education practitioners themselves, by school coaches who have a role in supporting others, or by psychologists who are working with school staff to support them in resolving problem situations. Knowledge of problem-solving approaches and processes represents part of the contribution that a coach can bring to support people in finding ways forward, even where the coach is non-expert in the nature of the specific problem being discussed. In addition, the coach's added value lies in the application of core skills (e.g. questioning, reflective listening, clarifying, summarizing, challenging) that facilitate the person's or team's thinking and support the problem-solving/solution-finding process.

What can we learn about how to help others to change?

As noted, we have seen how there are times when other people may benefit from taking a systematic problem-solving approach to address situations they may be facing. The case study also underlines the value of *collaboration* in problem-solving, since the participation of the stakeholders proved invaluable when generating ideas and considering consequences, while their involvement in the decision-making process also impacted on their commitment to the solution.

How could you apply these skills or principles in your own practice?

Reflection questions

1   In what circumstances might you be able to use the PRACTICE framework to support another person or team with problem-solving?
2   Are you facing an organizational problem for which involving the members of your team in generating a solution may be of help?

Suggested reading

Palmer, S. (2007). PRACTICE: A model suitable for coaching, counselling, psychotherapy and stress management. *The Coaching Psychologist*, 3 (2): 71–77.
Palmer, S. (2008). The PRACTICE model of coaching: Towards a solution-focused approach. *Coaching Psychology International*, 1 (1): 4–8.

Note

This chapter is an adapted version of a paper that was first published in *The Coaching Psychologist*, June 2012.

Chapter 12

Coaching for teams

> To work effectively with groups, we must harness their power to achieve change . . . At their best, groups offer a profound encounter with others that promotes collaboration, creative challenge and adaptation.
>
> (Thornton, 2010, p. 3)

While many of the case studies in this book have focused on coaching in a one-to-one context, coaching can also be applied to support the performance, development and wellbeing of *teams*. When working with a team or group of people we may need to attend to a number of factors that can influence their functioning, including the extent to which there is alignment over goals or agendas; the relative activity or inactivity on the part of the group members; the way in which the team members communicate with each other; and the degree to which the working of the group is guided by a structure. However, as noted by Thornton (2010), groups and teams possess tremendous potential for collaboration, learning and development. Coaches and coaching psychologists are well placed to support the functioning of groups or teams to unlock their potential through the application of core skills and the use of coaching frameworks (e.g. I-GROW or PRACTICE – see Chapters 4 and 11); in addition, an understanding of the psychology of group processes can further enhance our ability to support the group to function, perform and learn together more effectively.

While there are many ways in which a coach might work with a team, a solution-focused approach to team development can be very powerful in that it focuses the group on a common goal while eliciting, harnessing and further developing the members' existing resources. In the course of my coaching work with both individuals and teams I have come to represent some of the key stages of the solution-focused approach with the acronym ENABLE:

Elicit the preferred future
Notice exceptions
Activate strengths and resources
Build on what's working
Look for opportunities
Efficacy-supportive feedback

The stages of the ENABLE framework will be unpacked further, below, illustrating how the framework has been applied to supporting the performance and development of a team in an early years setting.

Managing group processes

While a coaching framework such as ENABLE is helpful for facilitating team development, it is not sufficient since we are working with a group of people who are invested in achieving the desired outcome or whose involvement is crucial in order to secure progress. It is therefore necessary for us to be able to attend to and manage group processes and dynamics in order to support those present in working together effectively. With this in mind, we can call upon Edgar Schein's (1988, 1999) work on group processes as a helpful complementary addition to the coaching toolbox.

Group processes

Edgar Schein describes a number of behaviours and processes that must occur in order for a group to function effectively, which include functions that are necessary for getting the job done (*task functions*) and those that are essential for the building and maintenance of good relationships (*maintenance functions*). These can be described as follows:

Table 12.1 Task functions and maintenance functions in groups

Task functions ('Getting the job done')	Maintenance functions (Building and maintaining relationships)
Initiating – Stating the goal or problem, making proposals, setting time limits.	*Harmonizing* – Managing dysfunctional levels of conflict or disagreement.
Information seeking and giving on issues related to the task.	*Compromising* – Two or more parties conceding their own interests slightly in the interests of reaching a workable agreement.
Opinion seeking and giving on issues related to the task.	*Gatekeeping* – Reducing the activity of overly active members and increasing the activity of overly passive members.
Clarifying – Testing the adequacy of communication by checking out understanding.	*Encouraging* – Helping a person to make a point in an atmosphere of acceptance.
Elaborating – Building on the ideas or contributions of others.	*Diagnosing* – Identifying what might have happened if the group has broken down to some degree.
Summarizing – Reviewing what has been covered.	*Standard setting* – Establishing norms for group behaviour.
Consensus testing – Testing whether the group is nearing a decision.	*Standard testing* – Reviewing the functioning of the group against established norms.

As coaches, we can attend to these processes throughout the conversation. Sometimes, the functioning of the group will flow with little need for intervention; at other times, it may be helpful for us to call on one of the above functions in order to facilitate the group's working.

A case study will now be presented to illustrate the application of the ENABLE framework in a team context.

Case study

The details of the engagement are described below, with headings used to identify the specific techniques applied.

Background

The coach was contracted to help a team of thirteen Early Years Practitioners to develop their practices for supporting children with complex Special Educational Needs (SEN). The team had previously been trained in the use of particular approaches or tools to support working with children with SEN, such as breaking tasks down into a series of small steps ('task analysis') and using structured assessment tools to measure increments of progress; now, the team wished to further consolidate, embed and extend their use of these practices, and to plan how they could further support the children and their families.

Team coaching session

The team coaching session progressed through the steps of the ENABLE framework as outlined above:

Elicit the preferred future

Key question: 'Imagine a time in the future when you have had the impact you want to have . . . What does that look like?'

Clarification of the team's preferred future was important to provide direction to the conversation, while reminding the team of the common purpose that united them. In this case the team imagined a future in which the children had social and life skills that would enable them to achieve their full potential and participate in their community.

Notice exceptions

Key question: 'What are the signs *now* of your preferred future already happening?

The next step was to ask the group to reflect on their experience in a search for *exceptions* – that is, times when the preferred future was already happening, even if only in part. This encouraged the team to remember real-life examples of where they had been able to have a positive impact on the children's development and participation. As well as providing material for the subsequent discussion about how they had achieved this, this had a positive impact on the team's feelings that – as predicted by Barbara Fredrickson's research (5.8) – would contribute to an atmosphere of creativity and expansion.

Activate strengths and resources

Key question: 'What helped to achieve those successes?'

Having brought a collection of success stories to their attention, it was now possible to trawl these examples for the *practices* the team had applied to achieve them. This led to the generation of a broad range of strategies that the team had used, including:

- Maintaining regular communication with parents.
- Successful use of task analysis to break goals down into a series of manageable steps.
- Using each other's knowledge and experience.
- Getting down to the child's level and joining the child in their play.

An extensive list of detailed strategies was generated, which again had a further visible impact on the confidence of the team. Confronted with this list of strategies, they began to realize how skilled they already were.

Build on what's working

Key question: 'How can you learn from your own or each other's successes to further develop your practice?'

At this point in the conversation, the focus shifted to how the team could learn from their existing successes in order to further develop their individual and collective practice. This placed the successful use of particular strategies under the spotlight and enabled the team to trawl learning that would support them in moving forward. In this way, effective practices were cross-fertilized across the team members.

Look for opportunities

Key question: 'How can you apply that learning in the coming days or weeks?'

A key part of the conversation is to support the team to translate ideas into a reality. To this end, the coach supported the group to look for opportunities in the coming days or weeks when they could apply their new learning, or apply their existing strengths in a new way. The focus was on identifying particular children and being specific about how the ideas generated could inform a practical strategy that they would get started on in the next few days, for example: 'I will use visual symbols to support [child] in understanding the morning routines.' Planning a clear, small step in this way can help to ensure that people get going quickly before momentum is lost, and also helps to put closure on the conversation.

Efficacy-supportive feedback

Throughout the session, the coach had attended to the team members' contributions and specifically listened for strengths and qualities shown by the individual team members and the team as a whole. The end of the session was an opportunity for the coach to give feedback about some of his observations to further enhance the practitioners' sense of self-efficacy, for example:

- 'I've noticed that you have the ability to tune in to where a child is at and change what you are doing to suit them.'
- 'You've demonstrated persistence and patience in supporting children to learn social behaviours that they have found difficult to acquire.'
- 'You have a team ethos where it is okay to make mistakes and if that happens you learn from it and move forward.'

Evaluation

All thirteen practitioners rated the session as 'very helpful' and all reported practical changes that they would incorporate into their practice as a result. It was also noted that the session had the added benefit of helping new members of the team to develop familiarity with the team's vision, approach and ethos.

Reflections and conclusions

How was coaching applied to support improvement of performance, development and/or wellbeing?

In this case a coaching approach was applied to support a team of Early Years Practitioners to develop their proficiency at providing for children with complex SEN. By asking the team to define their preferred future, and supporting them to elicit and clarify the resources they already possessed that would enable them to achieve it, a platform of strengths and successes was built that could be used to drive the development of future practice. Throughout this endeavour, the coach attended to group dynamics and processes in order to support the effective functioning of the team during the session. The approach facilitated the cross-fertilization of effective practices across team members, enabling them to learn from each other's real-world successes. Since the strategies generated were ones that had already been proven to work in the team's unique context, the team could be more confident in their subsequent application and experimentation. All this resulted in a team experience that strengthened their individual and collective efficacy, and left them feeling confident and empowered to move forward.

What coaching models, skills or techniques have we covered?

This chapter has presented a solution-focused coaching framework (ENABLE) that can be used to enhance the performance, development and wellbeing of individuals and teams. In a group context, application of the model in practice is supported by attention to the task and maintenance functions described by Edgar Schein (1988, 1999).

How else could this approach be applied?

The ENABLE model could be applied to support teams on a range of development themes, for example:

- Supporting a secondary school science faculty to improve student engagement at the beginning of lessons.
- Supporting a team of Learning Support Assistants to cross-fertilize and develop 'best and next' practices for supporting children in classrooms.
- Supporting a setting to move towards a shared vision.

The framework could also be called upon to support the performance and development of individuals.

What can we learn about how to help others to change?

This case study illustrates (and in some cases re-emphasizes) the value of the following principles:

- *Envisaging:* Eliciting and shaping a vision of a preferred future to provide focus, direction and emotional energy.
- *Structuring:* Providing flexible structures that support people's explorations.
- *Developing:* Planning small steps forward that move the team in the direction of their preferred future.
- *Appreciation:* Recognizing, valuing and building on that which is positive.
- *Collaboration:* Working *with* people rather than 'doing to' them, and supporting them to work effectively with each other.

The solution-focused approach thus provides us with a very positive way of working with people, resting on the fundamental assumption that they are competent and resourceful, and that it is the coach's role to support them in discovering and harnessing those resources. We listen for, and explicitly ask about, their strengths and achievements, and seek to uncover and nurture the small green shoots of success that already exist in their experience. In so doing we support them in constructing a solution that works for them as a unique individual/team in their own particular context and situation. Since the green shoots of emerging success are already surviving in the coachee's soil – that is, there is evidence that they work for the individual coachee and/or in their own unique context – the coach can be more confident that strategies built from them will take. In contrast, exotic blooms that thrive elsewhere may not readily transfer to new environments!

I hope that the ENABLE model proves helpful in supporting you to develop familiarity with some of the components of the solution-focused approach, and invite you to apply it in your own work with individuals, teams and/or groups.

How could you apply these skills or principles in your own practice?

Reflection questions

In what circumstances could you use the ENABLE coaching model to support the development of an individual or team? Who might benefit?

Suggested reading

Schein, E. (1988). *Process Consultation: Its Role in Organizational Development.* New York: Addison-Wesley.

Schein, E. (1999). *Process Consultation Revisited: Building the Helping Relationship.* New York: Addison-Wesley.

Thornton, C. (2010). *Group and Team Coaching: The Essential Guide.* Hove: Routledge.

Chapter 13

Developing resilience

Challenging times demand inner strength and a spirit that won't be defeated.
(Morris, 2004, p. 1)

Have you ever thought that some people seem to be more resilient than others? What do you think contributes to resilience? Is our resilience a fixed trait, or is it something that we can develop? In fact, resilience is – like many of our attributes – a malleable quality that we can work to shape. What's more, if we do so, it can benefit us both professionally and personally. Indeed, studies have demonstrated a positive relationship between resilience and performance outcomes (e.g. Luthans *et al.*, 2006), while recent research in the UK public sector has indicated that resilience coaching can impact positively on confidence in dealing with organizational change (Sherlock-Storey *et al.*, 2013). Certainly, my own experience as a coach of teachers convinces me of the value of such approaches in education settings. Education practitioners are likely to face many demands on their coping resources in the course of an academic year, and while we may not be able to predict and control the form that those demands might take, we can certainly equip people with resources and strategies to increase the likelihood of them dealing with such challenges effectively. As Morris (2004) notes, it is our inner resources that can make the difference in the face of challenging circumstances, and the application of coaching psychology can strengthen the resources we have at our disposal.

This chapter will demonstrate how the principles of cognitive-behavioural coaching (CBC – see 5.3 and Chapter 9) can be applied to support the members of an organization to develop resilience-enhancing strategies, leaving them better equipped to respond to current and future adversities at work and at home. The chapter concludes with a demonstration of how the principles can also be applied in self-coaching, drawing on my own experience of using such strategies in the course of a challenging life change.

What is resilience?

Resilience can be commonly conceived as 'bouncing back' from adversity; however, as noted by Neenan (2009), this conjures an image of a child's inflatable punch bag, being knocked down by force but then quickly reverting to an upright position. The trouble with this image is that it suggests that resilience is associated with a rapid and effortless return to normality, which may not be the case. It also implies that the person returns to their original state, and that may not be the case either. Sometimes resilient responses to change and adversity can stretch across many weeks, months or even years, while the individual may in fact never return to the exact way they were before adversity struck; some adversity experiences are truly life-changing and can be personally transformative. So 'bouncing back' doesn't cover it. Nor does narrowing the concept of resilience to focus on 'adversity', since resilience can be relevant in times of change and challenge (e.g. taking on new responsibilities at work). Therefore, we need a definition of resilience that can reflect these considerations. The definition of resilience that we will use is adapted from the work of Michael Neenan (2009): 'Resilience comprises a set of flexible, adaptive behavioural, cognitive and/or emotional responses to change, challenge or adversity.'

This definition recognizes that resilience is relevant to a number of life circumstances, and emphasizes that flexible, adaptive responses are the key to resilience – that is, we are able to adjust how we react to events that may place demands on our coping resources, changing the way we think, feel and behave in order to better deal with the challenge we are presented with. The tools and principles of CBC can support us to do just that.

Cognition and resilience

Remembering the lessons from Chapters 5 and 9, the way we think about events can significantly influence our feelings and behaviour. Albert Ellis's ABC model is again helpful in illustrating this:

Activating event	*Beliefs about the event*	*Consequences*
Get challenging performance feedback.	'That's it, I'm a useless practitioner!'	Anxiety, despondency.

When we experience change, challenge or adversity, our reaction at (C) is not entirely caused by the activating event in question (A–C thinking); rather, it is the beliefs we hold about the event at (B) that significantly influence our response. To illustrate the point, consider the above example but with a different thought process taking place at (B):

Activating event	*Beliefs about the event*	*Consequences*
Get challenging performance feedback.	'I would prefer it if I got better feedback but it's not the end of the world that I didn't on this occasion. I will learn from this and move on.'	Disappointed, determined.

In this example, a change of mind-set at (B) shifts the individual's emotional and behavioural reaction to one of healthy disappointment rather than despondency and a determination to move forward.

The key point here is that we can react differently to the same event depending very much on how we view it, and our thoughts and beliefs play a key role in determining our emotional and behavioural reaction. Crucially, while we may not be able to exert control over all of the events of our lives, we can exert a measure of control over our thoughts and beliefs. So how do we apply this principle to develop resilience?

Identifying resilience-undermining thoughts

There are a number of ways of thinking or interpreting that can undermine resilience. Box 13.1 contains some examples of resilience-undermining thoughts (RUTs – Palmer, 2013), adapted from the 'thinking errors' described in Chapter 9.

Box 13.1 Resilience-undermining thoughts

- *Resistance to reality:* 'This shouldn't be happening!', 'This shouldn't happen to me!'
- *Awfulizing/catastrophizing:* 'This is awful, nothing could be worse!' (it's as bad as it could be); 'It's wholly bad!' (there are no good aspects/no good can come from this); 'It's the end of the world!'
- *Personalization/blame:* 'It's all my fault/their fault!' (no other factors contributed).
- *Ignoring context:* Interpreting events in isolation, without considering the bigger picture.
- *Self-doubt/fortune-telling:* 'I won't be able to handle it!'
- *Low frustration tolerance:* 'I can't stand it!'
- *Avoidance:* Refusing to think about something as it's too uncomfortable.
- *Condemning (self or others):* 'I'm useless!', 'I'm a failure!', 'He's a total ***!'
- *Demands (musts, shoulds, oughts, have-tos):* 'I must achieve outstandingly well or else I am an inadequate person!'; 'Others must treat me fairly or else they are awful people!'; 'They should be different to the way they are!'; '(S)he shouldn't be in that role!'; 'My circumstances have to be favourable or else it's awful and I can't stand it!'
- *Negative filter:* Focusing only on what is wrong or lacking without acknowledging positives.
- *Resilience-undermining imagery (playing dodgy videos):* Mentally running images of, for example, not coping, bad outcomes.

Such thoughts reflect selective or distorted perception, and are extreme, illogical or irrational in nature. They can lead to unhelpful emotional consequences such as anxiety, anger, depression or shame, and counterproductive behavioural responses. However, armed with insight into such thought patterns, we can use the ABC model when we experience change, challenge or adversity to identify if we are holding any RUTs. Having located and identified RUTs, we can then apply the cognitive-behavioural method of *disputation* to challenge them.

Disputing resilience-undermining thoughts

Disputation was first introduced in Chapter 9. In disputation, we place the RUTs in the dock and seek to challenge them by calling on a number of questions:

- What is the evidence that supports that thought? What is the evidence against that thought? What are the *facts*?
- How logical is the thought?
- How helpful is the thought? What are the consequences of thinking that?
- Are there alternative ways of thinking about it? What would we say to a friend who said that?

Developing resilience-enhancing thoughts (RETs)

Through disputation, we can seek to challenge and undermine any RUTs we experience. However, we need to do more than simply weed out the poisonous thoughts; instead, to develop resilient responses, we need to be able to develop alternative ways of thinking and construing that are more balanced, logical and rational, and that keep things in perspective and in context. These can be considered to be resilience-enhancing thoughts (RETs – Palmer, ibid.), and are adapted from the 'thinking skills' also described in Chapter 9 (see also Neenan, 2009; Neenan & Dryden, 2012). They are summarized in Box 13.2.

Box 13.2 Resilience-enhancing thoughts

- *Acceptance of reality:* 'This is happening/has happened. Now what can I do?'
- *De-awfulizing/de-catastrophizing:* 'It is not as bad as it could be'; 'It's not 100 per cent awful. Some good may come from this'; 'It'll pass/I'll adjust'.
- *Broadening the picture:* Considering the range of factors influencing a situation (de-personalizing); considering the broader context in which an event/situation occurs.
- *Self-confidence:* 'I will handle it'.

- *High frustration tolerance:* 'I might not like it, but I can stand it'.
- *Facing your dragons:* 'What's the worst that could happen? If that happens, how will I handle it?'
- *Being realistic:* 'That's the worst that could happen . . . How likely is it?"
- *Compassion (to self or others)*: Focusing on specific behaviours. Not rating/labelling ourselves or others on the basis of specific actions. Accepting self/other as fallible.
- *Preferences (rather than demands)*: 'I would prefer to always achieve well but if I don't it's not awful and it doesn't make me an inadequate person'; 'I would strongly prefer it that . . . but if not . . .'
- *Gratitude/appreciation:* Keeping in touch with the positive aspects of a situation (or one's life more broadly).
- *Resilience-enhancing imagery:* Imagining oneself coping with difficulty or experiencing success.

By disputing RUTs, and transforming them into RETs, we can develop an effective new response that enables us to deal adaptively and constructively with the change, challenge or adversity we have encountered.

An ABCDE model for developing resilience

The full process can be summarized using Albert Ellis's ABCDE model, as follows.

Activating event	*Beliefs about the event*	*Consequences*	*Disputation*	*Effective new approach*
Get challenging performance feedback.	'That's it, I'm a useless practitioner!'	Anxiety, despondency.	'Where's the evidence? Is it logical to conclude that? What other ways of thinking about it are there?'	'This is just one piece of feedback in a bigger picture. It's not the end of the world.' Learning from the event and moving on.

In the above framework, we can identify RUTs at (B), challenge and dispute them at (D), thereby developing an effective new approach at (E). This can also involve calling upon the examples of RETs to guide our explorations.

Application in a school context

The members of staff of an urban primary school were provided with training in the approaches described in this chapter, the rationale being that this would develop individual and organizational capacity for responding to change, challenge and adversity. Twenty participants were encouraged to apply the ABCDE framework to their own lives and situations, and were supported to identify, dispute and transform RUTs. After the training, eighteen of the twenty participants indicated that they had found the session 'very helpful', with the remaining two participants indicating that it had been 'helpful'. Examples of qualitative feedback were as follows:

- 'It has made me think about situations I have recently been in, and know will occur again in the future, to help me reflect on how I coped and felt about them.'
- 'I intend to use ABCDE in future situations as a strategy for dealing with occurrences.'
- 'I will use this within my own teaching to support my pupils with understanding and wanting to learn.'
- 'Life-changing! I feel I now have a strategy to help me move forward and in effect become a better practitioner.'

Ten of the participants also agreed to provide three-month follow-up feedback about the extent to which they made use of the strategies in their lives and practice. The following are some of the responses obtained:

- 'I have given myself time to think about how I would face challenges/adversity. This has enabled me to put aside the "whispering voice" that gives me negative beliefs about my abilities and what others might think. This has in some part led to a more self-care approach to my thinking on a more regular basis.'
- 'Before the session I was a person who used to be negative. When it came to stressful situations I would always focus on how bad things were and this would make me feel worse. I am getting better. I still immediately go into my default mode when things happen but I now take a step back after my initial negativity and assess the situation better. I find now that I am no longer as stressed as I used to be and can manage situations better.'
- 'I have had to draw on inner strength and resilience in order to put things into perspective and not catastrophize the situation. The strategies shared and discussed on the training helped to further develop my understanding of this.'

In the above examples, we can see evidence of participants demonstrating insight into their responses to change, challenge or adversity, and evidence that this insight has had a positive impact on their coping style. Of course, as the comments suggest, such approaches are not a quick fix, and application requires work, effort and practice. Furthermore, this chapter has focused only on certain components of resilience, and there are other factors relevant to developing resilience that are beyond the scope of this exploration (e.g. clarity of values, problem-solving skills). However, if we can equip school practitioners with such tools, we can positively impact on their ability to handle the myriad challenges they may encounter in the course of a teaching year. This, in turn, will have corresponding benefits for the organization and, crucially, the children within it.

Developing resilience through self-coaching

Before bringing this chapter to a close, I would like to demonstrate how these principles can be applied in the context of self-coaching. Self-coaching is a good way to begin to develop familiarity with the cognitive-behavioural approach, and I would urge any coach or practitioner to start with themselves before attempting to use CBC with others. To illustrate, I will use an example from my own personal experience. Of course, this is another example of self-disclosure on my part; however, my hope is that sharing this example will be helpful in illustrating the application of the strategies. At the same time, I want to stand alongside the coachees who have allowed me to share the content of their sessions or feedback in the interests of supporting the learning of others.

In June 2013, I resigned from my full-time permanent contract as a local authority educational psychologist in order to set up my own independent practice and business. This was a move that I had planned and envisaged for some time, and I expected my final day to be a day of inner celebration and excitement. However, my reaction was somewhat different and unanticipated. Driving home from my final day, I was surprised to note that I felt deflated and anxious. As I became more and more focused on the empty spaces in my diary, these feelings intensified with a corresponding negative impact on my behaviour. I snapped at the children, was quiet and withdrawn at a party, and sought to numb my feelings with wine and television. For the next two nights, my sleep was disturbed, and I was troubled with recurring negative thoughts and images. Come the Sunday morning, I decided (for the sake of my family) that it was time to take hold of the situation and see if I could develop an alternative response. Rather than taking the ABCDE approach, I used the SPACE model (see Chapter 9) to attempt to develop some insight into what was happening. This enabled me to map out my reaction and to begin the process of searching for any RUTs (see Figure 13.1).

There were, in fact, many RUTs on my diagram, but I have selected the 'hottest' ones (i.e. those that seemed to cause me the most disturbance) for clarity of illustration. Those were:

- *Fortune-telling:* predicting that my move had been a mistake before even getting started.
- *Extreme thinking:* telling myself that I had given up all my security.
- *Self-condemnation:* condemning myself as an 'idiot'.

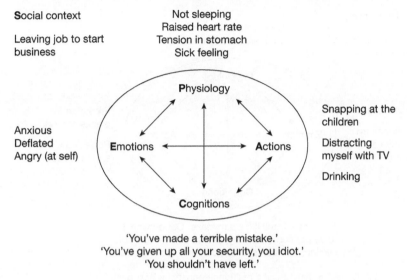

Social context

Leaving job to start
business

Not sleeping
Raised heart rate
Tension in stomach
Sick feeling

Anxious
Deflated
Angry (at self)

Snapping at the
children

Distracting
myself with TV

Drinking

Physiology

Emotions ←→ Actions

Cognitions

'You've made a terrible mistake.'
'You've given up all your security, you idiot.'
'You shouldn't have left.'

Figure 13.1 A SPACE diagram of a resilience-undermining reaction

- *Denial of reality/demanding-ness:* telling myself I shouldn't have left, as if it was possible to go back in time and change it.

Having developed some insight into the thoughts that were contributing to my feelings and behaviour, I was then able to begin disputing them and transforming them into more RETs. This proceeded as follows:

- *Challenging fortune-telling*: 'How can you judge it's a mistake when you haven't even started? That's not logical! It's too soon to tell.'
- *Challenging extreme thinking:* 'You haven't given up *all* your security. You have a contract to provide services to a client, and you've got some other pieces of work.'
- *Challenging self-condemnation:* 'You're not an idiot. That's harsh. Be a bit kinder to yourself.'
- *Challenging denial of reality:* 'What do you mean, you shouldn't have left? As if you can do anything about that now! No good dwelling on that! You have left, and that's it now. You can only move forward.'

As well as carrying out this self-reflection exercise, I was also able to access the support of others around me. This led to some changes in how I felt, and some more constructive behavioural responses (going over additional preparations for pieces of work, going through my list of reasons for leaving my job to remind myself of my vision and purpose). In turn, this impacted on the physical symptoms

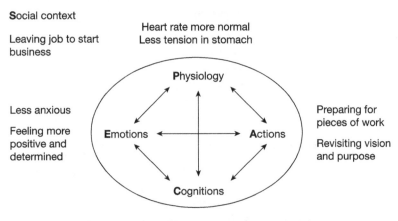

Social context

Leaving job to start
business

Heart rate more normal
Less tension in stomach

Less anxious

Feeling more
positive and
determined

Preparing for
pieces of work

Revisiting vision
and purpose

'Only time will tell if it's a mistake. Get on with it.'
'You've got some security, and you're not an idiot.'
'You've left, and that's it. You can only move forward.'

Figure 13.2 A SPACE diagram of a resilience-enhancing approach

I had been experiencing. The changes can be represented on a new SPACE diagram (see Figure 13.2).

The result of this was an effective new approach that enabled me to approach my first week of business in a much more positive state and mind-set.

Reflections and conclusions

How was coaching applied to support improvement of performance, development and/or wellbeing?

This chapter has demonstrated how the principles of CBC can be applied to support individuals to develop their levels of personal resilience. The case illustration has shown how such principles can be applied on a larger scale by providing school practitioners with training in CBC methods, thereby enabling them to coach themselves (and perhaps each other) in times of difficulty. The impact of this is enhanced capacity within the organization to deal with change, challenge or adversity – one of the factors that Luthans *et al.* (2007) refer to as constituting the 'psychological capital' of the organization. Applied in this way, psychology has the potential to support school practitioners to develop more adaptive responses to adversity, enabling them to sustain performance through times of change or difficulty. The latter part of this chapter has also demonstrated how you can apply coaching principles or techniques to your own life and situation in the context of self-coaching.

What coaching models, skills or techniques have we covered?

This chapter has illustrated the following tools and techniques:

- The ABCDE model for recognizing, disputing and transforming self-limiting thoughts.
- Identifying resilience-undermining thoughts (RUTs).
- Disputing RUTs.
- Developing resilience-enhancing thoughts (RETs).
- The SPACE model for developing insight into reactions to a situation and generating a multimodal intervention plan.

How else could this approach be applied?

The approaches described in this chapter could also be used with individuals in one-to-one coaching engagements. It would also be possible to provide older students with training in these approaches, equipping them with a valuable life skill for dealing with change, challenge and adversity. Indeed, this coheres with the current drive in the UK for schools to place teaching of 'character, resilience and grit on a par with academic learning' (DfE, 2014).

This chapter re-emphasizes the value of *enabling* others by equipping them with tools to effectively coach themselves. Again, the principles of *structuring* and *application* (supporting people to apply ideas or concepts to their own situations) are illustrated. Importantly, this chapter has demonstrated that we need not wait for adversity to strike in order to prepare people with such strategies; instead, we can proactively and preventatively equip them with resilience-enhancing strategies so as to build their capacity for responding to future challenges.

How could you apply these skills or principles in your own practice?

Reflection questions

1   When encountering a change, challenge or adversity, can you use either the ABCDE or SPACE models to understand and transform your reaction?

2   How can you use the methods outlined in this book to support you in taking a structured self-coaching approach to enhancing your own performance, development and/or wellbeing?

3   If you are a school leader, how would the principles described in this chapter be helpful to the members of your own organization?

Suggested reading

Neenan, M. (2009). *Developing Resilience: A Cognitive-Behavioural Approach.* Hove: Routledge.

Part 3

Reflections, conclusions and future directions

Chapter 14

Pulling it all together

Tell them what you're going to tell them. Tell them. Then tell them what you told them.

(Teaching proverb)

Introduction

So, having read the chapters in Part 2, where does that leave us? What do the case studies tell us about how coaching psychology can be applied in education, and the possible impact it can have? How do the case illustrations presented support *you* in becoming more effective at enhancing the performance, development and wellbeing of others? In this chapter we will pull together and summarize the learning from the preceding chapters, and begin to think about how you can start putting it into practice. The questions explored by each of the chapters in Part 2 will be revisited in turn, below.

How was coaching applied in schools to support the improvement of performance, development and/or wellbeing?

In each of the chapters in Part 2, we have seen how coaching can be successfully applied to address real-life issues faced in schools. Specifically, we have seen coaching applied in the following ways:

- Supporting the development of classroom practice (e.g. developing strategies for managing low-level disruption, improving the quality of teaching and learning).
- Supporting a practitioner to move towards specific performance standards that have been identified in a performance appraisal process.
- Providing a practitioner (in this case a school leader) with an individualized CPD opportunity that directly relates to their day-to-day reality.
- Improving practitioner confidence and wellbeing.
- Supporting a new-to-role practitioner to manage the practical and emotional demands of role change.

- Supporting practical problem-solving.
- Supporting the performance and development of a team.
- Developing individual and organizational resilience.

You might wish to reflect on whether any of these applications of coaching would be relevant to your own practice or situation. Additionally, you may be able to think of other applications that are specifically relevant to your own unique context.

In terms of the impact of the aforementioned applications, we have seen that coaching can give rise to the following:

- Development and implementation of concrete strategies that have a tangible impact on student learning and engagement.
- Improved practitioner performance, with corresponding benefits for the students.
- Enhanced commitment to the use of a particular teaching strategy and greater quality in its execution.
- Enhanced professional growth and development, with associated benefits for the children and organization.
- Increases in practitioner and team confidence, resilience and wellbeing.

Of course, we must be tentative in the conclusions drawn from a small number of case studies where the impact has been predominantly measured by the self-report of the participants immediately after the engagement has concluded. While in some cases the reported improvements have also been corroborated by third-party observers (Chapters 7, 8 and 11), there has been no rigorous follow-up study of impact over time and no comparison with others who have not received such interventions. To further investigate the value of coaching and coaching psychology in education, research is required that measures the impact of such work, for example: (i) over time; (ii) on a broader range of outcome measures; and (iii) in comparison to controls. Similar research that has already taken place in other professional domains has demonstrated the impact of coaching psychology on staff resilience, self-efficacy and work engagement (e.g. Ijntema, 2014), and the specific exploration of the extent to which this also holds true in educational contexts would be valuable. What these case studies *do* suggest, however, is the potential of coaching psychology to have an impact in schools in ways that can result in benefits for many children and young people.

What coaching models, skills or techniques have we covered?

In terms of broad methods that can be used to support the performance, development and wellbeing of education practitioners, we have covered the following:

- A non-judgemental approach to teacher observation.
- A nine-step performance coaching model.
- A six-step model for supporting practitioner development.

- A six-step model for supporting practitioner wellbeing.
- A framework for supporting practical problem solving (PRACTICE).
- A solution-focused framework for supporting individual and team development (ENABLE).

We have also seen how coaching practice can be supplemented by the application of the following psychological approaches:

- The principles of the person-centred approach to support the creation of a climate that is conducive to change by providing a relationship characterized by regard, empathy and genuineness.
- The four tasks of Motivational Interviewing (express empathy, enhance self-efficacy, develop discrepancy, roll with resistance) to elicit the coachee's motivation to change and develop.
- The principles of Self-Determination Theory to increase the likelihood of sustainable change occurring (enhancing the person's sense of competence in relation to a behaviour; respecting their autonomy; supporting them to reflect on the meaning of a behaviour and how it relates to their own goals and values; involving the coachee in devising their change plan or making strategies their own somehow).
- The principles and practices of solution-focused coaching (eliciting and shaping the coachee's preferred future, scaling, exception-seeking, exploring what is already working, planning small steps forward) that enable people to tap into and harness their own resources to move towards the future they want to create.
- Techniques informed by Self-Efficacy Theory (bridging from success to problem, facilitating efficacy-supportive processing) in order to enhance practitioner confidence.
- The principles and practices of cognitive-behavioural coaching (the SPACE model, ABCDE, identifying and disputing thinking errors, developing thinking skills), which enable people to recognize and transform thoughts and behaviours that may otherwise interfere with performance and goal achievement.

Evidently, psychology has much to offer to the practice of coaching in terms of providing principles and techniques that can enrich and enhance coaching practice. This illustrates the potential of psychology to make a positive contribution to schools and society by supporting people to achieve enhanced performance, development and wellbeing.

Reflection questions

Which of the aforementioned techniques or methods do you already use? Which might you like to develop further? How can you begin to further develop your proficiency?

As for how you can begin putting these methods into practice, it may be that you choose to narrow your focus to one or two particular approaches and then develop your proficiency with those until they feel more embedded. Another alternative would be to adopt an eclectic approach to practice in which you call on each of the above approaches as they seem appropriate to a particular engagement or situation. For this purpose we can embed some of the aforementioned psychological principles or techniques into the classic I-GROW coaching model. Table 14.1 is one example of how you might go about this.

Thus, the I-GROW model provides us with an easy-to-remember framework that can support the integration of many other techniques or approaches. However, we must remember that all the above must take place within the context of a sound collaborative alliance if coaching is to prove effective. It is also important to acknowledge that the approaches listed are only those that have influenced *my* practice, and there are other psychological approaches that could be incorporated into coaching (and, indeed, this framework) that are not covered here (see e.g. Palmer & Whybrow, 2007). Psychology has a much broader legacy of ideas and principles that we can draw upon, and there are many other possible applications to coaching that have not been explored in this volume. The possibilities are exciting for those interested in developing this aspect of their practice.

Table 14.1 An eclectic, psychology-informed, I-GROW coaching model

I-GROW stage	Approach
Issues	• Demonstrating the Rogerian core conditions of unconditional positive regard, genuineness and empathy (of course, this climate needs to be maintained throughout the engagement).
Goals	• Eliciting and shaping the coachee's preferred future.
Reality	• Using a cognitive-behavioural model such as SPACE or ABCDE to explore the coachee's current reality. • Developing the coachee's awareness of a discrepancy between how things are and how they want them to be. • Using scaling to explore the coachee's current reality. • Seeking exceptions. • Exploring what is already working, enhancing the coachee's sense of self-efficacy.
Options	• Exploring previous successes or strengths in other areas. • Using SPACE or ABCDE to generate new ways of thinking and acting. • Collaboratively generating practical alternatives and considering their consequences. • Bridging from previous success experiences to the current problem or goal.
Wrap-up	• Planning small steps forward. • Providing effectance-promoting feedback.

Table 14.2 Psychological and practical aspects of change

Psychological	Practical
Confidence	Goals
Motivation	Skills/behaviours
Resilience	Problem-solving
Beliefs	Decision-making
Emotions	Action planning
Self-acceptance	Support networks

The incorporation of psychological methods and principles into a classic coaching framework provides us with a *dual systems* approach, meaning that we are able to attend to both the practical and psychological aspects of a coachee's life or situation as is appropriate (see Table 14.2).

This leaves us with a versatile coaching toolbox that can be applied in a broad range of situations and contexts wherever any of the above factors may be relevant. Moreover, this enables us to target the factors that may be most relevant to a particular individual, team or situation.

How else could these approaches or principles be applied?

A range of further applications for the approaches and principles described has been suggested throughout each of the chapters in Part 2. At this stage you might wish to consider yourself if there are any further possible applications that have not been suggested.

What can we learn about how to help others to change?

Throughout this book we have learned (and/or relearned) a number of lessons that can inform how we can work with others in a way that makes change more likely. These lessons can be summarized as follows:

- The creation of a non-judgemental climate is crucial in that it allows the coachee(s) to engage fully and honestly and to genuinely explore the possibility of change.
- We cannot have a one-size-fits-all approach to change, and need to be able to modify our approach to match the needs of the situation and the coachee. The quality of the collaborative alliance between coach and coachee is a crucial factor.
- We can improve the quality of the collaborative alliance – and, indeed, the effectiveness of our work – by seeking feedback from the coachee about, for example, the extent to which our chosen approach has matched their particular needs.

- Motivation arises from a person's awareness of a discrepancy between how things are and how they want them to be. Without this discrepancy, there can be no motivation for change. As coaches, we can work so as to develop the coachee's awareness of such a discrepancy.
- Behaviour change is likely to be of better quality, and longer lasting, if the person experiences a sense of self-determination over their behaviour. This can be achieved by, for example, respecting the person's autonomy; involving them in devising their own change plan; supporting them to reflect on the underlying meaning or benefit of a behaviour; or encouraging consideration of how the behaviour relates to their own goals and values.
- We do not need to understand the origins of problems in order to support people to begin constructing solutions. The mental image of a preferred future can provide the necessary focus and direction to the engagement.
- When supporting people to articulate preferred futures, we need to be alert to whether the person is describing a particular outcome or a strategy for achieving it. Ensuring a focus on outcomes rather than strategies opens up more possibilities as to how the end destination might be reached.
- People bring strengths and resources to the engagement, and we can support them to tap into and harness these so they can move towards the future they want to create. Our role is less about the prescription of solutions and more about supporting people to uncover and nurture the small green shoots of success that already exist in their lives and situations.
- A person's sense of self-efficacy (their belief in their ability to produce desired results from their actions) may be a key factor to address. People may have a low sense of self-efficacy even if they objectively have skills that are relevant to their goals. We can support a person's sense of self-efficacy by drawing their attention to the skills they have that are relevant to a particular situation, and facilitating efficacy-supportive processing of success experiences.
- Sometimes the ways in which people think can be a crucial factor affecting their performance and wellbeing. We can support people to recognize ways in which their thinking may be limiting their progress, and enable them to find new ways of thinking and acting that will take them towards their goals.
- We may need to attend to psychological factors (e.g. confidence, motivation, beliefs) as well as being able to support the planning of practical actions.
- The flexible use of structures can support both individuals and teams to reflect on their experiences and any factors that may be relevant to them achieving their goals.
- We can have an enabling impact on people by supporting them to focus on the factors relevant to their situation that are under their control.
- A small change can lead to bigger changes. Therefore, we can be of help by supporting the person to plan a realistic small step forward from their present situation.
- Achieving change takes effort and persistence and the coachee will need to do work in between sessions in order to achieve their goals. If we equip

people with the necessary tools and strategies, they can make further gains through self-reflection outside of sessions.

•   It can be helpful to support people to take a systematic problem-solving approach to situations they are experiencing. We do not need to be expert in a particular problem area in order to support the person or team to think through and evaluate their options.

My contention is that if we can allow the above principles to guide our actions and decision-making, it will enhance the likelihood that people will benefit from our support. Stop to reflect for a moment: to what extent do these principles speak to you about your experience? Which of these principles are already reflected in your practice? Which might you seek to develop further?

I hope that this collated list of principles proves helpful to you in your work to support the performance, development and wellbeing of others. Of course, the list may change in time, and will continue to be shaped in response to experience. In this world, very little is fixed for long; however, if our business is growth and development, then this fluidity gives us cause for optimism. As Carl Rogers (1961) notes: 'Life is guided by a changing understanding of and interpretation of my experience. It is always in process of becoming' (p. 27). As are we all.

Chapter 15

Future directions

Coaching psychology has the potential to be a major force for the promotion of wellbeing and performance enhancement for the individual, for organizations, and society as a whole.

(Grant, 2007, p. 35)

Outcomes of this book

In Part 2 of this book we saw a range of ways in which coaching psychology has been applied to support the performance, development and wellbeing of education practitioners. Each case illustration has demonstrated how coaching psychology can support schools to address real-life day-to-day concerns, with corresponding benefits for the staff, the students and the organization. Crucially, we have seen that coaching is not just an intervention that meets the needs of the individual being coached; on the contrary, if set up and facilitated correctly, coaching is a robust intervention that can support the individual to move forward in directions that are aligned with school improvement priorities. This is achieved not through judgement, blame or condemnation, but by creating the conditions in which purposeful, lasting change can occur. By creating an interpersonal climate in which the person feels safe to speak openly and honestly, we increase the likelihood that they will engage genuinely and authentically with the process. Within this climate, coaching provides individuals or teams with a personalized learning experience that enables them to deeply engage with the subject of focus, resulting in specific action plans that are tailored to their unique context and circumstances. It is a supportive yet challenging way of working with people that demonstrates respect for their opinions and experience, values their strengths and qualities, and – hopefully – leaves them feeling more confident and energized to move towards their goals. The result of this is a practitioner who feels better, performs better, and is able to carry out their functions more effectively, all of which is good news for both the children and the organization.

As we have seen throughout this book, psychology is a tool that can enrich coaching practice and make it more effective by offering us theories, principles and models that can enhance our ability to work with others in a way that makes change more likely. My hope is that seeing the positive impact of working with people in this way will encourage more professionals to reflect these principles and values in their practice. Indeed, one of the central tenets of this book is that the methods described can be utilized by a range of professionals who have an interest or investment in helping others to move forward. As previously noted, coaching is a skill that has relevance to many roles in education, from in-school coaches to school leaders to classroom practitioners. I hope that in writing this book I have made such principles and methods clear and accessible so that many others in education can make use of them. The following are some of the possibilities I can envisage:

- Classroom practitioners using the non-judgemental observation approach as part of peer coaching to support their colleagues to develop classroom practices.
- School leaders using psychology-informed coaching principles and skills in their work with individual teachers and/or teams.
- School coaches using the methods described in order to support colleagues in their own or other schools to move forward.
- Special Educational Needs Co-ordinators drawing upon coaching principles when responding to requests for advice from staff.
- Specialist Leaders of Education or Local Leaders of Education applying psychology to enhance their own effectiveness at bringing the best out of colleagues in other schools.
- Practitioners using the principles of cognitive-behavioural coaching to support their own performance and wellbeing.

If you would like to further develop your practice in the ways described in this book, then you may wish to consider the following professional development activities:

- Practising some of the approaches described in the context of self-coaching.
- Practising with volunteer coachees.
- Getting going. There is no substitute for real-life practice and (supervised) reflection.
- Maintaining a reflective learning log about your coaching experiences (what was the context, what happened, what went well, what would you do differently, what key learning points emerged that will inform your future practice?).
- Reading some of the texts referenced in Chapters 2–5 of this book and seeking to embed the principles into your practice.
- Accessing a short course in coaching psychology (see, for example, www.centreforcoaching.com).
- Accessing regular supervision in relation to the development of your coaching skills.
- Joining a professional coaching psychology society (e.g. the British Psychological Society's Special Group in Coaching Psychology – see www.sgcp.org.uk).

If you intend to provide formal coaching services, I would recommend that you read the appendices of this book which will support you in thinking through some of the practical and ethical issues that can arise in coaching.

One of the outcomes I would like this book to achieve in the future is an increased demand for coaching psychology services in education, and an increase in the numbers of psychologists who offer coaching to schools as part of their professional services. With this aim in mind, I envisage that schools could make use of coaching psychologists in the following ways.

Direct coaching

A school could contract a coaching psychologist to carry out coaching work with individuals or teams, perhaps in relation to some of the themes identified in Part 2 of this book. Of course, there are resource implications here, and for some purposes the continued contracting of psychologists would arguably be less sustainable than supporting school staff to develop coaching proficiency themselves. However, there may still be some circumstances where the involvement of an external coaching psychologist would be desirable, for example:

- The coachee's sense of trust and safety would be enhanced by the use of an external professional.
- It is thought that there may be particular psychological factors that are relevant to the coachee's performance, development and wellbeing.
- It is thought that the coaching psychologist's particular approach and orientation may be well-suited to the needs of the prospective coachee(s).
- The school's capacity to provide coaching support from its existing resources is limited.
- Other attempts to support the prospective coachee to move forward have not resulted in the desired progress.

Training in coaching skills

Schools could arrange for coaching psychologists to provide school practitioners with training in coaching skills. Indeed, these skills are not just relevant for staff who occupy formal coaching roles, but all practitioners who have an interest or investment in helping others to move forward. Experienced coaching psychologists would be well placed to facilitate learning about core coaching skills and psychological approaches that can enrich and enhance coaching practice.

Supervision for in-school coaches

Supervision is a crucial aspect of the professional development of coaches. Coaching psychologists could be used to provide in-school coaches with a reflective space to support their ongoing development, enabling them to celebrate positives, problem-solve issues, and talk through ethical dilemmas or considerations.

Developing in-school coaching systems

As well as skill development, coaching psychologists could support schools to develop and embed their own in-school or between-school coaching systems. For some objectives (e.g. supporting the ongoing development of classroom practice) this may represent a more cost-effective and sustainable option than seeking the involvement of coaches who are external to the organization. Indeed, if you wish to read further about a school's journey in developing a coaching culture and the value it added to the organization, I refer you to Suggett (2012). Experienced coaching psychologists would also be able to support schools to manage some of the practical and ethical issues that can arise in the course of coaching (e.g. deciding the focus for coaching when the views of multiple stakeholders need to be considered, whether to use written action plans, establishing confidentiality parameters).

Building psychological capacity

Schools could make use of coaching psychologists to provide training for school staff and young people in particular psychological principles that can enhance their ability to achieve their own goals and deal with change, challenge and adversity (e.g. solution-focused coaching, cognitive-behavioural coaching). Equipping people with such tools so that they are able to effectively self-coach will increase both their professional and personal effectiveness.

If you work in a school, then what options are available to you in terms of contacting a coaching psychologist to arrange such services? The following are some of the options you might consider:

- You can contact your local Educational Psychology service to ask if any of the psychologists are able to provide coaching psychology services.
- The International Society for Coaching Psychology maintains a register of members from across the world (www.isfcp.net/membersregister.htm).
- The British Psychological Society also maintains a register of coaching psychologists (www.bps.org.uk).

Before closing this section, I would like to make it clear that I am in no way suggesting that psychologists are *uniquely* qualified to carry out coaching, or to provide coaching training. Indeed, one of the most talented coaches I have worked with was not a psychologist, and I am sure there are psychologists out there who would not be well-suited to deliver coaching services. My intention is to draw attention to the fact that the use of a coaching psychologist exists as an option for education practitioners to consider when planning how best to support the ongoing development of their staff and organizations.

Conclusion

Throughout this book we have seen how coaching can be applied in schools to enhance the performance, development and wellbeing of education practitioners. We have also seen how the application of psychology can enrich and bring depth to coaching practice, providing a range of frameworks, principles and techniques that can support practitioners in schools to move towards their goals and achieve enhanced wellbeing. By working with people in this way, we can support them to achieve higher standards of performance while leaving them feeling respected, valued, confident, energized and empowered. Coaching psychologists therefore potentially have much to offer to education in terms of supporting education practitioners and settings to unlock and maximize their potential for the benefit of the children they work with. However, perhaps the greatest contribution that coaching psychology can make in this respect is to equip those who work in education with a set of psychology-informed principles and tools so that they become more effective at helping themselves and each other. In so doing, as more and more practitioners improve their proficiency at supporting and challenging themselves and others to grow and develop, so the capacity for sustainable improvement within and between schools will increase.

Our children only get one go through the education system, and they need the adults who work with them to be supported, challenged and enabled to be the best that they can be. Coaching psychology provides us with the means to make this vision a reality.

Making coaching work

God is in the details.

(Ludwig Mies van der Rohe)

Structure of a coaching engagement

In this section I will outline the overarching structure of a typical coaching engagement. The structure comprises a number of key elements that map a progression through the piece of work, and reminds us of crucial details that need to be attended to at each stage. While at first glance some of the material may seem a little dry and procedural, in my experience it is attention to details like these that can make the difference in practice. The section will have most relevance to those who intend to formally provide coaching as service; however, a consideration of the underlying concepts may also be helpful to those who provide coaching as part of their roles.

The components of the framework are illustrated in Figure A.1.

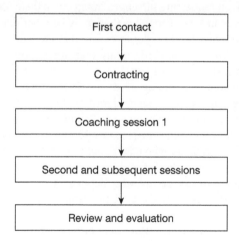

Figure A.1 A typical coaching engagement

First contact

This is the point at which a prospective client first makes contact with the coach to enquire about the possibility of a coaching engagement. It may be that the person is requesting coaching for themselves, or enquiring about the provision of coaching for another person in their school or organization. Either way, we can ask further questions to clarify the rationale for seeking coaching, the outcomes that are wanted from the engagement, and the possible client relationships that exist and will have a bearing on the piece of work.

Client relationships

In any given engagement there may be a number of people who have the potential to be in different 'client' relationships with the coach (see, for example, McMahon, 2005; Schein, 1999). In the context of coaching, these client relationships include:

- *Customer:* The person who wants something to happen as a result of the coaching engagement.
- *Coachee(s):* Those who will participate in the coaching sessions.
- *Sponsor:* The person who will 'foot the bill'.
- *Stakeholders:* Others who may have a vested interest in the outcome.

A key function of the initial conversation is to begin to determine the client relationships that exist in order to ensure that the coaching engagement is contracted correctly. In life coaching contexts, for example, this is typically more straightforward, as the person seeking coaching is usually the person who participates in the sessions, who benefits from the engagement and, ultimately, pays the bill. It is therefore possible in such circumstances for the coach to contract purely with the person requesting the engagement since there are no other parties to consider. However, in school contexts there may be other relationships that the coach needs to have regard to in order to ensure that the work satisfies the needs of those involved. Working towards goals that are important to the coachee but that do not meet the needs of the customer or other key stakeholders may ultimately result in someone ending up dissatisfied. Conversely, if the possible need for coaching support has been identified by a third-party sponsor or stakeholder (e.g. the teacher's line manager), then the question of how to enlist the coachee as a customer for change needs to be addressed – that is, how to enlist the coachee as a willing participant who has 'bought in' to the engagement and wants something to happen as a result of it. This can be achieved through, for example, a pre-coaching conversation or meeting between the coachee and their line manager to discuss the rationale for coaching and the potential benefits it may offer to them.

It is important to emphasize that one person or group of people may simultaneously occupy several of these client roles; alternatively, a particular role might be shared across several people, depending on the nature of the piece of work undertaken. While this may all seem a little pedantic, the aim of exploring and clarifying such relationships is, in the first instance, to ensure that the needs of all relevant parties are understood and met as far as possible. Moreover, a consideration of the client relationships in a given piece of work informs decision-making about who should be included in the contracting meeting (see below). For example, in Chapters 6, 7 and 8 of this book the contracting meetings took place with both the coachee and a third-party customer-sponsor who also had views and wishes with regard to the focus and goals of coaching that needed to be taken into consideration; in contrast, in Chapters 9 and 10 the customers and sponsors of the coaching (the head teachers) indicated that, once the logistical and financial matters had been agreed, the coachees were free to contract with the coach directly and to self-select their own goals for the engagement.

Throughout the 'first contact' conversation, you will begin to develop a sense of the degree to which coaching is a suitable intervention for achieving the desired outcomes; any approaches you are aware of that may be relevant to supporting the achievement of the stated aims; and whether your own personal involvement is appropriate (e.g. are there any relationship boundary issues that might impact on the engagement?). If it seems that the provision of a coaching engagement is a suitable course of action, then a contracting meeting can be arranged.

Objectives

- Clarify the rationale for seeking coaching as a form of support.
- Explore the hoped-for outcomes.
- Determine the relevant client relationships that exist.
- Determine whether it seems coaching is a suitable intervention.

Contracting

Contracting is a process through which the focus and goals of the engagement are agreed, ways of working are clarified, and the confidentiality parameters are established. The process may or may not involve a written agreement, but either way it is the psychological contract between the parties that is crucial (O'Broin & Palmer, 2010) – that is, the extent to which everyone is 'on the same page' in terms of their expectations of the process and each other. The contracting meeting is a key vehicle for beginning to build and develop the collaborative alliance that is so crucial for achieving positive outcomes (5.9).

When setting up a contracting meeting, the first question to consider is 'Who needs to be present?' In educational contexts, the contracting meeting typically takes place with both the coachee and the customer/sponsor; however, this is not always the case. The process can also be informed by the views of other key stakeholders (e.g. the coachee's line manager), although it may not be necessary for them to be physically present at the meeting. Once convened with the appropriate participants, the contracting meeting will address the following:

- The rationale for seeking coaching.
- The focus of coaching.
- Methods and principles of working.
- Roles and responsibilities.
- The parameters of confidentiality.
- Logistics, e.g. the number of sessions required, when and where the sessions will take place.
- How the coaching will be evaluated.
- Any questions or concerns those present may have.

The rationale for seeking coaching

It can be helpful at the beginning of the meeting to revisit the story of why coaching has been sought in order to ensure that there is transparency and mutual understanding regarding the rationale for the engagement.

The focus of coaching

There are two key areas of exploration in this part of the meeting:

- Any issues the coaching needs to address, perhaps informed by information from a range of sources about the coachee's performance, development and wellbeing.
- The hoped-for outcome of the engagement, and specific goals that might be worked towards.

As the clients offer their perspectives, the coach can seek to listen, understand, and to verify their understanding of what has been said by using the core skills of questioning, reflective listening, clarifying and summarizing. The aim is to generate a specific, clear focus for the work and, if it is not premature to do so, an outcome that the coachee is motivated to work towards. There may be a need for some negotiation with (or, indeed, between) the participants, depending on the nature of the issues or goals initially presented. In some engagements, the coachee may have the autonomy to entirely select their own goals; alternatively, the commissioning organization may wish to narrow the parameters of the coaching engagement to focus on particular themes or desired outcomes. Of course, the coachee may still have the freedom to choose their precise focus within the agreed parameters.

Methods and principles of working

The coach can provide information that clarifies the overall structure of the engagement, the coach's proposed ways of working and the principles that underpin their approach. An awareness of the 'big picture' is helpful in that it means that the coachee knows where it is all going and can add to the coachee's sense that the engagement has been thought through and will be purposeful. In turn, this can increase their sense of faith in both the process itself and in the coach as an agent of change, which can positively influence expectancy effects (5.9).

In engagements where changes to classroom practice are desired, it may be helpful to arrange to observe the practitioner at work prior to each coaching session taking place. If this is to happen, then the timing of the observation can be negotiated with the coachee so as to ensure that the session observed is relevant to the goals they wish to achieve from the engagement. The non-judgemental approach to teacher observation described in Chapter 6 can be used for this purpose.

Roles and responsibilities

The contracting meeting allows a discussion in which the roles and responsibilities of all parties can be clarified, for example:

*   *Coachee's role:* To engage honestly and openly; to commit to doing work in between sessions; and to voice concerns about the process if it is not meeting their needs.
*   *Sponsor's role:* To show an interest, to 'check in' with the coachee and to provide constructive feedback.
*   *Coach's role:* To adhere to confidentiality parameters; to create a safe space in which the person can reflect on their practice and situation; to bring frameworks that can support the coachee's exploration.

This degree of transparency is important for engaging the coachee as an equal participant and active collaborator, while clarifying the specific nature of any third-party involvement in the process. Coaching sessions are more likely to result in gains in the workplace in engagements where line manager involvement is supportive (Ogilvy & Ellam-Dyson, 2012).

A crucial outcome of this aspect of the meeting is that all parties are clear in terms of their expectations about what will and will not happen and what their respective roles will be. If there are differences of perception, then this gives the opportunity for them to be unearthed and aired at an early stage. Of course, it is not always possible to anticipate every eventuality in advance, and it may be that there is further work to do with regard to clarifying expectations once the reality of the engagement is experienced.

Parameters of confidentiality

It is in the contracting meeting/process that the parameters of confidentiality are established. This key ethical consideration is vital for ensuring that the coachee places trust in the process/the coach, and provides all parties with clarity with regard to the boundaries of any future conversations that may take place. Confidentiality parameters can be negotiated afresh for each new engagement undertaken, depending on the views and wishes of those involved and the purpose of the engagement. In my experience, it is often agreed for the content of the coaching sessions (and, if relevant, observation notes) to remain confidential; however, it is understood that at the end of the session the coachee will be given time to write an action plan that will be copied for other relevant parties (the sponsor, or another key stakeholder such as the coachee's line manager). This maintains the required degree of trust and safety, while adding a degree of accountability to the process for both coach and coachee. Moreover, the transparent sharing of actions that will be worked on enables subsequent in-school discussions regarding any support the coachee might require with putting them into place. There will also usually be an evaluation process and/ or form, which again may sit outside the parameters of confidentiality. The coachee can volunteer additional information beyond this if they wish, but the coach does not enter into communication about the coachee or the session with other parties. If such parameters are agreed, then it is important that they are adhered to for the sake of the engagement itself and for the trust placed in future engagements by other potential coachees. Additional enquiries from curious sponsors, however innocently ventured, must be politely but assertively rebuffed! If it transpires that more information is wanted by the sponsor, then that is not a mandate to breach the parameters of the present relationship; instead, it may be a cue to reconsider and renegotiate the confidentiality parameters of future engagements.

At the time of contracting, some exceptions to the confidentiality parameters may be agreed, for example:

- If the coach becomes concerned about the coachee's or other person's safety and/or wellbeing.
- If the coachee is not engaging in the process.
- If, during an observation, there is, for example, a child protection disclosure, an incident that breaches the Equalities Act (2010), or a serious health and safety incident.

In all the above cases, the coach will not act without first transparently declaring the perceived need to act to the coachee, and seeking their views as to how to proceed. Unambiguously clarifying these matters in advance allows the coachee to safely immerse themselves in the conversation and relationship (to the extent that they feel comfortable to do so), and can reduce the likelihood of doubts arising later in the process.

Logistics

A number of key logistical matters will be addressed during the meeting, such as the number of sessions in the engagement; when and where the sessions will take place; who will arrange 'cover' for the teacher if needed (i.e. if someone else needs to teach their class while they are in coaching); what happens in the event of a need to rearrange a session; and the terms and conditions of the engagement (if applicable).

How coaching will be evaluated

If there is to be a formal evaluation at the end of the coaching engagement (see later), then the contracting meeting provides an opportunity for the mechanisms by which that will be achieved to be discussed and agreed in advance.

Addressing questions or concerns

The clients' views are actively sought regarding the details of the engagement, and their expression of any concerns or questions is encouraged. The coach will endeavour to address any unresolved questions or concerns prior to the formal commencement of the engagement.

By the end of the contracting meeting, the goal is for all parties to be 'on the same page' about the focus of the engagement, the direction of the work, the parameters of confidentiality and the agreed ways of working. It is also hoped that the meeting will have begun the formation of a collaborative alliance between coach and coachee that will be conducive to change.

Once the above have been clarified, and all parties are in agreement about the details, the engagement can continue with the first coaching session.

Objectives

- Clarify any issues the coaching needs to address.
- Agree the outcomes and goals of the engagement.
- Transparently share methods and principles of working.
- Clarify roles and responsibilities.
- Ensure clarity regarding parameters of confidentiality.
- Attend to logistical matters.
- Clarify the outputs of coaching.
- Clarify the evaluation process.
- Address questions or concerns.

First coaching session

Facilitate reflection and learning

In the first coaching session, the coach will facilitate the coachee's active reflection on their practice or performance in relation to the identified focus of the engagement. A number of approaches or structures may be called on in service of this aim, depending on the situation and the needs of the coachee (see Chapter 5). The collaborative alliance is served by openly and transparently sharing the rationale for particular approaches with the coachee and enabling them to make an informed decision about the task(s) they wish to undertake. Irrespective of the specific approach being taken, the first coaching session is likely to involve some or all of the following:

- Revisiting and reclarifying the confidentiality parameters.
- Revisiting and reclarifying the goals of the engagement.
- Exploring aspects of the coachee's present reality.
- Considering options as to how the coachee might move forward.
- Translating possibilities into a specific action plan.

The session will usually move through the broad stages of the I-GROW model (see Chapter 4), albeit in a non-linear and dynamic fashion. Throughout, the coach will utilize the range of core coaching skills (Chapter 3) within the context of an approach that is broadly characterized as collaborative, non-directive, facilitative and future-focused (see Chapter 2).

Develop an action plan

In most cases, the end result of the session will be a written action plan that documents the goals that the coachee is working towards, and any actions they plan to take which will take them in the direction of the desired outcomes. The plan usually comprises no more than three discrete actions so that it is realistic and manageable to achieve before the next session. The important thing is to obtain some forward movement, and over-ambitious plans can be a barrier to realizing this aim. The confidentiality parameters of the action plan will have been negotiated and agreed at the contracting stage, and it can be useful to remind the coachee of those prior to them completing the plan.

Evaluate the alliance

Remember: the quality of the collaborative alliance between coach and coachee is one of the most crucial factors that will influence the outcomes of the coaching engagement (5.9). Therefore, it can be helpful at the end of the first session to evaluate the extent to which that alliance has been established. This enables any difficulties to be picked up at an early stage, and informs any ways in which the coach might need to adjust their approach in the second session. To do this, inspired by the work of Scott Miller, John Murphy and Barry Duncan, I personally ask coachees to complete a version of the following form shown in Table A.1.

Table A.1 Evaluating the collaborative alliance

	Strongly agree (1)	*Agree (2)*	*Disagree (3)*	*Strongly disagree (4)*
We had a good rapport.				
We were working on goals I wanted to work towards.				
I got the sense we were 'on the same page'.				
The things we did were helpful.				

You will notice that the questions refer directly to the key components of the collaborative alliance, enabling a discussion between coach and coachee if there is any work to be done in any of these areas.

Objectives

- Facilitate the coachee's active reflection on their practice.
- Generate a manageable action plan that the coachee will put into practice between sessions.
- Evaluate the collaborative alliance.

Second and subsequent sessions

Second and subsequent sessions are an opportunity to review and celebrate progress, to further build on things that are working, and to problem-solve any obstacles to change. Goals can be refined, and action plans reshaped to reflect the learning that has taken place as a result of active experimentation. New methods can be called on if needed. As previously, the emphasis is on supporting the coachee's active reflection, with the coach utilizing the range of core coaching skills to this effect. If change has been achieved, then the coach can support the coachee to reflect on what helped them to achieve it – and, indeed, what they have learned about themselves as a result – before allowing the coachee to determine the next matter to be worked on.

Objectives

- Review and celebrate progress.
- Build on what is working.
- Problem-solve obstacles to change.
- Identify next goals (if applicable).

Review and evaluation

After coaching through this type of model, it is important for the success of the engagement to be reviewed and evaluated. Depending on the specific contract, this may take place as a separate meeting, or it may take place as part of the final coaching session. A review meeting may be held with just the coach and coachee, or it may also involve another key person (e.g. the customer or other stakeholder). A tripartite meeting like this provides an opportunity for all parties, for example, to share stories about successes and review progress; to reflect on what has helped or hindered that progress; to share views regarding the impact of the work; to consider any possible obstacles to change; to collectively trawl the key learning points that have occurred; and to plan additional support routes now that the coaching engagement has concluded.

The engagement can then be evaluated to determine the extent to which coaching has had a discernible impact on the coachee's performance, development and/or wellbeing. The views of both the coachee and the third-party customer or sponsor can be sought so as to gather different perspectives on this crucial point. This captures evidence about the effectiveness or otherwise of coaching, introduces a further element of accountability to the customer/sponsor/stakeholders, informs consideration as to whether further or alternative forms of support are required, and serves as a valuable mechanism for driving the professional development of the coach. Evaluation also represents a means of putting *closure* on the relationship.

Objectives

- Review and celebrate progress.
- Reflect on learning that has occurred during the engagement.
- Identify further support routes (if required).
- Evaluate the impact of the coaching engagement.

Summary

A typical coaching engagement comprises the following components:

- First contact.
- Contracting.
- First coaching session.
- Second and subsequent sessions.
- Review and evaluation.

This sequence of stages provides an overarching framework in which the application of other approaches can take place. As you can see, there are a number of details to consider which, if attended to, will greatly enhance the likelihood of the coaching engagement having a positive impact, encompassing matters such as client relationships, roles and responsibilities, and confidentiality parameters. My hope is that after reading this appendix you will feel better equipped to set up coaching engagements or conversations that are more likely to succeed.

Ethics in coaching

> Ethical codes are standards of conduct that define the essentials of honourable behaviour within the particular field or organization.
>
> (Brennan & Wildflower, 2014, p. 431)

Ethical principles and the coach

Throughout this book, I have argued that psychology can be utilized by anyone who has an interest or investment in helping others to change, and I stand by that claim. However, if I am to encourage you to utilize psychological principles and practices in your coaching work with others (or indeed as part of your other functions), then that needs to be balanced by drawing your attention to the crucial matter of ethics.

As the above quote from Brennan & Wildflower indicates, a code of ethics defines the moral standards that are expected of someone undertaking a particular professional activity. In the context of coaching, ethical principles embody the values of the coach and justify the coach's moral judgements and actions (Law, 2013). If you are already a professional coach, then you may well be a member of one of the various organizations with their own defined codes of ethical practice, such as:

- The Association for Coaching (AC).
- The European Mentoring and Coaching Council (EMCC).
- The International Society for Coaching Psychology (ISCP).
- The International Coach Federation (ICF).

If that is the case, you will need to ensure that you adhere to the ethical standards of your own particular professional body (see, for example, www.isfcp.net/ethics.htm). If you are a professional coach (or aspiring coach) who is not yet a member of one of these (or similar) organizations, then you would be advised to join one. However, this book is also aimed at the broader audience of education practitioners, so it is possible that you may be a practitioner with another formal role designation where coaching others is one of your functions (e.g. a head teacher, a teacher coach, or a specialist leader of education). If that is the case, then there are certain ethical principles that are common to the different organizations' codes (even if they are described differently) that it would be important for you to be aware of and have regard to. These include the following.

Rights and respect

Respecting the rights of coachees as human beings; respecting the right to privacy and confidentiality; establishing clear confidentiality parameters, including what feedback (if any) will be given to whom; respecting the coachee's right to self-determination; being sensitive to individual and cultural differences (age, gender, disability, race, religion, sexual orientation, etc.); respecting the coachee's right to end the engagement at any time.

Recognition

Recognizing the limits of your competence and practising within them; being open and honest about the limits of your competence; referring coachees on to other services (e.g. a psychologist or counsellor) if they seem more appropriate to their needs.

Responsibility

Maintaining a commitment to your own continuing professional development; engaging in reflective practice and supervision; maintaining personal and professional integrity; evaluating the outcomes of coaching.

Representation

Representing your competence and experience accurately.

Relationship

Establishing trusting relationships with coachees; managing potential conflicts where the coach has multiple relationships with the client, or where the coach is in a relationship with more than one member of the client system (e.g. working with a teacher in a school where the head teacher has contracted the coaching engagement).

Adhering to the above principles enhances the integrity of coaching practice and, moreover, ensures that the coachee's needs and safety are protected.

Ethical dilemmas

Reflection question

You have just finished coaching a teacher in a secondary school to develop his behaviour management skills. The 'host' school has paid for your time and services. As you are leaving the building, the head teacher sees you and asks: 'Well? How did that go?' What do you do?

Here, the coach has found him-/herself in a difficult situation whereby he/she wants to respect the privacy of the coachee but is also feeling a pressure to impart information to the commissioner. In this example the key is to prevent yourself from ending up in such an uncomfortable situation by agreeing clear confidentiality parameters at the start of the engagement. This can include, for example, what (if anything) can be fed back to whom and how that will be fed back. With clear agreements in place, the coach can respond with confidence.

Reflection question

You are in a coaching session with a teacher, supporting her to identify resilience-undermining thoughts that might be impacting on her wellbeing. In the process of this exploration, she discovers that she holds a core belief that she is incompetent, and says that she thinks that this may have arisen during her childhood. She would like to talk about it further. What do you do?

There are a number of questions to consider in this example. The key question is: What is the limit of your competence? Have you had training in supporting people to challenge and manage dysfunctional core beliefs? Or would it be better to refer on to another professional? If that is the case, are you going to just stop the coachee in their tracks and abruptly end the session? Or is there another way of responding? Assuming that you have not had training in this particular area, one option would be to transparently share that with the coachee while clarifying what you can offer – e.g. careful listening and attention; then, the coachee can make an informed decision about whether or not they wish to proceed.

There are very often multiple possible responses to an ethical dilemma, and sometimes ethical principles can come into conflict with each other. Therefore, navigating our way through ethical minefields is not necessarily a straightforward task. It is therefore important to discuss ethical dilemmas with others, perhaps in supervision, in order to seek different perspectives and to enable our thinking to be challenged.

Summary

- Ethics are the moral standards that define what is expected of someone undertaking a particular professional activity.
- Professional coaches will most likely adhere to the code of ethical practice of one or more of the professional coaching organizations.
- Ethical principles can guide our decision-making and safeguard the interests of our clients.
- Some common ethical principles are: rights and respect; recognition; responsibility; representation; and relationship.
- It is advisable to talk through ethical dilemmas with others, perhaps in the context of supervision.

References

Allan, J. & Whybrow, A. (2007). Gestalt coaching. In S. Palmer & A. Whybrow (eds), *Handbook of Coaching Psychology: A Guide for Practitioners*. Hove: Routledge.

Association for Coaching (AC) (2014). Coaching defined. Available at: www.associationforcoaching.com/pages/about/coaching-defined (accessed 9 March 2014).

Bachkirova, T., Cox, E. & Clutterbuck, D. (2014). Introduction. In E. Cox, T. Bachkirova & D. Clutterbuck (eds), *The Complete Handbook of Coaching* (2nd edn). London: SAGE.

Bandura, A. (1977). Self-efficacy: Toward a unifying theory of behavioral change. *Psychological Review*, *84 (2)*: 191–215.

Bandura, A. (1997). *Self-Efficacy: The Exercise of Control*. New York: Freeman.

Beck, A. T. (1967). *Depression: Clinical, Experimental and Theoretical Aspects*. Philadelphia, PA: University of Pennsylvania Press.

Beck, A. T. (1976). *Cognitive Therapy and the Emotional Disorders*. New York: International Universities Press.

Beck, J. S. (2011). *Cognitive Therapy: Basics and Beyond* (2nd edn). New York: Guilford Press.

Beere, J. & Broughton, T. (2013). *The Perfect Teacher Coach*. Carmarthen: Independent Thinking Press.

Berg, I. K. & De Jong, P. (2002). *Interviewing for Solutions*. Pacific Grove, CA: Brooks/Cole.

Biswas-Diener, R. & Dean, B. (2007). *Positive Psychology Coaching: Putting the Science of Happiness to Work for Your Clients*. New Jersey: John Wiley & Sons.

Bordin, E. S. (1979). The generalizability of the psychoanalytic concept of the working alliance. *Psychotherapy: Theory, Research & Practice*, *16 (3)*: 252–260.

Bransford, J. D., Brown, A. L. & Cocking, R. R. (eds) (1999). *How People Learn: Brain, Mind, Experience and School*. Washington, DC: National Academy Press.

Brennan, D. & Wildflower, L. (2014). Ethics in coaching. In E. Cox, T. Bachkirova & D. Clutterbuck (eds), *The Complete Handbook of Coaching* (2nd edn). London: SAGE.

Briner, R. & Dewberry, C. (2007). *Staff Wellbeing is Key to School Success: A Research Study into the Links between Staff Wellbeing and School Performance*. London: Worklife Support.

Chamberlain, P., Patterson, G., Reid, J., Kavanagh, K. & Forgatch, M. (1984). Observation of client resistance. *Behaviour Therapy*, *15*: 144–155.

Cox, E. & Jackson, P. (2014). Developmental coaching. In E. Cox, T. Bachkirova & D. Clutterbuck (eds), *The Complete Handbook of Coaching* (2nd edn). London: SAGE.

Creasy, J. & Paterson, F. (2005). *Leading Coaching in Schools*. London: National College for School Leadership.

Curwen, B., Palmer, S. & Ruddell, P. (2000). *Brief Cognitive Behaviour Therapy.* London: SAGE.

Deci, E. L. & Ryan, R. M. (1985). *Intrinsic Motivation and Self-Determination in Human Behavior.* New York: Plenum.

de Haan, E. & Page, N. (2013). Outcome report: Conversations are key to results. *Coaching at Work, 8 (4)*: 10–13.

Department for Children, Schools and Families (DCSF) (2008). *Improving Practice and Progression through Lesson Study: Handbook for Headteachers, Leading Teachers and Subject Leaders.* London: DCSF.

Department for Education (DfE) (2014). Press release: England to become a global leader of teaching character. Available at: www.gov.uk/government/news/england-to-become-a-global-leader-of-teaching-character (accessed 17 January 2015).

de Shazer, S. (1985). *Keys to Solution in Brief Therapy.* New York: W. W. Norton.

de Shazer, S. (1988). *Clues: Investigating Solutions in Brief Therapy.* New York: W. W. Norton.

DiClemente, C. C. & Prochaska, J. O. (1998). Toward a comprehensive, transtheoretical model of change: Stages of change and addictive behaviours. In W. R. Miller & N. Heather (eds), *Treating Addictive Behaviours* (2nd edn). New York: Plenum Press.

DiClemente, C. C. & Velasquez, M. M. (2002). Motivational interviewing and the stages of change. In W. Miller & S. Rollnick (eds), *Motivational Interviewing: Preparing People for Change.* New York: The Guilford Press.

Downey, M. (2003). *Effective Coaching: Lessons from the Coach's Coach.* Thomson-Texere.

Dryden, W. (2011). *Dealing with Clients' Emotional Problems in Life Coaching: A Rational-Emotive and Cognitive-Behaviour Therapy Approach.* Hove: Routledge.

D'Zurilla, T. J. & Nezu, A. M. (2006). *Problem-Solving Therapy: A Positive Approach to Clinical Intervention* (3rd edn). New York: Springer.

Edgerton, N. & Palmer, S. (2005). SPACE: a psychological model for use within cognitive-behavioural coaching, therapy and stress management. *The Coaching Psychologist, 2 (2)*: 25–31.

Egan, G. (2002). *The Skilled Helper: A Problem-Management and Opportunity-Development Approach to Helping.* Pacific Grove, CA: Brooks/Cole.

Elliot, A. J. & Harackiewicz, J. M. (1996). Approach and avoidance achievement goals and intrinsic motivation: A mediational analysis. *Journal of Personality and Social Psychology, 70 (3)*: 461–475.

Ellis, A. (1962). *Reason and Emotion in Psychotherapy.* New York: Lyle Stuart.

Ellis, A. (1988). *How to Stubbornly Refuse to Make Yourself Miserable About Anything, (Yes, Anything!).* New York: Citadel.

Ellis, A. (2001). *Overcoming Destructive Beliefs, Feelings and Behaviours.* New York: Prometheus.

Frankl, V. ([1959] 2004). *Man's Search for Meaning.* London: Rider.

Fredrickson, B. L. (1998). What good are positive emotions? *Review of General Psychology, 2*: 300–319.

Fredrickson, B. L. (2005). Positive emotions. In C. Snyder & S. Lopez (eds), *Handbook of Positive Psychology.* New York: Oxford University Press.

Gordon, T. (1970, 2000). *Parent Effectiveness Training.* New York: Three Rivers Press.

Govindji, R. & Linley, P. A. (2007). Strengths use, self-concordance and well-being: Implications for strengths coaching and coaching psychologists. *International Coaching Psychology Review, 2 (2)*: 143–153.

Grant, A. M. (2007). Past, present and future: The evolution of professional coaching and coaching psychology. In Palmer, S. & Whybrow, A. (eds), *Handbook of Coaching Psychology: A Guide for Practitioners.* Hove: Routledge.

Grant, A. M. & Cavanagh, M. J. (2007). Coaching psychology: How did we get here and where are we going? *InPsych, 29:* 6–9.

Grant, A. M. & Stober, D. (2006). Introduction. In D. R. Stober & A. M. Grant (eds), *Evidence Based Coaching Handbook: Putting Best Practices to Work for your Clients.* New Jersey: John Wiley & Sons.

Green, L. S., Oades, L. G. & Robinson, P. L. (2012). Positive education programmes: Integrating coaching and positive psychology in schools. In C. van Nieuwerburgh (ed.), *Coaching in Education: Getting Better Results for Students, Educators and Parents.* London: Karnac.

Greene, J. & Grant, A. M. (2003). *Solution-Focused Coaching.* Harlow: Pearson Education.

Gross Cheliotes, L. & Reilly, M. (2010). *Coaching Conversations: Transforming Your School One Conversation at a Time.* Thousand Oaks, CA: Corwin.

Gyllensten, K. & Palmer, S. (2012). Stress and performance coaching. In M. Neenan & S. Palmer (eds), *Cognitive Behavioural Coaching in Practice: An Evidence Based Approach.* Hove: Routledge.

Harris, R. (2008). *The Happiness Trap.* London: Constable & Robinson.

ICF & PricewaterhouseCoopers (2012). ICF Global Coaching Study – executive summary. Available at: www.coachfederation.org/coachingstudy2012 (accessed 9 March 2014).

Ijntema, R. (2014). Coaching enhances staff wellbeing over time. *Coaching at Work, 9 (2):* 12.

Iveson, C., George, E. & Ratner, H. (2012). *Brief Coaching: A Solution-Focused Approach.* Hove: Routledge.

Jackson, P. Z. & McKergow, M. (2007). *The Solutions Focus: Making Coaching and Change Simple.* London: Nicholas Brealey Publishing.

Knowles, M. (1978). *The Adult Learner: A Neglected Species.* Houston, TX: Gulf.

Kolb, D. A. (1984). *Experiential Learning: Experience as the Source of Learning and Development.* Englewood Cliffs, NJ: Prentice-Hall.

Law, H. (2013). *Coaching Psychology: A Practitioner's Guide.* Chichester: John Wiley & Sons.

Lazarus, A. (1977). Towards an egoless state of being. In A. Ellis & R. Grieger (eds), *Handbook of Rational-Emotive Therapy.* New York: Springer.

Linley, P. A. (2008). *Average to A+: Realising Strengths in Yourself and Others.* Coventry: CAPP Press.

Linley, P. A. & Harrington, S. (2007). Integrating positive psychology and coaching psychology: Shared assumptions and aspirations? In S. Palmer & A. Whybrow (eds), *Handbook of Coaching Psychology: A Guide for Practitioners.* Hove: Routledge.

Locke, E. A. (1999). Motivation through conscious goal-setting. *Applied and Preventive Psychology, 5 (2):* 117–124.

Lofthouse R., Leat, D. & Towler, C. (2010). *Coaching for Teaching and Learning: A Practical Guide for Schools.* CfBT Education Trust.

Luthans, F., Avolio, B. J., Avey, J. B. & Norman, S. M. (2006). Psychological capital: Measurement and relationship with performance and satisfaction (Working Paper No. 2006-1). Gallup Leadership Institute, University of Nebraska-Lincoln.

Luthans, F., Youssef, C. M. & Avolio, B. J. (2007). *Psychological Capital.* New York: Oxford University Press.

Maddux, J. (2005). Self-efficacy: The power of believing you can. In C. Snyder & S. Lopez (eds), *Handbook of Positive Psychology.* New York: Oxford University Press.

McKenna, D. & Davis, S. (2009). Hidden in plain sight. *Industrial and Organizational Psychology: An Exchange of Perspectives on Science and Practice, 3 (2)*: 244–260.

McMahon, G. (2005). Behavioural contracting and confidentiality in organizational coaching. *Counselling at Work,* Spring: 10–12.

Michael, J. (2006). Where's the evidence that active learning works? *Advances in Physiology Education, 30*: 159–167.

Miller, G. (1969). Psychology as a means of promoting human welfare. *American Psychologist, 24*: 1063–1075.

Miller, R. (2007). Foreword. In S. Palmer & A. Whybrow (eds), *Handbook of Coaching Psychology: A Guide for Practitioners.* Hove: Routledge.

Miller, W. & Rollnick, S. (2002). *Motivational Interviewing: Preparing People for Change.* New York: The Guilford Press.

Morris, T. (2004). *The Stoic Art of Living: Inner Resilience and Outer Results.* Chicago, IL: Open Court Publishing.

Murphy, J. J. & Duncan, B. L. (2007). *Brief Intervention for School Problems: Outcome-Informed Strategies.* New York: The Guilford Press.

National Union of Teachers (2008). *The A to Z of Peer Coaching.* Available at: www.teachers.org.uk/node/10470 (accessed 10 August 2014).

Neenan, M. (2009). *Developing Resilience: A Cognitive-Behavioural Approach.* Hove: Routledge.

Neenan, M. (2012). Understanding and tackling procrastination. In M. Neenan & S. Palmer (eds), *Cognitive Behavioural Coaching in Practice: An Evidence Based Approach.* Hove: Routledge.

Neenan, M. & Dryden, W. (2002). *Life Coaching: A Cognitive Behavioural Approach.* Hove: Routledge.

Neenan, M. & Dryden, W. (2012). Understanding and developing resilience. In M. Neenan & S. Palmer (eds), *Cognitive Behavioural Coaching in Practice: An Evidence Based Approach.* Hove: Routledge.

Neenan, M. & Palmer, S. (eds) (2012). *Cognitive Behavioural Coaching in Practice: An Evidence Based Approach.* Hove: Routledge.

O'Broin, A. & Palmer, S. (2010). Introducing an interpersonal perspective on the coaching relationship. In S. Palmer & A. McDowall (eds), *The Coaching Relationship: Putting People First.* Hove: Routledge.

O'Connell, B. (2002). *Solution-Focused Therapy.* London: SAGE.

O'Connell, B. & Palmer, S. (2007). Solution-focused coaching. In S. Palmer & A. Whybrow (eds), *Handbook of Coaching Psychology: A Guide for Practitioners.* Hove: Routledge.

O'Connell, B., Palmer, S. & Williams, H. (2012). *Solution-Focused Coaching in Practice.* Hove: Routledge.

Ofsted (2011). Barton Hill Primary School Inspection Report. Report no. 130997.

Ogilvy, H. & Ellam-Dyson, V. (2012). Line management involvement in coaching: Help or hindrance? A content analysis study. *International Coaching Psychology Review, 7 (1)*: 39–54.

Padesky, C. (1993). *Socratic Questioning: Changing Minds or Guiding Discovery.* Keynote address delivered at the European Congress of Behavioural and Cognitive Therapies, London, 24 September 1993.

Palmer, S. (2007). PRACTICE: A model suitable for coaching, counselling, psychotherapy and stress management. *The Coaching Psychologist, 3 (2)*: 71–77.

Palmer, S. (2008). The PRACTICE model of coaching: Towards a solution-focused approach. *Coaching Psychology International, 1 (1)*: 4–8.

Palmer, S. (2011). Revisiting the 'P' in the PRACTICE coaching model. *The Coaching Psychologist, 7 (2)*: 156–158.

Palmer, S. (2013). Resilience Enhancing Imagery: A cognitive behavioural technique which includes Resilience Undermining Thinking and Resilience Enhancing Thinking. *The Coaching Psychologist, 9 (1)*: 48–50.

Palmer, S. & Cooper, C. (2000). *How to Deal with Stress*. London: Kogan Page.

Palmer, S. & Dryden, W. (1995). *Counselling for Stress Problems*. London: SAGE.

Palmer, S. & Dunkley, C. (2010). A behavioural approach to BIG Problems encountered in coaching: Behaviour Incompatible with Goals. *The Coaching Psychologist, 6 (1)*: 32–37.

Palmer, S. & Szymanska, K. (2007). Cognitive behavioural coaching: An integrative approach. In Palmer, S. & Whybrow, A. (eds), *Handbook of Coaching Psychology: A Guide for Practitioners*. Hove: Routledge.

Palmer, S. & Whybrow, A. (eds) (2007). *Handbook of Coaching Psychology: A Guide for Practitioners*. Hove: Routledge.

Ramsden, P. (1992). *Learning to Teach in Higher Education*. London: Routledge.

Rivkin, S. G., Hanushek, E. A. and Kain, J. F. (2005). Teachers, schools and academic achievement. *Econometrica, 73 (2)*: 417–458.

Rogers, C. ([1951] 2003). *Client-Centred Therapy: Its Current Practice, Implications and Theory*. London: Constable & Robinson.

Rogers, C. (1961). *On Becoming a Person: A Therapist's View of Psychotherapy*. London: Constable & Robinson.

Rosenberg, M. (2003). *Non-Violent Communication: A Language of Life*. Encinitas, CA: PuddleDancer Press.

Ryan, R. M. & Deci, E. L. (2000). Self-determination theory and the facilitation of intrinsic motivation, social development, and well-being. *American Psychologist, 55*: 68–78.

Schein, E. (1988). *Process Consultation: Its Role in Organizational Development*. New York: Addison-Wesley.

Schein, E. (1999). *Process Consultation Revisited: Building the Helping Relationship*. New York: Addison-Wesley.

Seligman, M. (2003). *Authentic Happiness*. London: Nicholas Brealey Publishing.

Seligman, M. (2011). *Flourish: A New Understanding of Happiness and Wellbeing – and How to Achieve Them*. London: Nicholas Brealey Publishing.

Seligman, M. & Csikszentmihalyi, M. (2000). Positive psychology: An introduction. *American Psychologist, 16*: 126–127.

Sherlock-Storey, M., Moss, M. & Timson, S. (2013). Brief coaching for resilience during organisational change – an exploratory study. *The Coaching Psychologist, 9 (1)*: 19–26.

Skiffington, S. & Zeus, P. (2003). *Behavioural Coaching: How to Build Sustainable Personal and Organizational Strength*. London: McGraw-Hill.

Snyder, C. & Lopez, S. (eds) (2005). *Handbook of Positive Psychology*. New York: Oxford University Press.

Spinelli, E. & Horner, C. (2007). An existential approach to coaching psychology. In S. Palmer & A. Whybrow (eds), *Handbook of Coaching Psychology: A Guide for Practitioners*. Hove: Routledge.

Starr, J. (2003). *The Coaching Manual*. London: Prentice Hall.

Suggett, N. (2012). Coaching in primary schools: A case study. In C. van Nieuwerburgh (ed.), *Coaching in Education: Getting Better Results for Students, Educators and Parents*. London: Karnac.

Sutton Trust (2011). *Improving the Impact of Teachers on Pupil Achievement in the UK – Interim Findings*. London: Sutton Trust.

Thornton, C. (2010). *Group and Team Coaching: The Essential Guide*. Hove: Routledge.

van Nieuwerburgh, C. (2012). *Coaching in Education: Getting Better Results for Students, Educators and Parents*. London: Karnac.

Wasik, B. (1984). Teaching parents effective problem-solving: A handbook for professionals. Unpublished manuscript. Cited in Palmer, S. (2007), PRACTICE: A model suitable for coaching, counselling, psychotherapy and stress management. *The Coaching Psychologist, 3 (2)*: 71–77.

Whitmore, J. ([1992] 2002). *Coaching for Performance: GROWing People, Performance and Purpose*. London: Nicholas Brealey Publishing.

William, D. & Black, P. (2006). *Inside the Black Box: Raising Standards through Classroom Assessment*. London: NFER Nelson.

Williams, H., Palmer, S. & Edgerton, N. (2014). Cognitive behavioural coaching. In E. Cox, T. Bachkirova & D. Clutterbuck (eds), *The Complete Handbook of Coaching* (2nd edn). London: SAGE.

Young, D. & Anderson, K. (2011). Reflections of a coaching psychologist – new hire, on-boarding & transition: A role for coaching psychologists. *Coaching Psychology International, 4 (1)*: 19–21.

Zeus, P. & Skiffington, S. (2000). *The Complete Guide to Coaching at Work*. Sydney: McGraw-Hill.

Index